Cuisines of Portuguese Encounters

Expanded Edition

Recipes from

Portugal

Angola

Brazil

Cape Verde

East Timor

Goa

Guinea-Bissau

Macao

Malacca

Mozambique

São Tomé and

Príncipe

The Hippocrene Cookbook Library

Afghan Food & Cookery
African Cooking, Best of Regional
Albanian Cooking, Best of
Alps, Cuisines of the
Aprovecho: A Mexican-American Border Cookbook
Argentina Cooks!, Exp. Ed.
Austrian Cuisine, Best of, Exp. Ed.
Bolivian Kitchen, My Mother's
Brazil: A Culinary Journey
Burma, Flavors of
Cajun Women, Cooking with
Calabria, Cucina di
Caucasus Mountains, Cuisines of the
Chile, Tasting
Colombian Cooking, Secrets of
Croatian Cooking, Best of, Exp. Ed.
Czech Cooking, Best of, Exp. Ed.
Danube, All Along The, Exp. Ed.
Dutch Cooking, Art of, Exp. Ed.
Estonian Tastes and Traditions
Egyptian Cooking
Filipino Food, Fine
Finnish Cooking, Best of
French Caribbean Cuisine
French Fashion, Cooking in the (Bilingual)
Germany, Spoonfuls of
Greek Cooking, Regional
Greek Cuisine, The Best of, Exp. Ed.
Gypsy Feast
Haiti, Taste of
Havana Cookbook, Old (Bilingual)
Hungarian Cookbook, Exp. Ed.
Icelandic Food & Cookery
India, Flavorful
Indian Spice Kitchen, The, Exp. Ed.
International Dictionary of Gastronomy
Irish-Style, Feasting Galore
Italian Cuisine, Treasury of (Bilingual)
Japanese Home Cooking
Jewish-Iraqi Cuisine, Mama Nazima's
Korean Cuisine, Best of
Laotian Cooking, Simple
Latvia, Taste of
Lithuanian Cooking, Art of
Macau, Taste of

Malta, Taste of, Exp. Ed.
Middle Eastern Kitchen, The
Mongolian Cooking, Imperial
New Hampshire: from Farm to Kitchen
New Jersey Cookbook, Farms and Foods of the Garden State:
Norway, Tastes and Tales of
Persian Cooking, Art of
Pied Noir Cookbook: French Sephardic Cuisine
Piemontese, Cucina: Cooking from Italy's Piedmont
Poland's Gourmet Cuisine
Polish Cooking, Best of, Exp. Ed.
Polish Country Kitchen Cookbook
Polish Cuisine, Treasury of (Bilingual)
Polish Heritage Cookery, Ill. Ed.
Polish Traditions, Old
Portuguese Encounters, Cuisines of
Pyrenees, Tastes of
Quebec, Taste of
Rhine, All Along The
Romania, Taste of, Exp. Ed.
Russian Cooking, Best of, Exp. Ed.
Scandinavian Cooking, Best of
Scotland, Traditional Food From
Scottish-Irish Pub and Hearth Cookbook
Sephardic Israeli Cuisine
Sicilian Feasts
Smorgasbord Cooking, Best of
South American Cookery
South Indian Cooking, Art of Healthy
Spanish Family Cookbook, Rev. Ed.
Sri Lanka, Exotic Tastes of
Swedish Kitchen, A
Swiss Cookbook, The
Syria, Taste of
Taiwanese Cuisine, Best of
Thai Cuisine, Best of, Regional
Trinidad and Tobago, Sweet Hands: Island Cooking from
Turkish Cuisine, Taste of
Tuscan Kitchen, Tastes from a
Ukrainian Cuisine, Best of, Exp. Ed.
Uzbek Cooking, Art of
Warsaw Cookbook, Old
Vietnamese Kitchen, A

Cuisines of Portuguese Encounters

Expanded Edition

Cherie Y. Hamilton

Recipes from

Portugal

Angola

Brazil

Cape Verde

East Timor

Goa

Guinea-Bissau

Macao

Malacca

Mozambique

São Tomé and

Príncipe

HIPPOCRENE BOOKS INC.
NEW YORK

Jacket and book design by Acme Klong Design, Inc.
Photography by Tom Wallace

For more information, address:
HIPPOCRENE BOOKS, INC.
171 Madison Avenue
New York, NY 10016

ISBN-10: 0-7818-1181-3
ISBN-13: 978-0-7818-1181-1

Library of Congress Cataloging-in-Publication Data

Hamilton, Cherie Y.
  Cuisines of Portuguese encounters : recipes from Portugal, Angola, Brazil,
Cape Verde, East Timor, Goa, Guinea-Bissau, Macao, Malacca, Mozambique,
Sao Tome, and Principe / Cherie Y. Hamilton. -- Expanded ed.
    p. cm.
  Includes bibliographical references and index.
  ISBN 0-7818-1181-3
  1. Cookery, Portuguese. 2. Cookery, International.   I. Title.
  TX723.5.P7H36 2007
  641.59469--dc22

                                    2007023331

Printed in the United States of America.

To my husband Russell,
with whom I traveled to the Portuguese-speaking
world of wonderful cuisines.
Without his love, support, and encouragement,
this book would not have been possible.

Contents

Acknowledgments

my odyssey through much of the Portuguese-speaking world began some forty-five years ago. In 1960, along with my husband, Russell, then a graduate student at Yale and a Fulbright fellow, and Cherie Andrea, our three-year-old daughter, I arrived in Brazil. It was in the city of Salvador, in the northeastern state of Bahia, that I was introduced to the cuisine of Portuguese, African, and Indian influence.

So felicitous was my introduction to Brazilian food, especially the African-influenced dishes of Bahia, that I resolved at that time to learn to prepare as many of them as I could. Jorge Amado, one of Brazil's premier novelists, was so taken with my interest in the cuisine of his native Bahia that he encouraged me to write a cookbook. Although I took his encouragement to heart, many, many years passed before the dream became a reality.

On the other hand, in between the birth and realization of that dream, I not only had the opportunity to become familiar with the dishes of Bahia, where I lived for two years, but with the delicacies of the other regions of Brazil that I was fortunate enough to visit. In 1968, during a three-month stay in Bahia, this time with our four children, I had the opportunity to travel to Rio de Janeiro and the state of Alagoas. My interest in the varied cooking of Brazil had not waned, and I continued to collect recipes and learn how to prepare dishes under the tutelage of countless Brazilian friends.

In 1970–1971, my husband, by then a university professor, and I spent a sabbatical year in Portugal with our four children. We lived in the Lisbon area, but traveled throughout Portugal from Trás-os-Montes to Alentejo to the Algarve. As had been the case with Brazilian cuisine, Portugal's national and regional cooking whetted my appetite, both literally and figuratively. I really began to understand how the Portuguese had served as intermediaries for the spread of crops, food cultures, and recipes to the far reaches of their old colonial empire and to other parts of the world.

While living in Portugal I was fortunate enough to receive a grant from the Lisbon-based Gulbenkian Foundation. This grant allowed me, in the company of my husband, to make the first of many trips to Africa, specifically to the then-Portuguese colonies of Mozambique and Angola. That trip was an eye-opener and, I might say, a delectable mouth-opener. As I had done first in Brazil and then in Portugal—with my taste buds ready and paper and pen in hand—I delved into new culinary worlds. I sampled many amazing dishes and assiduously wrote down dozens of compelling recipes.

In 1978 my husband took another sabbatical from the University of Minnesota, and we set off with three of our four children for an unforgettable year in Cape Verde, Angola, and Mozambique. I was able to contrast and compare the cuisines of the newly independent countries of Portuguese-speaking Africa as well as how they differed from, and were similar to, many of the dishes of Brazil and Portugal. What fascinated me were the prevailing commonalities among so many of the dishes found in the seven Portuguese-speaking countries on three continents. This culinary interrelationship motivated me to extend my original idea for a cookbook. What had started out as a Bahian, then a Brazilian, and later a Luso-Brazilian cookbook, had grown into the ambitious project of the cuisines of the entire Portuguese-speaking world, including African and Asian countries and territories.

In the 1980s, I got my first chance to visit São Tomé and Príncipe and Guinea-Bissau. In São Tomé and Príncipe, the two-island, Portuguese-speaking country in the Gulf of Guinea, I learned to prepare a number of sumptuous dishes with the help of several prominent citizens, including the mother of the outstanding poet Alda Espirito Santo. Likewise, in the tiny West African country of Guinea-Bissau, I experienced one gastronomic delight after another, and after conferring with local cooks, I dutifully recorded recipes.

By the late 1980s, I had completed my sojourn in all five of the Lusophone African countries, as well as Brazil and Portugal. What was lacking was a visit to the former territories in Asia. Although I still have not been to Goa, Malacca, or East Timor, my husband and I did get to Macao in 1987, which has since reverted to mainland China. Moreover, I have been able to count on the culinary experiences of friends who have visited Goa, Malacca, and East Timor, and who have shared their knowledge with me.

Over the past forty years so many friends have aided me that it would take several pages to list them by name. Needless to say, I am extremely grateful to all those who helped make this book possible. In the brief remarks that precede many of the individual recipes in this volume, I do refer to those who played especially key roles by introducing me to, or teaching me how best to prepare, a given dish.

In these prefatory remarks I would be remiss, however, if I did not acknowledge by name those players as well as others not mentioned who contributed to the completion of this project. I must thank my esteemed Brazilian friends Norma Sampaio, Carybé and Nancy, Jorge Amado and Zélia Gattai, Waldeloir Rego, Silvio and Lia Robatto, Mário and Lúcia Cravo, Deoscóredes Maximilliano dos Santos (a.k.a. Didi), João Reis, and Mariangela Nogueira.

I also express my heartfelt appreciation to the Carelli family from the city of São Paulo. Antônio and Isabel Carelli had lived in the United States back in the 1960s when he was a graduate student. We had not seen them in over thirty years. But in August of 1999, during our stay in São Paulo, they graciously invited my husband and me to stay at their home. During that memorable visit they and their three children, Fabiana, Gabriela, and Ernesto, welcomed us with friendship and a number of unforgettable *Paulista* dishes.

In Lisbon, I was warmly received and aided by the Santos Pinto and Pinheiro families. Also in Lisbon, my heartfelt thanks to my dear friends Manuel Ferreira, the Portuguese writer and expert on Lusophone African culture, and his wife, Orlanda Amarílis, who taught me how to prepare dishes from her native Cape Verde. Other friends in Lisbon who treated me to wonderful meals are Luisa d'Almeida and Ana Maria Mão de Ferro Martinho. My warm thanks to Dr. Miguel Natal, an Angolan living in Portugal. On three memorable occasions, Dr. Natal invited us to share *consoada* (Christmas supper) with his family, including Lutice Diniz, his Portuguese mother-in-law, whose prowess as a chef is equaled by her talent as a singer of *fados*. Also in Lisbon, many thanks to my good friends Joaquin and Ana Soares da Costa, who shared many recipes and Portuguese customs with me.

In the Cape Verde city of Mindelo, I send thanks to my friend Ivone, the sister of Orlanda Amarílis. Warm thanks are also due to poet Oswaldo Osório and his wife Dinah Custódio, cherished friends and food connoisseurs in Praia, Cape Verde's capital.

On the African continent, in Guinea-Bissau, I thank Deolinda Rodrigues for her invaluable advice, some of it offered while she was living in the Washington, D.C., area as the wife of her country's ambassador to the United States.

In Luanda, I express my appreciation to José Maria and Sara dos Santos, in whose home I was a guest for several months and who daily taught me something new about Angolan cuisine. I also thank Arnaldo Santos and his spouse, Teresa Cohen, who took our three children in and helped teach them to love Angolan cooking.

On the eastern coast of the continent, in Mozambique, I recall the memorable dishes served up by Naly Honwana, the mother of the famous writer Luis Bernardo Honwana. I also have fond memories of the meals eaten in the Maputo home of Luis and his wife, Suzette. I likewise shall always remember the Mozambican delicacies prepared back in the 1970s by Maria, wife of José Craverinha, Mozambique's poet laureate, and in the 1980s and 1990s by her daughter-in-law.

In Maputo, I also received valuable tips on Mozambican, Goan, and Portuguese cooking from my cherished friends Célia Dinis and Blandina Barbosa. And I am indebted to the poet Rui Nogar, who in 1979 shared with me his insights on Goan cooking.

Many people in the United States helped me in this enterprise. My friends Shep and Leona Forman, who spent some time in East Timor, were able to give me some useful hints about cuisine from that Indonesian island. I am also indebted to José Ramos Horta, the Nobel Peace Prize laureate from East

Timor, whom I met during his visit to Nashville and who, by way of his mother, provided me with useful information on the cuisine of his homeland. Thank you also to Yolande Zahler, a transplanted Brazilian living in New York, with whom I traveled so often to Portugal and Lusophone Africa, and who has been an unfailing source of encouragement.

My heartfelt gratitude to António Matinho, director and editor-in-chief of *Luso-Americano*, Newark, New Jersey's, Portuguese-language newspaper, and Maria do Carmo Pereira, associate news editor. Over the years they have promoted the first edition of this book in their newspaper.

Across the river from Newark, in the Big Apple, dwells an individual for whom words are not sufficient to express the extent of my gratitude and affection. That person is Dalia Carmel, a cookbook maven and world culinary connoisseur extraordinaire. Dalia encouraged me, guided me, and provided me with valuable leads, and ultimately acted, pro bono, as my agent. And I would be remiss if I did not express my gratitude to Maria Luisa Nunes. It was Maria Luisa, a Cape Verdean-American from Rhode Island, a professor of Portuguese, and my longtime friend, who brought Dalia and me together. Also in New York, I'd like to express my gratitude to Nahum Wachman, owner of Kitchen, Arts, and Letters, for his sound advice and support.

My love and gratitude to my four children: Cherie Andrea, Russell Malcolm, Melissa Elena, and David Dean, for their unfailing encouragement and for taste-testing so many of the dishes. I am also pleased to include black-and-white photos shot in Portugal by Lucinda Hamilton, my dear mother-in-law.

A special expression of Brazilian *saudade* to Ginga, my oldest grandchild, who so enjoyed those scrumptious Bahian dishes when, in 1997, she accompanied her grandfather and me to Salvador. And in 2003 Ginga spent a month with us in Lisbon and Maputo, Mozambique, where, of course, she enjoyed the cuisines of Portugal and Mozambique.

Introduction

When, in 1415, a military force led by Prince Henry the Navigator crossed the Strait of Gibraltar and landed in Morocco, the Portuguese became the first Europeans to gain a foothold in Africa. In 1460, Portuguese mariners sailed west to discover the Cape Verde Islands, some 400 miles off the coast of Senegal. By the 1480s, Portuguese explorers had penetrated sub-Saharan Africa from the Senegambia to the Congo and Angola in the south-eastern region of the continent. Then in 1497, Vasco da Gama rounded the Cape of Good Hope at the southern tip of Africa, and sailed north to the Indian Ocean, where his fleet made port in Mozambique and Mombasa.

The four ships under Vasco da Gama's command continued up Africa's east coast and eventually reached Calicut on the west coast of India. Not only did this historic voyage open the way to European control of the spice trade, it also set the stage for another momentous Portuguese sea adventure. In 1500, in the wake of Columbus's trip across the Atlantic Ocean, Portugal's Pedro Álvares Cabral sailed west to the vast territory that would become known as Brazil. By the late sixteenth century, Fernão Mendes Pinto had extended the Portuguese presence in Asia to include China. And eventually, the Portuguese would be the first Europeans to reach Japan.

The Portuguese, in effect, established the first "empire" upon which the sun never set. By virtue of this early presence in Africa, Asia, and South America, the Portuguese became the first carriers of language, social norms, culture, and agricultural products to different parts of the globe. Not only were the Portuguese the first intercontinental and interregional carriers of agricultural products, they were also the purveyors of food cultures, including specific cuisines. Moreover, the mingling of ingredients, food cultures, and culinary customs resulted in the creation of unique cuisines in the colonies, as well as in Portugal itself and its Atlantic islands of Madeira and the Azores.

According to the order in which they became part of the old Portuguese "empire," the African territories were Guinea-Bissau, Cape Verde, São Tomé and Príncipe, Angola, and Mozambique. The Portuguese territories in Asia and South America, in the order in which they became colonies, were Goa, Brazil, East Timor, and Macau. Brazil became independent in 1822, and today all of the former colonies in Africa are sovereign nations, having gained their independence in 1974 and 1975. In 1961 Goa, along with the two other small Portuguese territories of Damian and Diu, were returned to India. East Timor

1

became part of Indonesia in 1974 and then achieved its independence in 2002. Macao reverted to mainland China in 1999. All of these former colonies and possessions have a culinary legacy that stems from those early and centuries-long Portuguese encounters.

Although the Portuguese controlled Malacca on the Malay Peninsula from only 1511 until 1641 (the latter being the year in which it was occupied by the Dutch), even today there are significant traces of the Lusitanian presence in the local cuisine. To this day the descendents of the Malaccan Portuguese are known as *Cristangs*. This term derives from the Portuguese adjective *cristã*, as in *gente cristã*, meaning "Christian people." *Cristã* also refers to the Portuguese-based Creole language still spoken in Malacca.

Portuguese cuisine, already in great part molded by the Moors and Sephardic Jews who inhabited the Iberian Peninsula, quite naturally influenced the culinary cultures of the indigenous peoples in the overseas provinces. At the same time, these indigenous peoples exerted their own influence on each others' cuisine as well as on that of the Portuguese themselves. Portuguese explorers returned home with new food products and new ways of preparing them, and introduced them not only to their own country but to Europe in general.

One of the many examples of this is the sweet potato, which the Portuguese brought from its native South America to Africa. From Africa, the sweet potato spread to Europe, North America, and Asia. There are several recipes in this collection that exemplify how the Portuguese fostered the use of the sweet potato as a food in Africa and Asia.

Another fascinating example of the initially Portuguese-induced spread of crops is that of the peanut. This legume, native to South America, traveled in the cargo of Portuguese merchant vessels to Africa. African slaves then brought the peanut back across the Atlantic and introduced it in North America. As a matter of fact, in Kimbundu, a Bantu language of Angola, the word for peanut is *nguba*. Few Georgians, Virginians, and other residents of the United States know, however, that "goober," the popular regional word for peanut, derives from an African word.

Yet another noteworthy example is that of the okra, a vegetable also native to Africa that was taken by the Portuguese to Brazil. Interestingly enough, both the English word okra and *quiabo* (the Portuguese equivalent), as well as *gumbo*, are all words of West African origin. When okra was transplanted to Brazil, it resembled a local thick-leaf plant called *caruru* grown by the Tupi-Guarani Indians. And, indeed, okra (or *quiabo*) is the main ingredient of a now classic Afro-Brazilian dish first concocted in Bahia. This stew-like shrimp and okra dish is known, however, as *caruru*. The story does not end here. Caruru was taken to Africa under that Native American name, and became a part of Angolan cuisine. Contract workers, known as Angolares, took the dish to São Tomé and Príncipe. On those islands in the Gulf of

Guinea, the original Tupi word became *calulu*, the name of a fantastic chicken and okra dish. The Brazilian-Indian word *caruru* spelled *calalu*, *kalulu*, or *callaloo*, emigrated to Jamaica and to Louisiana as the names of a variety of leafy greens used in Creole cooking, particularly soups. Wherever the word, its spelling variants, and the dishes to which it refers appear, the Portuguese were the original propagators of caruru.

Portuguese mariners were also responsible for the dissemination of one of the world's best-known and most appreciated cereal crops—corn—a crop that American Indians cultivated long before the arrival of Europeans. *Milho*, the Portuguese word for corn, was introduced to Europe and Africa in the early seventeenth century. It became such an important staple of the Cape Verdean diet that when that African archipelago achieved political independence in 1975, their new official flag sported ears of corn as a national emblem.

Rice, which originated in China and India, is a most important and versatile grain that is eaten worldwide. By virtue of their early arrival in Asia, the Portuguese can be credited with having carried rice to Europe, Africa, and the Americas, where it was adapted to varying cuisines. Also with respect to Asia, the Chinese word for "bread" comes from the Portuguese *pão*. And *tempero*, Portuguese for "seasoning," became Japanese *tempura*.

This cookbook contains a number of recipes that call for sweet potatoes, peanuts, okra, corn, rice, and other foods that make the *Cuisines of Portuguese Encounters* so historically fascinating and gastronomically compelling. These recipes offer you the opportunity to prepare a diversity of dishes from a range of geographical locales and a variety of distinctive cultures. At the same time, the common denominator of the Portuguese presence gives the adventuresome cook the chance to prepare several varieties of the same dishes, with sometimes only subtle, and other times very pronounced differences in ingredients and flavors. For example, in this volume you will find several recipes for *feijoada*. This basic bean stew comes in several regional varieties in Brazil, where it is the national dish. There are also national and territorial versions of feijoada in Portugal, Mozambique, Goa, and East Timor. Then there is *cachupa*, the Cape Verdean version of feijoada. Some believe that the name of Cape Verde's signature dish derives from "ketchup." What everyone who tastes it will agree is that cachupa is a delectable medley of corn, beans, meats, and seasonings.

This book is intended for the serious cook and for any food lover who also has a bent for culinary adventure. I hope that in preparing, serving, and savoring these dishes you will share in the adventure that I have experienced throughout the years of my *Portuguese Encounters*.

CUISINE OF
Portugal

as we consider the cuisine of Portugal today, there are many ingredients that have come from the age of exploration. Cinnamon and curry spices were brought to Portugal by Vasco da Gama and became a staple for many of the egg sweets influenced by the Moors. Pineapples were brought from Brazil, and Brazilian chili peppers (*pimenta malagueta* peppers) came by way of Angola and Mozambique. Other exchanges were coffee from Africa, transplanted to Brazil; Brazilian cashews, which were transplanted in Africa and India; and tomatoes and potatoes, which were taken from South America to Portugal. Onions and garlic were brought to Portugal by the Romans, who established colonies there. They also brought wheat, olives, and grapes. The Moors who occupied Portugal for 500 years, were responsible for planting almond, fig, apricot, lemon, and orange trees. They invented the *cataplana*, a clam-shaped pan for cooking. A famous dish that has resulted from this is *Ameijoas na Cataplana* (clams tossed with sausages and pork). The dish was created during the Inquisition to test adherence to Christianity, since the consumption of pork and shellfish was forbidden by Orthodox Judaism and Islam. The Moors are also credited for the egg desserts so popular in Portugal and throughout the Portuguese-speaking world. The nuns in convents were responsible for making these sweets and are credited for taking them to Brazil in the sixteenth century.

Present-day Portugal is a cosmopolitan banquet of the foods and moods of neighboring countries and far-off colonial ports—from char-grilled sardines to *bacalhau* and beer; this small country of roughly ten million has made its mark on the culinary globe. As we look at the cuisine of Portugal today, we find there are certain foods, such as fish and seafood, that are popular throughout the country. But each region has its own way of preparing them. Salt cod, known as the "*fiel amigo*" (faithful friend), along with grilled sardines, are two types of fish most popular throughout Portugal, particularly in the area around Lisbon. It is said that there are 365 ways to prepare salt cod. Dishes like *Bacalhau à Gomes de Sá* (Salt Cod and Potato Casserole) and *Bacalhau à Bras* (Codfish Brás Style) are two of the salt cod dishes savored nationwide. In the early sixteenth century, Portuguese sailors discovered Newfoundland's great banks of fresh cod, sparking a fathomless fishy love affair that endures to this day. Sardines grilled over coals with green tomatoes and served with a green salad is another dish that is enjoyed by all. Dishes like *açorda*, a bread-based soup made with fish or seafood, is an experience not to be missed.

Caldo Verde, the national soup made with collard greens, potatoes, and *chouriço* (Portuguese sausage); and *pãezinhos*, the delicious small rolls served warm for breakfast with coffee; and the cheeses from the Serra (mountain) region are all examples of foods enjoyed in all regions of Portugal.

The islands of the Azores and Madeira are Portugal's autonomous archipelagos located about 900 miles west of the mainland, in the middle of the Atlantic Ocean. Each island has its own traditions and distinctive cuisine. Some of the recipes have the same names as those in mainland Portugal, but they have different ingredients. On some of the islands, cattle of the highest quality are raised, along with pigs, chickens, turkeys, ducks, and rabbits, and all are fed on corn and vegetables. The islands are rich in fish and seafood, and many of the tropical fruits grown there, such as *maracujá*, *goiabada*, and *araça*, are found in Brazil. That's why some Madeirans call their islands "Brazil in Miniature." As in Cape Verde, corn is a Madeiran staple. Although an important crop, very little is actually grown on the islands. The majority is imported and is of the white variety because yellow corn ferments quickly and is thus used mainly for fodder.

One of the dishes that is famous on the islands of both the Azores and Madeira is *Carne de vinha-d'alhos* (Pork in Wine and Garlic Sauce), which is traditionally served on Christmas Day, Boxing Day, and the day after. Another dish is *Bolo de Mel* (Walnut and Honey Cake). Tradition has it that the cake be prepared on the eighth of December, the feast of the Immaculate Conception, to be ready for Christmas festivities.

Almost all of the dishes of Portuguese cuisine have among their ingredients garlic and olive oil. The classical national dish *caldeirada*, is similar to the French *bouillabaisse* and is made from various types of fish and popular throughout the country. In the north, pork is the preferred meat. And dishes like *Carne de porco à alentejana* (Pork Alentejo Style) and goat meat roasted on skewers are found on dinner tables throughout the country. Portuguese cheeses are known throughout the world, such as *queijo do Alentejo* and *queijo da Serra da Estrela*, both made from goat milk. Finally, but not least, there are the famous sweets made from egg yolks and sugar by the nuns.

Stuffed Squid in Tomato Sauce

Lulas Recheadas
8 to 10 servings

S quid is a mollusk that is plentiful from Peniche, just north of Lisbon, to Sagres on the southern tip of the country. People from the Algarve, Portugal's sunny, southernmost province, have a special liking for dishes made with squid. This is one of my favorite dishes—squid stuffed and baked in a tomato and olive oil sauce. The best size squid to use for stuffing are about four inches in length. The larger ones tend to be tougher, take longer to cook, and are best used in caldeiradas (stews).

Stuffing these tiny sacs can be quite tedious, but the end result is well worth the effort. You can find squid cleaned and frozen in some super-markets and most Asian grocery stores. If you buy them fresh, wash carefully, removing the purplish skin that covers the body, leaving them completely white. Pull off the head and tentacles and remove the purplish skin from the larger suction cups. Save the tentacles. Remove the transparent cartilage that runs down the back of the sac. Clean out the sac and rinse well. Do not salt the squid while raw as they will become tough.

FILLING:

- 3 pounds small squid, cleaned (see above)
- 1 medium onion, minced
- ½ cup finely chopped lean ham (see note)
- ¼ cup chopped parsley
- ¼ teaspoon salt
- ⅛ teaspoon black pepper
- 1 tablespoon olive oil
- 3 egg yolks, or ⅓ cup egg substitute

FOR THE FILLING: Remove the fins from the sides of the squid sacs, chop the fins finely and place them in a measuring cup. Chop the tentacles finely and add to the fins to make 1 cup. In a small bowl, mix the chopped squid, onion, ham, parsley, salt, and pepper.

Heat the olive oil in a small skillet. Add the squid mixture and sauté for about 3 minutes or until the onions are soft. Remove the mixture from the heat and add the egg yolks. Mix well and cool for about 15 minutes.

(CONTINUED)

½ cup olive oil
½ cup white wine
3 tablespoons tomato paste
¼ teaspoon salt
¼ teaspoon black pepper

Preheat the oven to 350 degrees F. Stuff the squid sacs two-thirds full with the squid mixture and close each with a toothpick. Place the squid sacs in a nine by eleven inch baking dish in one layer.

FOR THE SAUCE: In a small bowl, blend together the olive oil, white wine, tomato paste, salt, and pepper. Pour over the squid and bake for 45 minutes.

Serve as an appetizer with toothpicks; with thick-cut French-fried potatoes for lunch; or with peas and potatoes cooked together, drained, and seasoned with a little of the squid sauce for dinner.

NOTE: Turkey ham or turkey pastrami can be substituted for pork ham in the filling.

Codfish Croquettes

Pastéis de Bacalhau
8 to 10 servings

O riginally this was a dish prepared and eaten exclusively in northern Portugal. Years ago these croquettes were served with rice, tomatoes, or greens. Nowadays they are usually served as part of a cocktail buffet or as a snack with afternoon tea and are enjoyed in all regions of Portugal as well as in most of the former colonies.

1 pound salt cod
12 ounces white potatoes
1 medium onion, chopped
4 cloves garlic, halved
2 eggs, separated
2 tablespoons minced
    parsley
1 tablespoon olive oil
1 teaspoon salt
¼ teaspoon black pepper
Vegetable oil for frying

Soak the salt cod in cold water to cover in the refrigerator for 24 hours, changing the water frequently.

Peel the potatoes, put in a medium pot, cover with water. Bring to a boil, and simmer for 20 minutes. Drain and cool.

Drain the salt cod, break into pieces, and remove any skin and bones. In a meat grinder or food processor, grind the salt cod, potatoes, onion, and garlic, and transfer to a large bowl. Add the egg yolks, parsley, olive oil, salt, and pepper; mix well with a wooden spoon until all the ingredients are incorporated and smooth. Beat the egg whites into firm peaks and fold them into the codfish mixture.

Pour the vegetable oil into a deep frying pan or heavy skillet to a depth of two inches. Heat it over medium-high heat to 365 degrees F on a deep-frying thermometer.

Shape the cod mixture into croquettes using two tablespoons for each, and fry in the hot oil until golden on all sides, about two minutes. Drain on absorbent paper towels. Arrange the croquettes on a serving platter and serve with toothpicks.

Sephardic Turnovers

Bourekas
Makes 20 turnovers

bourekas *belong to the rich food culture of the Sephardic Jews from Portugal. Expelled during the Inquisition, they took this dish to the four corners of the world.* Bourekas *are usually served on the Sabbath and festive occasions such as weddings, bar and bat mitzvahs, and in some countries on the evening preceding a circumcision. The Portuguese serve these turnovers for holiday breakfasts, afternoon teas, late suppers, or as part of an appetizer buffet. Almost anytime is perfect to enjoy these savory delights. They are often accompanied by olives, grapes, melon, cheese, and coffee or wine. Today, in many cafés in Lisbon, you will still find bourekas on the menu.*

DOUGH:

2½ cups all-purpose flour
1 teaspoon salt
½ cup shortening
2 eggs

FOR THE DOUGH: Sift the flour and salt together. Using a pastry blender or two knives, cut the shortening into the flour until it is the size of rice. Add 1 beaten egg and work it into the dough. Gradually add 2 tablespoons of water and mix the dough until it forms a ball and leaves the sides of the bowl. Cover with plastic wrap and let rest for 1½ hours.

Preheat the oven to 375 degrees F. Roll out the dough on a lightly floured board to one-eighth inch thickness. Cut into 3-inch rounds. Put a teaspoon of filling on each round and fold it over to form a half moon. Pinch the edges together to seal.

Beat the remaining egg and 1 teaspoon of water together. Brush the turnovers with this egg mixture. Place the turnovers on ungreased baking sheets and bake for 30 minutes or until golden. Serve at room temperature.

Fillings for Bourekas

POTATO AND CHEESE FILLING:

1 cup grated Monterey jack or Swiss cheese

¾ cup crumbled feta, farmer, or pot cheese

1 cup mashed potatoes

2 eggs, lightly beaten

½ teaspoon salt

SPINACH AND ONION FILLING:

3 tablespoons olive oil

1 medium onion, chopped

1 package (10-ounce) frozen chopped spinach, thawed and squeezed dry

½ cup finely chopped walnuts

¼ cup chopped fresh parsley

2 eggs, lightly beaten

½ teaspoon salt

POTATO AND CHEESE FILLING:

Combine all the ingredients and use as filling for *bourekas*.

SPINACH AND ONION FILLING:

Heat the olive oil in a large skillet over medium heat. Add the onion and sauté until translucent, about 5 minutes. Let cool. Stir in the remaining ingredients and use as filling for *bourekas*.

Black-Eyed Pea Salad

Salada de Feijão Frade
6 to 8 servings

his hearty salad is popular along the western coast of Portugal and, according to legend, originated in the historic town of Óbidos, about twenty miles north of Lisbon. The Moors occupied much of this area between the seventh and fifteenth centuries and left their mark on the culture and cuisine. This salad is a nice accompaniment for Codfish Croquettes (page 9), grilled sardines, or Minced Meat Croquettes (page 273).

2 cups dried black-eyed peas, washed and sorted
6 whole cloves
2 yellow onions (1 whole, 1 chopped)
5 tablespoons olive oil
½ cup chopped fresh parsley or coriander
2 tablespoons cider vinegar
Salt and black pepper to taste
1 hard-boiled egg, finely chopped

rinse the black-eyed peas and refrigerate them in water to cover for 2 hours. Drain the peas; put them in a large saucepan, add 6 cups of cold water, and place over medium heat. Stick the cloves into the whole onion and add to the pot. Add 1 tablespoon of the olive oil, stir, and cook, covered, for 1 hour and 15 minutes.

Drain the peas and pour them into a heatproof serving bowl. Season with the chopped onion, remaining 4 tablespoons of olive oil, parsley, vinegar, salt, and pepper. Mix well, cover, and marinate in the refrigerator for 6 hours or overnight. To serve, sprinkle chopped egg over all.

NOTE: I sometimes substitute fresh coriander for the parsley—it enhances the flavor.

Portuguese Salad

Salada à Portuguesa
4 servings

although there are other salads that are considered national treasures, this is the one you will find served with grilled sardines at outdoor cafés in the Alfama district of Lisbon. Alfama is one of the three Lisbon neighborhoods that was not destroyed by the earthquake of 1755, and thus retains much of its historic charm. This part of the city has quaint, narrow cobblestone streets, fado nightclubs, and houses the traditional Moorish and Jewish quarters.

1 large cucumber
1 tablespoon kosher salt
2 green bell peppers
4 medium tomatoes
2 medium white onions
½ cup olive oil
2 tablespoons white wine
    vinegar
1 teaspoon salt

preheat the broiler. Bring a medium pot of water to a boil.

Peel the cucumber, leaving thin stripes of the peel lengthwise down the cucumber. (This makes it more digestible.) Cut the cucumber crosswise into ¼-inch slices. Place the slices in a colander and sprinkle with the kosher salt; let drain for 20 minutes.

Roast the peppers under the broiler until blackened, turning them often. Remove the blackened skin and seeds, and slice the peppers into circles. Rinse the salt from the cucumbers and place them in a salad bowl along with the peppers.

Scald the tomatoes by dipping them in the boiling water, then peel off the skins. Cut the tomatoes lengthwise into circles and add them to the cucumbers. Peel the onions and slice them very thinly; add to the salad bowl. Beat the olive oil, wine vinegar, and table salt together. Pour over the vegetables and toss. Serve with grilled sardines or fish.

Chickpea and Salt Cod Salad

Meia-Desfeita
4 appetizer servings

meia-desfeita *comes from the Estremadura region of Portugal, which runs north along the coast from Lisbon to the little fishing village of Nazaré. Meia-desfeita translates literally as "half an insult." The half of this dish that is an insult is the inclusion of the chickpeas which, according to legend, remind the Portuguese of the Moorish invasion. Another belief is that the dish originated in the nineteenth century in Lisbon in one of the old restaurants called João do Grão. The name for the dish comes from the fact that the cliental asked for "half an order" or "meia (dose) de desfeita."*

1 pound salt cod
1 cup dried chickpeas,
  washed and sorted
1 cup olive oil
1 medium onion, chopped
¼ cup chopped fresh parsley
3 large garlic cloves,
  minced
2 tablespoons white vinegar
½ teaspoon salt
¼ teaspoon black pepper
3 large hard-boiled eggs
½ teaspoon paprika

Soak the cod in cold water to cover for 24 hours in the refrigerator, changing the water frequently.

Refrigerate the chickpeas overnight or for 6 hours in cold water to cover. Rinse the chickpeas and place them in a medium pot with ¼ cup of the olive oil and eight cups cold water. Bring to a boil, reduce the heat, and simmer for about 2 hours. Drain.

Preheat the oven to 350 degrees F. Meanwhile, remove the salt cod from the water. Remove any skin and bones and divide the cod into 4 equal pieces. Place them in a large skillet and add water to barely cover. Simmer the fish about 10 minutes.

Place the cod in an ovenproof dish and top with the chickpeas. Sprinkle the onion, parsley, and garlic on top. Mix together the remaining ¾ cup olive oil, the vinegar, salt, and pepper and pour over the salad. Decorate with hard-boiled egg slices (use only white if you wish) and sprinkle with paprika. Cover the dish and bake for 30 minutes. Serve warm.

Azorean Fish Salad

Salada de Peixe Açoreana
4 appetizer servings

t he waters around the Azores abound with a variety of fish, such as mackerel, cod, limpets, swordfish, tuna, bass, and many types of shellfish. This recipe calls for a pound of an assortment of fish. You can use all of the above-named fish or just one or two. This appetizer recipe can be doubled for a main course.

4 medium white potatoes, peeled
2 medium carrots, peeled
8 ounces string beans
2 teaspoons salt
1 pound fish steaks or fillets
¼ cup olive oil
½ teaspoon black pepper
4 to 8 Romaine lettuce leaves
2 hard-boiled eggs, sliced
½ cup sliced black olives

p lace the potatoes, carrots, and string beans in a large pot and barely cover with water. Add one teaspoon of the salt, bring to a boil, and cook for 10 minutes. Add the fish steaks and continue to cook until the fish flakes easily, about 10 minutes.

Remove the fish and vegetables. Cube the potatoes and carrots and cut the green beans into 2-inch pieces; place the vegetables in a bowl and set aside. Remove the skin and bones from the fish and flake. Add the fish to the bowl with the vegetables. Drizzle with olive oil, sprinkle with the remaining salt and the pepper and toss.

Spread the lettuce leaves on a serving platter. Mound the salad on the lettuce leaves and decorate with the hard-boiled egg slices and olives.

Eggs in Cotton

Ovos em Algodão
4 servings

t his dish is as popular in Portugal as it is in the Luso-American community of southern New England. It is usually served as a light meal for brunch, lunch, or an early supper. The cotton in the title refers to the baked egg whites that look like cottonballs.

WHITE SAUCE:
2 tablespoons butter
3 tablespoons flour
1½ cups cold milk
Salt and black pepper to
taste

EGGS:
4 eggs
1 teaspoon butter or
margarine
4 slices buttered toast
4 teaspoons grated
Parmesan cheese
½ teaspoon paprika
Salt and black pepper to
taste

FOR THE WHITE SAUCE: Melt the butter in a medium saucepan. Add the flour and cook for about 2 minutes, stirring constantly. Slowly pour the milk into the saucepan, stirring, until the sauce thickens. Add salt and pepper to taste.

FOR THE EGGS: Preheat the oven to 350 degrees F. Separate the eggs, being careful not to break the yolks. Place the yolks into a separate bowl. Beat the whites until very stiff. Grease a baking sheet with the butter. Heap 4 mounds of egg whites onto the baking sheet. Make an indentation with a tablespoon in each mound. Place a yolk in each indentation. Bake for 20 minutes until the yolks are cooked and the whites are firm.

Place a slice of toast on each plate and pour ¼ cup of the sauce over each slice. Place an egg mound on top and pour the rest of the sauce over the egg. Sprinkle with the grated cheese, paprika, salt, and pepper. Serve immediately.

Green Eggs

t his is not the recipe from Dr. Seuss's Green Eggs and Ham. *Even though* ovos verdes *originated in the Middle East, Portugal has claimed the dish as its own. The original recipe (and my preference) calls for olive oil, but some cooks substitute butter.*

10 eggs
¼ cup chopped fresh parsley
2 tablespoons olive oil
2 teaspoons lemon juice
1 teaspoon Dijon mustard
½ teaspoon salt
¼ teaspoon white pepper
Oil for frying
Flour for dusting
2 bunches watercress
½ cup mayonnaise

h ard-boil 8 of the eggs; place them under cold running water and store in the refrigerator to cool.

Peel the hard-boiled eggs and halve lengthwise. Remove the yolks and place them in a small bowl. Add the chopped parsley, olive oil, lemon juice, mustard, salt, and pepper. Mix well and re-stuff the egg whites with the yolk mixture, mounding the filling to resemble a whole egg.

Pour the oil into a deep fry pan or heavy skillet to a depth of two inches. Heat it over medium high heat to 365 degrees F on a deep-frying thermometer.

Beat the remaining 2 eggs until frothy. Dip the filled egg halves in the beaten eggs, then roll them in the flour and dip again in the beaten eggs.

Fry the eggs in the hot oil, a few at a time, until golden, about 2 minutes. Remove and drain on absorbent paper. Serve the fried eggs on a bed of watercress that has been topped with the mayonnaise.

Salt Cod Omelet with Tomato Sauce

Omeleta de Bacalhau com Tomate
4 servings

*t*his is yet another of the fabled 365 ways to prepare salt cod. Serve this omelet, along with a green salad and rolls, for lunch or a light supper.

8 ounces salt cod
4 cups boiling water
6 tablespoons butter
1 onion, minced
2 tablespoons tomato
    sauce
2 tablespoons chopped
    fresh parsley
¼ teaspoon black pepper
¼ teaspoon salt
12 eggs
4 tablespoons whole milk

Soak the salt cod in cold water to cover for 24 hours, changing the water frequently. Drain; remove the skin and bones. Place the salt cod in a large dish or pot. Pour boiling water over the fish to cover completely. Cover the dish and let stand for 15 minutes to cook the fish. Pour off the water, cool, and flake.

In a large skillet, place 2 tablespoons of the butter and the onion. Sauté the onion until golden. Add the tomato sauce, parsley, pepper, and salt, and simmer for 12 minutes. Add the salt cod and stir for about 2 minutes.

Whisk together 6 of the eggs and 2 tablespoons of the milk. Heat 2 tablespoons of the butter in a large skillet. Pour the egg mixture into the skillet and cook over medium heat. When the omelet is almost set, add half of the codfish mixture and fold the omelet over. Cook until the omelet is done to your liking. Repeat with the remaining ingredients for a second omelet. Cut each omelet in half and serve warm.

Eggs with Navy Beans and Beef

Ovos com Feijão Pérola e Picado

5 to 6 servings

*t*his is a traditional recipe from the city of Abrantes in the Beira Litoral region of Portugal. It is typically served as a substantial lunch accompanied by a good regional red wine. There are some who fry the eggs separately in olive oil and then place them in the dish. The dish is then heated in the oven for five minutes.

2 cups (1 pound) navy beans
1 pound cooked roast beef and juice
1 large onion, chopped
2 tablespoons butter
½ cup plus 3 tablespoons fresh bread crumbs
½ cup milk
½ cup chopped fresh parsley
½ cup olive oil
10 to 12 eggs
1 teaspoon salt
¼ teaspoon black pepper

*r*efrigerate the beans overnight or for 6 hours in cold water to cover. The following day, drain the beans; cover with fresh cold water, place over medium heat, and bring to a boil. Reduce the heat and simmer for 2 hours or until tender. Drain and set aside.

Grind the roast beef in a meat grinder or food processor and place in a large bowl. In a medium skillet, sauté the onion in the butter until translucent and add to the ground beef. Soak the ½ cup of bread crumbs in the milk. Add to the meat with the parsley.

Heat ¼ cup of the olive oil in a large skillet and sauté the beef mixture, adding any juice from the roast as needed to moisten.

Heat the oven to 350 degrees F. Spread one-third of the beans over the bottom of a 9 x 11-inch greased baking dish. Top with half of the ground meat mixture. Spread one-third of the beans over the ground meat, then a layer of the meat mixture, and top with the remaining beans.

Pour the remaining ¼ cup olive oil over the beans and make 10 to 12 indentations in the mixture with a large spoon. Carefully break the eggs, one at a time, into each indentation. Sprinkle the whites of the eggs with salt and pepper. Place the dish in the oven and bake for 15 minutes. Sprinkle the remaining 3 tablespoons bread crumbs over the top and bake 5 minutes longer, until the eggs are cooked.

Azorean Holy Ghost Soup

Sopa do Espírito Santo
10 to 12 servings

during Easter week, church members traditionally offer this soup to the poor, who are allowed to keep the bowl in which the soup is served. Inscribed on the bowls is Em Louvor do Divino, which translates as "In Praise of the Lord." The original recipe calls for the meats and vegetables to be cooked together. More recently, however, Azorean cooks tend to prepare the onions, red peppers, and cabbage separately, and to add other vegetables like carrots, collards, and potatoes. Some cooks even add pork sausages (chouriço). For dessert after this soup, I usually serve the traditional Rice Pudding (page 49).

2 tablespoons olive oil
4 pound beef bottom round rump roast
2 medium onions, quartered
4 cloves garlic, crushed
2 small, dried chili peppers
1 sprig mint
1 cinnamon stick
1 bay leaf
1 teaspoon salt
2 pounds beef bones for soup
2 chickens (3 to 4 pounds each), or parts
1 medium cabbage, quartered
1 day-old loaf French-style bread
¼ cup fresh mint leaves
1 tablespoon ground cinnamon

heat the olive oil in a very large soup pot. Add the beef roast and brown on all sides. Add 2 cups of water to the pot and simmer for 5 minutes or until the liquid is reduced to 1 cup. Pour off the liquid from the pot and save.

Place the onions, garlic, chili peppers, mint sprig, cinnamon stick, and bay leaf in a piece of cheesecloth and tie with a string. Pour 3 quarts of water over the beef and add the salt. Lower the cheesecloth sack into the water and bring to a boil. When the water begins to boil, add the beef bones, reduce the heat, cover, and simmer for 1 to 1½ hours.

Add the chickens and cook for another 45 minutes.

When the beef is tender, add the cabbage and simmer for another 30 minutes.

Remove the beef from the pot and place it in the center of a large platter. Slice the beef into ⅛-inch-thick slices. Cut each chicken into 8 pieces and arrange around the beef. Place the cabbage in a separate large serving bowl.

Cut the bread lengthwise in half and then cut each half crosswise into 6 equal pieces. Place the bread pieces in a large, deep dish, cut side up. Sprinkle the mint leaves and ground cinnamon over the bread.

Add the 1 cup of reserved broth to the soup pot, mix well and simmer for 5 minutes. Pour the broth over the bread, cover, and let stand for 3 minutes.

Each guest should have a large, deep soup dish, into which is placed cabbage, chicken, and beef. Then top all with a ladleful of bread and broth. Some cooks, however, prefer to serve the broth first and then have the meat and vegetables as a main course.

NOTE: Reducing the liquid from the browned roast will give you a richer broth for the soup.

Collard Green Soup

Caldo Verde

4 to 6 servings

C aldo Verde, *considered Portugal's signature soup, is served in clay mugs with a slice of chouriço, a custom as remote as the time when spoons didn't exist and mugs were used to drink soup. It originated in the northern province of Minho and is said to reproduce the emerald color of the countryside. The green is provided by* couve galega, *a type of cabbage similar to collards that has large, flat green leaves. The* couve galega, *or collards, must be finely shredded to look like mounds of grass. Tender spring greens, when in season, can be substituted for the collards. In Portugal,* caldo verde *is traditionally served as a first course with slices of corn bread.*

1 pound Yukon potatoes, peeled and cubed
1 onion, chopped
2 cloves garlic, smashed
1 tablespoon salt
2 pounds collard greens
¾ cup olive oil
1 pound cooked chouriço, sliced ½-inch thick

b ring 2 quarts of water, the potatoes, onion, garlic, and salt to a boil in a large pot. Simmer until the potatoes are tender, about 15 minutes.

Meanwhile, wash the greens and remove the center stems. Stack the greens, roll tightly like a cigar, and slice as thinly as possible. Set aside.

Remove the potatoes, onions, and garlic from the broth. Mash well or place in a food processor, adding a little liquid to form a purée. Return the potato mixture to the broth; add the olive oil and the greens. Return the broth to a boil, reduce the heat, and simmer uncovered for only 5 minutes so as to maintain the bright green color.

In each soup bowl, place 2 slices of sausage. Pour the soup over the sausages and serve with African Corn Bread (page 317) or Peasant Corn Bread (page 47).

Bread and Cilantro Soup from the Alentejo Region

Sopa de Coentros à Alentejana
4 servings

this dish was originally created to provide peasant workers with a hearty noon meal and was made with bread, eggs, potatoes, and garlic. Today it is made with olive oil, fresh coriander, and eggs, and is enjoyed by rich and poor alike. This soup represents the best of Alentejo cuisine.

1 day-old round loaf whole wheat or multigrain bread
1 cup fresh cilantro, coarsely chopped
8 cups chicken broth, or 8 cups water with 1 teaspoon salt
4 eggs
½ cup olive oil

tear or cut the bread into large pieces and place them in a soup terrine. Sprinkle the cilantro over the bread.

Heat the chicken broth (or water with salt) to a simmer. Break the eggs, one at a time, into a saucer and carefully slide each into the simmering broth. Poach the eggs for about 3 minutes or until they are set. Remove the eggs one at a time and carefully set aside. Add the olive oil to the broth and bring to a boil. Pour the broth over the bread. Cover and let stand for 5 minutes. Using a ladle, spoon the soup into 4 bowls and top each serving with a poached egg.

NOTE: You can substitute beef or fish broth for the chicken broth. The original recipe calls for the eggs to be poached in the tureen. To do that, slide the raw eggs on top of the bread; heat the broth to boiling and pour carefully over the bread so as not to break the yolks. Cover and let stand for 5 minutes. This method is a little more difficult than poaching the eggs first, but worth a try.

Seafood and Bread Soup

Açorda de Mariscos
4 to 6 servings

a çordas *are bread-based soups originally from the Alentejo region of Portugal. Even though this particular type of açorda doesn't have a long history—only about fifty years—it has become a part of Portugal's typical cuisine. This recipe from the town of Ericeira won first prize in a cooking contest at the Pinta dos Mariscos, a three-star restaurant. It also won "The Best Dish at the Best Price," in the 1960s. In the Alentejo, this soup is a complete meal. Açorda made with just shrimp is very popular in Lisbon.*

1 pound medium raw
   shrimp
1 pound littleneck clams,
   scrubbed
1 pound mussels, well
   scrubbed and de-bearded
1 pound day-old peasant-
   style bread
¼ cup olive oil
3 cloves garlic, minced
6 egg yolks
¼ cup fresh cilantro leaves
1 teaspoon salt
¼ teaspoon black pepper
Piripiri or hot pepper
   sauce to taste

C ook the shrimp in water to cover until they turn pink. Remove the shrimp, peel, and set aside. Save the liquid.

Place the clams and mussels in a large skillet, add 2 cups of water, and simmer until the shells open. Discard any that do not open. Save the liquid.

Pour the liquid from the shrimp, clams, and mussels into a pot (there should be about 5 cups). Heat the liquid until warm. Break the bread into rough cubes and add to the liquid.

Heat the olive oil in a saucepan and sauté the garlic until soft. Add the olive oil and garlic to the soup and bring to a boil. Add the yolks and stir quickly to cook and incorporate. Add half of the seafood and season with half the cilantro leaves, the salt, and pepper.

Remove the pan from the heat and add the rest of the seafood and coriander leaves. Season the soup with the hot sauce to taste. Mix well and serve immediately.

Fried Pumpkin, Eggplant, and Parsnips

Abobora, Beringelas, e Xerovias Fritas

4 side-dish servings

these fried vegetables are especially prized in Portugal's Beira Baixa region, which borders Spain's western frontier. Parsnips are native to this area and are very much a part of the local diet. In taste, it is like a mixture of carrots and turnips but stronger. Because of its characteristic features, it is usually boiled in salted water before being dipped in the batter. The Portuguese word abobora refers to both squash and pumpkin. Since squash is more readily available, I have used it in this recipe. But fresh pumpkin, in season, is also good. This tasty side dish goes well with fried or grilled fish or chicken.

1 (2-pound) butternut squash or pumpkin
1 medium eggplant, long and narrow
2 large parsnips
2 teaspoons salt
1 cup all-purpose flour
1 egg, or ¼ cup egg substitute
Olive oil for frying

Peel the squash and cut in half lengthwise, remove the seeds, and cut each half into ¼-inch slices crosswise. Cut the eggplant in ¼-inch round slices. Peel the parsnips and cut into ¼-inch slices lengthwise. Place all the vegetables in a bowl of cold water to cover with 1 teaspoon of the salt. Cover and refrigerate until the following day.

Remove the vegetables from the water, drain, and dry with paper towels. Bring 8 cups of water to a boil in a large pot. Add the parsnips and cook for about 10 minutes. Drain and set aside to cool.

Preheat the oven to 250 degrees F. Beat together the flour, egg, ½ cup water and remaining 1 teaspoon salt to make a batter. If the batter is too thick, add a tablespoon of water. Pour the olive oil into a medium skillet to the depth of two inches. Heat it over medium-high heat to 365 degrees F on a deep-frying thermometer. Dip the vegetables into the batter and fry in small batches until golden. Drain on several layers of paper towels. Keep warm in the oven, uncovered, while you fry the rest of the vegetables. Serve hot or at room temperature with grilled or roasted meats.

Fried White Cornmeal, Madeira-Style

Milho Frito
4 to 6 side-dish servings

Y ears ago, this dish was the staple of the rural population of
Madeira and was eaten with slices of cooked onion. Today it
often serves as a side dish for Swordfish in Wine Sauce (page
34). Cooks often prepare large quantities of this dish so that leftovers
are always on hand for frying at a moment's notice. In Madeira, fresh
fava beans are sometimes substituted for the collard greens. For this
variation, during the last five minutes, add cooked, finely chopped
fava beans to the cornmeal mixture and continue with the recipe. Serve
with grilled meats or Fried Pork with Clams, Mariner's-Style (page 43)
for a holiday treat.

1½ cups white cornmeal
2 tablespoons margarine
1 teaspoon salt
1 cup firmly packed, finely
    minced collard greens
Vegetable oil for frying

d issolve ¾ cup of the cornmeal in a large saucepan with 5 cups cold water. Add the margarine
and salt and place over medium heat. Bring to a boil
and add the collards; stir well. Return to a boil and
cook for about 10 minutes, stirring occasionally.

Add the remaining ¾ cup of the cornmeal in a slow
but steady stream, whisking briskly. Reduce the heat
to a simmer and cook, uncovered, about 20 minutes,
stirring often until the mixture thickens. Pour the
mixture into a buttered 9 x 13-inch baking dish and
let it cool to room temperature. Cover and refrigerate for 4 hours or overnight.

Turn the chilled cornmeal out onto a board and cut
into 2-inch squares. Pour the oil into a medium skillet to the depth of two inches. Heat it over medium-
high heat to 365 degrees F on a deep-frying
thermometer. Fry the cornmeal squares in batches
of 3 or 4, being sure not to crowd them, until
golden on all sides. Drain on paper towels.

Smashed Potatoes

Batatas à Murro
4 to 6 side-dish servings

Several years ago, I saw this dish on the menu of the Torre restaurant located on the north bank of the Tagus River near the town of Oeiras, about ten miles west of Lisbon. The name of the dish so intrigued me that I felt compelled to order it. The name derives from the fact that originally, cooks prepared the roasted potatoes by smashing them with their fists after roasting them over coals. Today, most prefer to roast them in the oven and use a wooden mallet to achieve the desired result. Be sure to choose potatoes that are even in size. Serve with grilled salt cod, roast pork, or beef.

2 pounds small, round
  white potatoes
2 tablespoons kosher or
  sea salt
¾ cup olive oil
6 cloves garlic, crushed

Preheat the oven to 400 degrees F.

Wash the potatoes and scrub with a brush. Dry them and roll in the salt. Place in a clay roasting pot or baking pan and bake for 15 minutes, or until tender.

Heat the olive oil with the garlic in a small saucepan over medium heat. Remove the potatoes from the oven, and when ready to serve, use the side of a mallet or your fist to smack each potato lightly to split it open. Pour the warm garlic oil over the potatoes.

Puréed Turnip Greens

Esparregado
2 to 4 side-dish servings

e sparregado, *which originated in Portugal, has traveled to all of the Portuguese-speaking countries and territories and is favored as an accompaniment to roast leg of goat or pork. In Guinea-Bissau, it is served with Guinean Fish Stew (page 229), and in East Timor it is served with Boneless Stuffed Chicken (page 184).*

2 pounds turnip greens
8 cups boiling water
1 teaspoon kosher or sea
    salt
½ cup olive oil
3 cloves garlic, halved
2 slices whole wheat bread,
    cut into 1-inch strips
2 tablespoons whole wheat
    flour
3 tablespoons lemon juice
    or vinegar
2 hard-boiled eggs

r emove the stems from the turnip greens and place them in a large pot with the boiling water and salt. Keep the greens submerged and cook uncovered over medium heat until the greens are tender, about 15 minutes. Drain in a colander and rinse with cold water. Squeeze dry. Place the leaves on a board and chop finely or place them in a food processor and process until they resemble a purée.

In a large skillet, over medium heat, place the oil and garlic. When the garlic begins to sizzle, add the bread strips and fry until golden on all sides. Remove the bread strips and keep warm.

Remove the garlic from the oil and add the greens to the oil. Mix well but do not let them fry. Sprinkle with the flour, mix well, and cook the greens for 5 minutes. Sprinkle with the lemon juice and place on a platter. Decorate with sliced hard-boiled eggs and the bread strips, and serve.

St. John's Tuna

Atum de São João
4 to 6 servings

St. John's Day falls on June 24th, right after Midsummer Night. Although celebrated in Portugal and elsewhere in the Portuguese-speaking world, St. John's Day is especially popular in Brazil and on the island of Madeira. According to Catholic folk belief, John the Baptist is the "marrying saint." Traditionally, on St. John's Day night, the young, unmarried women hold hands while they dance around bonfires and sing: "Bring me a bridegroom, St. John, bring me a bridegroom, bring me a bridegroom so that I may be wed." It is also traditional to celebrate St. John's Day by eating corn prepared in a variety of ways, from the traditional Brazilian canjica and green corn soufflé, to the typical corn-on-the-cob roasted over a bonfire.

In Madeira, island cooks combine tuna with corn and other vegetables to create this very special St. John's Day dish. After eating this meal, diners often walk down to the docks to look for their shadows reflected in the water. Seeing their shadows guarantees at least another year of life.

1 whole tuna loin (2 to 3 pounds), or 4 to 6 tuna steaks
4 large cloves garlic, minced
1 tablespoon chopped fresh oregano
1 teaspoon kosher or sea salt
4 to 6 medium onions, peeled
1 pound pole beans, ends trimmed
4 to 6 medium sweet potatoes, peeled
4 to 6 medium white potatoes, peeled
4 to 6 ears corn, shucked
¾ cup olive oil
¼ cup white vinegar

Two days prior to preparing this dish, place the tuna in a glass dish and score the flesh 3 times on top and bottom. Press the garlic, oregano and salt well into the meat. Cover and place in the refrigerator, turning once each day.

Remove the tuna from the dish and place in a large pot. Add 4 cups of water. Place the pot on medium heat and add the onions and beans. Simmer for 20 minutes or until beans are tender.

In another pot, cook the sweet and white potatoes in water to cover for 10 minutes. Add the ears of corn to the potatoes and cook an additional 10 minutes or until the potatoes are tender.

(CONTINUED)

Remove the tuna from the pot and place it in the center of a large warm platter. Drain the vegetables and place them around the tuna. Combine the oil and vinegar by stirring with a whisk and drizzle over the tuna and vegetables. Carve the tuna into slices as you would a roast beef. Each person takes a slice, some vegetables, and a little of the vinaigrette. Despite the fact that this is a fish dish, a good red, not white, is the wine of choice in Portugal.

NOTE: This dish can also be served with a cucumber, tomato, and sliced onion salad drizzled with vinegar and olive oil. St. John's Tuna is also served for lunch on Good Friday. On this occasion, yams are substituted for the beans and corn cobs.

Salt Cod and Potato Casserole

Bacalhau à Gomes de Sá
8 to 10 servings

there are several versions of this very popular Portuguese dish. However, this recipe is the original one that Mr. Gomes de Sá Jr. offered to the owner of the Lisbonense Restaurant in the city of Porto. Gomes de Sá was a fishmonger who supplied the restaurant with codfish. The chef of the restaurant prepared this dish for him on many occasions and finally named it after him. The dish became a local favorite as word spread about this wonderful combination. Soaking the cod in warm milk is the secret behind its mild and incomparable flavor. Many Portuguese cooks prepare this dish a day or two before, refrigerate it to let the flavors meld, and reheat the day it's to be served.

2 pounds salt cod
8 cups boiling water
2 cups hot milk
¾ cup olive oil
8 cloves garlic, minced
4 medium onions, sliced thin
2 pounds medium Yukon or new potatoes, boiled, peeled, and sliced thin
4 hard-boiled eggs, quartered
1 cup whole, small, black pitted olives
¼ cup minced fresh parsley

In a large bowl, soak the salt cod in cold water to cover for 24 hours in the refrigerator, changing the water frequently. Drain the cod and place in a deep pot. Pour the boiling water over the cod, cover, and let sit for 15 minutes. Drain the cod; remove the skin and bones. Flake and return it to the large bowl. Pour the hot milk over the fish to cover and let stand for 1 hour, covered.

Preheat the oven to 400 degrees F. Heat the olive oil in a large skillet over medium heat and sauté the garlic and onions. Stir occasionally and remove from the heat when the onions are translucent.

In an ovenproof casserole, place one-third of the sliced potatoes, top with one-third of the codfish, followed by one-third of the onions. Repeat the layering, ending with the onions. Decorate with the egg wedges, black olives, and parsley. Pour any remaining olive oil over the eggs and olives. Cover and bake for 30 minutes or until the dish begins to bubble. Let the dish cool for at least 30 minutes before serving.

Grilled Sardines

Sardinhas Assadas na Brasa
4 to 6 servings

according to James Beard, *"There is no one fish called a sardine."*
*The name probably came from the fact that these small fish with
weak bones were first canned in oil on the island of Sardinia. In
the Mediterranean the pilchard is used, and in Norway it's the brisling.
In Portugal, sardines are quite a bit larger than the canned variety
commonly found in the United States. This recipe is for fresh sardines,
abundant in Portugal's offshore waters. Fresh sardines can be grilled,
fried, stuffed, or baked. The traditional preparation is to grill them
over coals along with green tomatoes.*

24 (6- to 8-inch) fresh or
    frozen sardines (see note)
1 tablespoon kosher salt
2 pounds Yukon potatoes
6 green bell peppers
12 medium tomatoes
2 medium onions
1 cup olive oil
¼ cup white wine vinegar
1 teaspoon salt
½ tablespoon black pepper

preheat the coals in a grill until they turn white.

Scale the sardines and wash in salted water. Sprinkle them with the kosher salt and set aside for 1 hour.

Meanwhile, cook the potatoes in water to cover for 15 minutes or until tender; peel, slice, and keep warm. Wash the bell peppers, dry them, and grill over hot coals until blackened; peel and cut into strips. Peel the tomatoes and onions and cut into thin slices. Beat together the olive oil, vinegar, salt, and pepper. Set aside.

Rinse the sardines; pat dry, and place on the grill for about 4 minutes on each side. Serve the sardines accompanied with the bell pepper, potatoes, and a salad of tomatoes and onions, all drizzled with the vinaigrette.

NOTE: Fresh sardines are difficult to find in this country, but many specialty shops and supermarkets sell packages of frozen sardines. The ones measuring 6 to 8 inches long are the tastiest.

French fries can be substituted for the boiled potatoes.

Christmas Eve Codfish

Bacalhau da Consoada
6 to 8 servings

C odfish prepared for the consoada *(the traditional Christmas Eve dinner) is an alternative to the codfish cooked with todos (literally "all"), which is traditionally served for supper on December 25. This particular recipe, besides being very enticing, appeals to those who like their codfish served in large pieces. In some homes it is served as a second course, preceded by boiled crabs, shrimp, and lobster, and followed by roast turkey or Roast Suckling Pig (page 44) and the trimmings.*

2 pounds thick salt
   cod fillets
6 medium onions, peeled
6 carrots, peeled
2 pounds medium white
   potatoes, peeled
3 pounds collard greens,
   stems removed
1 teaspoon salt
1 cup olive oil
8 cloves garlic, smashed
6 to 8 hard-boiled eggs
   (1 per person)

S oak the salt cod fillets in cold water to cover for 24 hours in the refrigerator, changing the water frequently.

Drain the salt cod and place in a large pot with the onions, carrots, potatoes, greens, and salt. Cook over medium heat until the vegetables are tender, about 30 minutes.

Heat the olive oil in a small saucepan and sauté the garlic cloves until lightly golden. Keep warm.

Arrange the codfish, onions, carrots, potatoes, collards, and eggs on a large platter or several platters. Serve the warm olive oil with garlic in a bowl on the side to drizzle over the fish and vegetables.

Swordfish in Wine Sauce

Espada de Vinho-d'alhos
4 servings

this is a very popular way to prepare fish on the Madeira Islands. It is quick and easy. Serve with Fried White Cornmeal, Madeira-Style (page 26) or white potatoes cooked with onions.

4 thick swordfish steaks
   (6 ounces each)
4 cloves garlic, crushed
1 teaspoon salt
¼ teaspoon black pepper
1 bay leaf
1 large tomato, chopped
⅔ cup white wine or
   vinegar
1 cup all-purpose flour
¼ cup olive oil

place the swordfish in a glass dish and season with the garlic, salt, pepper, and bay leaf. Set aside for ½ hour. Sprinkle the swordfish with the tomato and wine and marinate for ½ hour.

Place the flour in a shallow dish. Remove the swordfish from the marinade and flour each piece lightly.

Heat the olive oil in a large skillet and fry the swordfish until golden, about 4 minutes on each side. Remove to a warm platter. Add the marinade to the skillet and bring to a boil. Pour the marinade over the swordfish and serve immediately.

Mussel and Vegetable Kabobs

Espetadas de Mexilhão
4 servings

according to legend, this dish originated about 200 years ago in Cascais, a picturesque fishing village located just west of Lisbon where the Tagus River empties into the Atlantic Ocean. I learned how to prepare this dish in 1970 while living in Nova Oeiras, a town along the coast not far from Cascais. What follows is my adaptation of a recipe given to me by Mrs. Santos Pinto.

16 large mussels
1 cup olive oil
3 cloves garlic, minced
Salt and black pepper to
    taste
8 slices bacon, halved
2 firm tomatoes, quartered,
    or 8 cherry tomatoes
2 medium green bell
    peppers, quartered
    and seeded
4 large Romaine lettuce
    leaves

SAUCE *VILÃO*:
    (makes 1 cup)
1 medium onion, quartered
¼ cup fresh parsley leaves
3 cloves garlic
2 hard-boiled eggs
1 cup olive oil (see note)
¼ cup white vinegar
½ teaspoon salt
¼ teaspoon black pepper

preheat a gas grill or heat coals until white hot. Wash and scrub the mussels in their shells and remove the beards. Place the mussels in a large skillet with the olive oil, garlic, salt, and pepper. Sauté the mussels; as they open, remove from the pan and set aside; save the oil. Discard any mussels that do not open. Remove the mussels from their shells and wrap a half slice of bacon around each one. On each of 4 medium skewers, place 1 mussel, ¼ tomato, another mussel, and ¼ bell pepper. Repeat until there are 4 mussels on each skewer.

PREPARE THE SAUCE: Mince the onion, parsley, and garlic in a food processor or blender. Mash the egg yolks and add to the mixture. Beat the oil and vinegar together in a small bowl. Add the salt, pepper, and onion mixture. Blend well.

Grill the kabobs, turning until the bacon is crisp and the tomatoes and peppers are cooked. Serve the skewers over lettuce leaves with the sauce and rice.

NOTE: Instead of using 1 cup olive oil for the sauce, you can strain the oil from cooking the mussels, cool it, and then add more oil, if needed, to make 1 cup.

Clams, Mariner's-Style

Amêijoas à Marinheira
4 to 6 servings

*t*his dish is very popular in the Ribatejo region of Portugal. It can be served with a simple omelet or with fried and marinated pork cubes (see Fried Pork with Clams, Mariner's-Style, page 43). Begin preparation of this dish at least twelve hours before serving.

4 pounds littleneck clams
4 tablespoons cornmeal
4 teaspoons salt
½ cup olive oil
2 medium onions, thinly
    sliced
4 cloves garlic, smashed
4 large ripe tomatoes,
    peeled, seeded, and
    chopped
1 tablespoon all-purpose
    flour
½ teaspoon black pepper
1 cup minced fresh parsley

Wash the clams well and scrub with a brush. Place the clams in a pot with water to cover. Add the cornmeal and salt. Refrigerate for 10 hours. This will whiten the shells and give the clams a sweeter taste.

In a large heavy pot, heat the olive oil and add the onion slices and garlic. Sauté over medium heat until the garlic is lightly browned. Remove the garlic. Add the tomatoes, flour, and pepper and continue cooking over medium-low heat until the vegetables are tender.

Remove the clams from the water and rinse well. Place the clams over the tomatoes, cover, and cook for about 10 minutes. Remove any clams that don't open. Sprinkle the parsley over the clams and season to taste with salt and pepper. Let simmer for 1 minute. Serve with fried marinated pork cubes, or remove the shells and serve the clams over scrambled eggs.

Rice with Chicken, Minho-Style

Arroz com Frango à Moda do Minho
6 to 8 servings

t his recipe dates back to the seventeenth century and is often a
menu item at weddings in the northern region of Minho. It is also
similar to the dish that the Portuguese introduced to Macao called
Fat Rice (page 254), which calls for chicken, sausage, and other meats.

1 fryer chicken
   (2 to 3 pounds)
4 cloves garlic, smashed
1 teaspoon salt
4 slices bacon, minced
5½ cups beef broth, hot
3 medium tomatoes,
   peeled, seeded, and
   chopped
2½ cups rice
2 cups frozen peas
8 small cabbage leaves
1 medium onion, minced
1 pound lingüiça sausage,
   cut into ½-inch slices

C ut the chicken into 8 pieces.

Mash the garlic and salt together in a mortar to a
purée; mix the garlic with the bacon and rub the mixture into the chicken pieces. Sauté the chicken in a
large skillet until the bacon is browned.

Add the broth, tomatoes, rice, peas, cabbage leaves,
onion, and sausage. The broth should be 4 inches
higher in the pot than the ingredients. Cover and
cook for 20 minutes over low heat, or until the rice
is tender. Serve hot.

Chicken with Banana Sauce from Madeira

Frango com Bananas
4 servings

C hicken and bananas make for a very tasty combination. In the final preparation, the bananas make a thick sauce that covers the chicken pieces and gives them an exotically distinctive flavor.

1 whole chicken (3 pounds), or 4 chicken breast quarters
¼ cup butter
12 green onions, chopped
2 cloves garlic, chopped
4 slices extra lean bacon, diced (turkey bacon can be substituted)
1 teaspoon salt
¼ teaspoon black pepper
4 large green bananas
⅓ cup chopped fresh parsley or cilantro

I f using a whole chicken, cut it into quarters. Heat the butter in a large pot. Add the chicken and brown on all sides. Add 2 cups water, the green onions, garlic, bacon, salt, and pepper. Cover the pot and cook on low heat for 45 minutes (20 minutes for breasts).

Meanwhile, peel the bananas and cut each into 4 pieces. Place in a strainer or colander and immerse in a pot of boiling water for 15 minutes. Drain and mash.

Add the bananas to the chicken; mix well and continue cooking the chicken uncovered for 10 more minutes. Taste for seasonings. Arrange the chicken and banana sauce on a serving platter; sprinkle with the chopped parsley and serve.

Moorish Chicken

Galinha Mourisca
4 to 6 servings

t his recipe dates back to the sixteenth century, when the Portuguese incursions into Asia allowed Europeans to control the precious spice trade. Because of this trade, cinnamon became a popular spice for dishes with poultry and game. This particular recipe, with its cinnamon, was influenced by the Moors during their occupation of the Iberian Peninsula.

1 chicken (3 to 4 pounds), or 8 boneless chicken breasts
2 medium onions, sliced
4 ounces salt pork
2 tablespoons butter
1 tablespoon minced fresh parsley
1 tablespoon minced fresh cilantro
1 tablespoon minced fresh mint
3 tablespoons lemon juice
1 teaspoon salt
¼ teaspoon black pepper
6 slices country bread
6 eggs, poached
1 tablespoon ground cinnamon

i f using a whole chicken cut it into 8 pieces. Place the chicken pieces or breasts in a large deep skillet. Add the onions, salt pork, butter, and herbs, and brown the chicken on all sides over medium heat. Add 2 cups water and the lemon juice and cook until the chicken is tender. Season with the salt and pepper.

Arrange the bread on a deep platter and place the chicken pieces on top of the bread. Top the chicken with the poached eggs and the sauce from the pan. Sprinkle cinnamon over all and serve.

Sautéed Liver with Potatoes

Iscas com Elas

2 to 3 servings

*t*his is one of Lisbon's classic dishes. By the end of the nineteenth century, this dish had reached the level of popularity that it has today. It can be found on the menu of some of the best restaurants in Lisbon. Enjoy it with a glass of Dão or other Portuguese red wine.

1 pound calf's liver, thinly sliced

3 cloves garlic, thinly sliced

1 teaspoon salt

¼ teaspoon black pepper

1 bay leaf

3 tablespoons white wine

1 tablespoon white vinegar

1 pound Yukon potatoes

1 tablespoon lard or shortening

4 slices lean bacon, chopped

*p*lace the slices of liver in a deep dish and season with the garlic, salt, pepper, and bay leaf torn in half. Pour the wine and vinegar over all and marinate in the refrigerator for 12 hours or overnight.

The following day, peel the potatoes, cover with water in a medium pot, and cook over medium heat for about 20 minutes or until tender.

Heat the lard in a large skillet. Remove the liver slices from the marinade, do not dry, and fry them in the lard until brown on one side. Turn with a fork and cook 30 seconds more. Remove immediately from the pan to prevent the liver from becoming tough. Work in batches if necessary.

In the same pan cook the bacon pieces until crisp and add the marinade, removing the bay leaf. Turn off the heat and continue stirring to thicken the sauce. Add the liver pieces to the sauce, stirring to cover completely. Cut the potatoes into 1-inch slices and place them on a platter. Arrange the liver over the potatoes and pour the sauce over all.

Steak, Dom Pedro-Style

Bife Dom Pedro I
4 servings

i n 1971, we dined in the town of Cascais at a small restaurant called Dom Pedro I. I ordered the house specialty, a dish named for the restaurant. After tasting it, I called for the chef and requested the recipe. He was most gracious and shared the recipe with me and I have enjoyed it on subsequent visits to the restaurant. Serve this steak with French fries and a green salad.

4 large eggs
1 teaspoon white vinegar
8 filet mignon medallions,
    or 4 boneless top
    sirloin steaks,
    1-inch thick
¼ cup (½ stick) butter
Salt and black pepper to
    taste
2 teaspoons all-purpose
    flour
½ cup white wine
½ cup red wine
½ cup heavy cream,
    low-fat cream, or
    half-and-half

p our 3 cups water into a large skillet and bring to a boil. Break the eggs and slide them carefully one at a time into the boiling water. Add the vinegar and poach the eggs to the desired doneness. Remove the eggs from the water and keep warm.

Wipe the beef with a paper towel. Heat the butter in a large skillet over medium heat until just barely golden. Add the steaks and brown on each side, cooking to the desired doneness. Remove from the pan; salt and pepper to taste and keep warm on a covered platter. There should be about 3 tablespoons of butter left in the skillet. If not, add more to make 3 tablespoons.

Heat the butter over medium heat and stir in the flour. Cook until the mixture is a light brown, stirring constantly. Slowly add the wines; mix well, then add the cream and simmer for 2 minutes, stirring occasionally. Place 2 of the medallions or 1 sirloin steak on each plate. Place a poached egg on top of the beef and pour the sauce over all. Serve immediately.

Beef and Pork with Vegetables

Cozido à Portuguesa
8 to 10 servings

*t*his one-dish meal is one of Portugal's best-loved national recipes. The number and kinds of ingredients vary from region to region. Trás-os-Montes, in the northeastern corner of Portugal, is said to have the best and the richest cozido. This meat stew is a favorite during Carnival. In the summer, when string beans are plentiful, they are often used instead of cabbage.

1½ pound beef roast
1 pound pork roast
1 whole chicken, or 8 pieces with bone-in
8-ounce ham steak
1 pound smoked pork sausages
8 ounces smoked beef sausages
8 ounces blood sausage (optional)
2 pounds collard greens
1 medium head cabbage, cored and cut into 8 pieces
8 medium Yukon potatoes, peeled and quartered
3 turnips, peeled and cut into 3 pieces each
5 large carrots, peeled and cut into 3 pieces each
3 cups raw white rice
1 medium onion, minced
2 cloves garlic, minced
2 tablespoons olive oil

*i*n a large pot, place the beef roast, pork roast, chicken, and ham; cover with water and bring to a boil. Cook for 30 minutes or until the meats are tender, removing each one as it is cooked; save 6 cups of the water.

In another pot, scald the sausages in boiling water for 10 minutes. Remove the sausages and save the water. Remove the large stems from the collard greens and cut into pieces. Place all the vegetables in the large pot with the water from the sausages. Bring to a boil, reduce the heat, and cook for 10 minutes. Add the sausages and continue cooking for another 15 minutes.

Place the 6 cups of reserved water from the meats in a large pot and bring to a boil. Add the rice, onion, garlic, and olive oil, cover and cook over low heat for 25 minutes, or until the rice is tender.

On a large deep platter, arrange the meats, except for the beef sausages, around the edge. Mound the potatoes, carrots, turnips, and collards in the center. On another platter, mound the rice into a pyramid and arrange the beef sausages around the edge. Pour a little hot broth over the meats and serve.

Fried Pork with Clams, Mariner's-Style

Carne de Porco Frita com Ameijoas à Marinheira
4 to 6 servings

*f*or years, food specialists have disputed the origin of this dish. Some say it comes from the Ribatejo. Others believe it originated in the Algarve; still others maintain that it is a variation of that classic dish Pork Loin with Clams, which is obviously from the Alentejo region. Each region wants to claim it for its own. The recipe that appears here definitely comes from the Ribatejo region. Begin preparation the day before serving so that the pork and clams can marinate overnight.

MARINADE:

1 head garlic, peeled and chopped
1 teaspoon salt
½ cup white wine (see note)
6 tablespoons lemon juice
¼ cup white vinegar
1 teaspoon paprika
½ teaspoon black pepper
1 bay leaf

PORK:

2 pounds pork tenderloin
2 tablespoons olive oil
2 tablespoons bacon fat or lard
1 large yellow onion, chopped
4 cloves garlic, minced
2 tablespoons tomato paste
Clams, Mariner's-Style (page 36)

FOR THE MARINADE: With a mortar and pestle, purée the garlic and salt. Add the wine, lemon juice, vinegar, paprika, pepper, and bay leaf. Cut the pork into 1-inch cubes, rub well with the mixture and marinate overnight in the refrigerator.

FOR THE PORK: The following day, heat the olive oil and bacon fat in a large, heavy skillet over high heat until almost smoking. Drain the pork from the marinade, set the marinade aside, and in the skillet brown the pork quickly in small batches. Transfer the browned pork to a dish and keep warm. In the same oil sauté the onion and garlic until limp and golden, about 3 minutes. Add the tomato paste, reserved marinade, pork cubes and any juice that has accumulated. Mix well, cover, and simmer on low for 45 minutes. Add the clams to the pork mixture and simmer for 15 minutes to meld the flavors. Serve with fried potatoes and white rice.

NOTE: Some cooks use red wine instead of the white for the marinade.

Roast Suckling Pig

Leitão Assado

8 to 10 servings

i n August of 1970, I recall walking down Almirantes Avenue in central Lisbon and stopping to gaze at several suckling pigs, roasted a golden brown and hanging in a butcher shop window. I wondered what the meat tasted like. A few months later, at Christmas Eve dinner at the home of Mr. and Mrs. Pinheiro, in-laws of my friend Maria de Fatima Pinheiro, my curiosity was deliciously satisfied.

Upon my return to my home in Minnesota the following year, I wanted to replicate what I had enjoyed on several occasions during my year in Portugal. Fortunately, I discovered a nearby farm that provided me with a suckling pig. In the dead of winter, with about two feet of snow on the ground, we cooked the pig on a Weber grill in the backyard. The end result was very similar to what I remembered. Since then we have frequently enjoyed this gourmet treat. Serve it on Christmas Eve as is the tradition in Portugal, or on New Year's Day.

½ cup lard

3 slices smoked bacon, minced

10 cloves garlic

¾ cup white wine

2 tablespoons kosher or sea salt

2 tablespoons black pepper

2 tablespoons olive oil

1 tablespoon chopped fresh parsley

1 bay leaf, crushed

1 (12-pound) suckling pig

5 pounds small white potatoes

1 red apple

i n a mortar or food processor, grind the lard, bacon, garlic, 2 tablespoons of white wine, salt, pepper, olive oil, parsley, and bay leaf until the mixture resembles a purée. Rub the cavity of the pig with half of this mixture. Make cuts in the skin and press the remaining purée into the slits and rub into the flesh. Fold the legs under and tie together.

Let the coals burn until white hot in a grill or preheat the oven to 425 degrees F. Crush a piece of foil into a ball and place it in the pig's mouth. Cover the ears with foil so that they do not burn. Place the pig over the coals or in a roasting pan on a rack in the oven. If grilling, place a drip pan under the pig to catch the drippings before grilling. Baste frequently (about every 15 minutes) with the remaining wine. After 30 minutes, reduce the heat to 375 degrees F.

After the pig has been cooking for 2 hours, wash and prick the potatoes and add them. Cook the pig for an additional hour; the skin should be golden and crisp.

Drain any liquid from the belly into the pan juices. Pour the mixture into a pot and bring to a boil; cook until it thickens a bit. Taste for seasonings and place the sauce in a gravy boat. Remove the aluminum ball from the pig's mouth and replace it with an apple. Return the pig to the grill or oven for 20 minutes. Place on a serving platter and garnish with the roasted potatoes. Traditionally, the suckling pig is served whole, hot or at room temperature, then carved at the table with gravy on the side.

Home-Style Bread

Pão de Mesa
Makes 3 large or 10 small rolls

i n the Azores, pão de mesa *refers to the bread that people eat at lunch and supper on workdays. One also finds this bread on the menu during the* Espirito Santo *celebration. This bread is very popular in continental Portugal and several of the former African and Asian colonies. During festivals and on Sunday, sweet bread is substituted for the* pão de mesa.

7 cups all-purpose flour
½ to ¾ cup milk, or enough to form dough
2 eggs
¼ cup sugar
3 ounces baker's yeast, or 3 tablespoons baking powder
1 tablespoon butter, melted

p lace the flour in a bowl and make a hole in the center. Pour in ½ cup milk, eggs, sugar, yeast, and butter. Mix well. Add ¼ cup milk if the dough is too dry. Roll into a ball and place in a greased bowl. Cover with a cloth and let the dough rise for 1 hour in a draft-free place.

Form the dough into 10 small rolls or 3 small loaves. Place on a greased baking sheet dusted with flour and let rise for 50 minutes in a warm place.

Heat the oven to 350 degrees F. Bake the rolls for 40 minutes, or until lightly golden. Remove the rolls from the oven and place on wire racks to cool. Serve at room temperature.

Peasant Corn Bread

Broa Caseira
Makes one 3-pound loaf

t raditionally, broa *is made on a weekly basis. In the Trás-os-Montes and Alto Douro regions, yellow cornmeal is used, but in the Minho region, white cornmeal is the norm. Either cornmeal can be used in this recipe.*

7 cups yellow or white
    cornmeal
5 teaspoons salt
5 cups boiling water
3 cubes fresh active yeast,
    or 3 packets dry yeast
3 cups all-purpose flour

p lace the cornmeal and salt in a large bowl. Pour the boiling water over the cornmeal. Let it cool for about 5 minutes. Knead with your hands folding from the edge inward and from the bottom to the top (about 2 minutes) until lump free. Add the yeast and continue kneading for 3 minutes. Add 2½ cups of the flour and knead for an additional 3 minutes until smooth. Place in a large wooden bowl, cover with a linen cloth, and let rise in a warm place for 1 hour.

Heat the oven to 450 degrees F. Heat a baking sheet in the oven for 10 minutes. Shape the dough into a large round (see note). Dust the baking sheet with the remaining ½ cup flour and place the dough on the flour. Bake for 40 to 45 minutes, or until the loaf sounds hollow when tapped on the bottom and the top is golden brown and crusty. Transfer to a wire rack and cool.

NOTE: The dough can be divided to make 3 small loaves. The baking time would be 30 to 35 minutes.

King Cake

Bolo-rei
10 to 12 servings

uring the Christmas holiday season, the king cake can be found in just about every bakery in Portugal. Its flavor is a combination of cake and sugar rolls with crystallized fruits, nuts, and raisins. Each cake contains a fava bean and a small gift wrapped in greaseproof paper. Whoever finds the fava bean is supposed to buy or prepare next year's bolo-rei.

1 tablespoon baking powder
¾ cup warm milk
2½ cups all-purpose flour
¾ cup crystallized
    (candied) fruits
24 walnut halves
¼ cup butter, softened
½ cup sugar
¼ cup white brandy or
    aguardente
2 eggs
¼ cup raisins
1 fava bean
1 small heatproof gift,
    wrapped in greaseproof
    paper
1 egg yolk, beaten
¼ cup pine nuts
½ cup apple jelly, melted
    for glaze

issolve the baking powder in the warm milk. Add ¼ cup of the flour to the mixture and form into a ball. Set aside in a warm dry place to rise.

Meanwhile, chop ½ cup of the crystallized fruit and all the walnut halves.

Pile the remaining 2¼ cups of flour in a mound. In a bowl, mix together the butter, ¼ cup of the sugar, the brandy, and eggs. Make a hole in the center of the flour and pour in the egg mixture. Add the baking powder mixture and incorporate all the ingredients. Knead the dough until it doesn't stick to your hands and forms a ball. Knead in the chopped crystallized fruit, walnuts, and raisins.

Place the dough in a greased bowl and let rise in a warm place for 4 hours. After the dough rises, remove from the bowl and form it in the shape of a donut on a baking sheet. Place an aluminum glass or a ball of foil in the center to keep the hole open. Make 2 holes in the dough and place a fava bean in one and the gift in the other. Close up the holes and decorate the top with the remaining crystallized fruit. Set aside for 30 minutes.

Heat the oven to 300 degrees F. Brush the top of the cake with the beaten yolk. Sprinkle with pine nuts and ¼ cup sugar. Bake the cake for 25 minutes or until a toothpick comes out clean. As soon as the cake comes out of the oven, brush with the melted jelly or sugar water to give it a glaze.

Rice Pudding

Arroz Doce
8 to 10 servings

his dessert is almost obligatory at wedding receptions. In certain regions of Portugal and the Madeira Islands it has been the custom for the bride's mother, the groom, and the bridesmaids to visit close friends and family and offer them this pudding. Normally, the pudding is presented in a basket covered with a napkin. Custom also calls for the party to return a week later to collect the basket and dish and for the bride to receive a wedding gift. This pudding is also enjoyed on holidays and special occasions throughout the Portuguese-speaking world.

1¼ cups white rice
4 cups milk
1 lemon peel
1¼ cups sugar
3 egg yolks, lightly beaten
2 tablespoons ground
   cinnamon

lace the rice in a large pot, add the milk, and bring to a simmer. Add the lemon peel and the sugar. Cook over low heat, stirring occasionally, until the rice is cooked, about 25 minutes. Remove the rice from the heat and let cool for 30 minutes.

Add the egg yolks to the rice one at a time, mixing well after each addition. Return the rice mixture to the stove and bring to a boil, stirring constantly. Pour into a serving dish, cool, and chill in the refrigerator for at least 4 hours.

Sprinkle the pudding with the cinnamon before serving, using a doily over the rice to create a pattern.

Wedding Cookies

Biscoitos de Casamento

Makes 55 to 60 cookies

this cookie recipe has traveled halfway around the world from Portugal to Hawaii where there was an early and fairly sizable Portuguese community. These are served at wedding receptions in the Portuguese Hawaiian community. Individual cookies are either wrapped in white crepe paper, tied with narrow white satin bows at each end, or they are served in individual silver cups. In Brazil, they also serve these cookies at weddings, but they attach orange blossoms to the satin bows. In Portugal, they are served as part of a dessert tray.

1 cup (2 sticks) butter or margarine, softened
2¼ cups sifted confectioners' sugar
1 tablespoon grated lemon peel
2½ cups sifted all-purpose flour
55 to 60 whole blanched almonds

preheat the oven to 350 degrees F. Cream the butter until light and fluffy. Beat in ¼ cup of the sugar, the lemon peel, and 1 tablespoon water. Add the flour, ½ cup at a time, and mix in well with your hands. Continue kneading until the dough forms a ball.

Pinch off a piece of dough (about the size of a Brazil nut). Push a whole almond into the center of the dough. Press the dough around the almond to cover completely and mold into an oblong or round shape. Repeat until all the dough is used.

Place the cookies on a lightly greased and floured cookie sheet. Bake for 15 minutes, or until the cookies are lightly golden. Do not overcook. Remove from the cookie sheet and cool for 2 to 3 minutes on a wire rack.

Roll the cookies in the remaining 2 cups confectioner's sugar, return to the rack, and let cool completely. Roll again in sugar for a thick white coating. These cookies will keep for about a week, tightly covered.

Cream Tartlets

Pastéis de Natas
Makes 20 tartlets

Pastéis de Natas *were originally known as* Pastéis de Belém; *the name comes from a bakery in an area near Lisbon's Tower of Belém. These pastries are so popular that there is scarcely a bakery in Portugal where they are not sold. They are usually served with tea or coffee in the afternoon or as an after-dinner dessert.*

DOUGH:
1½ cups all-purpose flour
1 teaspoon salt
1 cup (2 sticks) butter or
    margarine, softened

FILLING:
2½ cups heavy cream
9 egg yolks
9 tablespoons sugar

FOR THE DOUGH: Place the flour in a bowl. Stir in the salt and ½ cup cold water, a little at a time, until it resembles soft dough, adding more water if necessary. Divide the butter into 3 portions. Take one-third of the butter and cut into small pieces. Roll out the dough and sprinkle the cut butter over the dough. Fold the dough in half; press to incorporate the butter. Fold in half again; press again. Roll out the dough and repeat the process with the other two portions of the butter, one-third at a time. Let the dough rest for 20 minutes.

Meanwhile, beat the cream, egg yolks, and sugar together until creamy. Place in a double boiler and cook over medium low heat, stirring until it resembles thick custard. Set aside to cool.

Heat the oven to 475 degrees F. Roll out the dough into an oblong shape and cut it into strips ½ inch wide. Beginning at the bottom of one of the sections of the tartlet or muffin pan, wind the dough in a spiral to cover the entire inside. Press the dough with your fingers to make it smooth. Repeat with the remaining dough.

Place 1 tablespoon or more of the custard in each tartlet, then place the tartlets on a baking sheet. Bake about 20 minutes, or until the custard is a light gold color and the pastry is golden. A toothpick inserted in the center should come out clean. Cool the tartlets for about 5 minutes. Run the blade of a knife around the edges to loosen them slightly. Lift out with a spatula and cool to room temperature. *Pastéis de Natas* are best eaten the day they are cooked. However, day-old pastries can be warmed in a hot oven for 5 minutes.

Sweet Toast

Rabanadas
10 to 12 servings

e *ven though this recipe originated in the northern part of Portugal, it is enjoyed throughout the country, especially during the Christmas Eve* consoada *meal. Most cooks prepare this dish the day before.* Rabanadas *are served at room temperature and by standing overnight the bread dries a little and the flavors meld. This dish is also known as* fatias-de-parida, *translated literally as "slices of bread for the mother-of-the-newborn."*

1 day-old loaf peasant-style
   bread (Portuguese or
   French)
½ cup port wine (see note)
3 tablespoons sugar
5 eggs, beaten
½ cup (1 stick) butter
½ cup confectioners' sugar
1 tablespoon cinnamon

Cut the bread into 1-inch-thick slices. Mix the port wine with the sugar and stir into 2½ cups warm water. Dip the bread slices into the mixture, covering all sides, and set aside on a rack to drain. Then dip the slices in the beaten eggs to cover completely.

Melt the butter in a skillet and fry the bread slices on both sides until golden brown. Remove the slices to a serving dish. Combine the confectioners' sugar and cinnamon and sprinkle over the bread, or top with Sweet Syrup (page 53).

NOTE: In Brazil, cow's milk or coconut milk is substituted for port wine, except during Christmas, when port is essential.

This toast also makes excellent sandwiches; you can omit the confectioners' sugar and cinnamon and instead use cheese, beef, chicken, or a seafood salad as filling for 2 pieces of toast.

Sweet Syrup

Caldo para Doces
Makes about 1½ cups

t his sweet syrup is used as a sauce for Sweet Toast (page 52), Dreams (page 132), and other fried dough desserts, particularly during the Christmas holidays, in most of the Portuguese-speaking world.

2 cups sugar
Peel of ½ lemon or orange
1 stick cinnamon

p lace all the ingredients in a pot with 1¼ cups water and bring to a boil. Boil for 5 minutes. Remove the peel and serve at room temperature.

NOTE: A variation of this recipe, Red Wine Sauce, calls for 1½ cups wine to be added to the mixture instead of water before bringing it to a boil. Boil until the mixture is a thin syrup (8 to 10 minutes). Remove the syrup from the heat and cool. Serve cold or at room temperature.

Mulled Wine

Vinho Quente
6 servings

t his drink is very popular during the Christmas holidays in the Minho region of Portugal. It is usually served after midnight mass with a plate of Portuguese Sweet Toast (page 52), or fried dough fritters.

6 egg yolks
1 cup plus 2 tablespoons
  sugar
¼ teaspoon sea salt
1¼ cups red wine
1¼ cups Madeira wine
1¼ cups port wine

b eat the egg yolks with 1 cup of the sugar until fluffy, about 4 minutes. Set aside.

Bring 4 cups water to a boil and add the salt. Remove the water from the heat. Add the red and Madeira wines and return to the heat. Bring to a boil, then gradually add the egg mixture a little at a time, returning the liquid to a boil. Remove from the heat and add the port. Stir and taste for sugar. If necessary, add another 2 tablespoons of sugar.

When ready to serve, heat the wine punch in a double-boiler, stirring occasionally. Ladle the warm wine into cups. Dip pieces of toast into the wine, if desired.

Punch

Ponche
6 servings

ponche *is a tropical drink from rural Madeira. When ordered in an eatery, the drink is prepared on the spot. Lately the punch has become popular among tourists and can now be found in taverns, cafés, and hotel restaurants. In Madeira, the punch is prepared with a special wooden utensil that beats it into a foam. It looks something like a wooden whisk with a long handle and the end is shaped like a ball. One holds the whisk between the palms of both hands and agitates it in the liquid until it foams.* Ponche *is also very popular in Cape Verde. And on the island of Santo Antão, it is prepared with brown sugar, cinnamon sticks, and lemon peel.*

2 cups aguardente or white brandy
½ cup lemon juice
¼ cup honey
1 tablespoon sugar

mix all the ingredients together in a large jar or bowl. Beat with a wire whisk until foam appears around the edges. Serve immediately in red wine glasses.

CUISINE OF
Angola

a ngola, in land mass the largest and the second most populous of the five countries in Africa where Portuguese is spoken, is situated on the west coast of the continent. It was "discovered" by the Portuguese navigator Diogo Cão, after his first voyage of exploration in 1482–1483. Before the arrival of the Europeans, from the thirteenth century until 1520, Angola was inhabited by the peoples from the Congo region in the area known as *Rio Kuanza* (the Kuanza River region). The principal work of these people was agriculture. They cultivated cereals such as sorghum. The tools used to harvest these crops were iron hoes and hatchets. These crops were grown on large farms and when the fields became overworked and would no longer cultivate crops, the workers simply moved to another area and replanted them. Both men and women worked the fields, but the men cleared the forests and the women did the planting. Besides raising crops, they fished and hunted to supplement their diet. Hides provided by hunted animals also served as clothing.

In 1490, Portuguese ships returned bringing presents from the king of Portugal to the king of the Congo, and laborers to construct a brick church. The ships then returned to Portugal with ivory, beautiful Congolese fabrics made by local artisans, and sadly, some slaves.

In 1575, Paulo Dias de Novais arrived in the Bay of Luanda with one-hundred Portuguese families to cultivate sugar and tobacco and extract salt and palm oil for export. The salt was used as money to trade for other necessities. Cattle, pigs, and goats were raised in the central and southern region. They drank the milk and used it to make cheese. The goat skins were used for clothing, rugs, pocketbooks, and bags. Various cereal crops were grown, including wheat, which was also used to make alcoholic beverages. By 1667, Brazil, already a Portuguese colony (1530), was an important player in the culture and cuisine of Angola. Angola provided Brazil with palm oil, salt, peanut oil, and coffee. Brazil supplied Angola with sugar, brandy (*aguardent*), rice, flour, dried beef, bacon, manioc flour, and beans. And both of these colonies supplied Portugal with these products. By 1796, most of the food products originally imported from Brazil were being produced in Angola.

Today, Angolan cuisine is largely based on fish, seafood, and poultry that sometimes is served with *fuba* (a type of purée) made from corn or manioc flour and known as "the poor man's bread." Olive, vegetable, peanut, and especially palm oils are used for cooking. Chief among the vegetables are manioc leaves, pumpkin, and beans.

The leaves of sweet potatoes, okra, green beans, tomatoes, and purslane (*beldroega*) plants are also used in cooking. Angolans also consume okra and various types of squash.

Today in the urban areas, breakfast (*matabicho*) consists of coffee or tea with bread and fruit. In the suburban (rural) areas, breakfast usually consists of leftovers from the night before such as dried beef, fish, or stewed vegetables. Lunch is usually eaten anytime from 1:00 pm to 3:00 pm, with a snack (usually sweet) eaten in the late afternoon. In homes, dinner is served around 9:00 pm. Dinner can be light, such as soup, bread, and dessert; or more elaborate, such as soup, fish, meat and vegetables, dessert, and coffee.

Angola stands out among Portugal's former colonies in Africa because of its culinary contributions to the so-called New World, especially Brazil. Slaves from the Congo-Angola region introduced such traditional Brazilian dishes as *caruru* and *vatapa*, as well as such condiments as *gindungo* (pimenta malagueta).

It is well-known that in the domain of culinary contributions, but also with respect to certain social customs, cultural practices, and such loan words as *moleque*, *samba*, and *macambuzio*, Angola is indeed "the mother of Brazil."

Giblet Canapés

Pipas
Makes 2 cups

*t*his is a wonderful way to use the giblets that you have collected from chickens. This recipe is a very popular appetizer in Angola as well as other countries in the Portuguese-speaking world. In Portugal, the tomatoes are eliminated and paprika and garlic are added. In Macao, this dish is served as a main course with cucumbers and ginger added. In Angola, it is served with toasted bread rounds.

Giblets from 4 chickens
(about 10 ounces)
¼ cup olive oil
1 medium onion, minced
2 medium ripe tomatoes,
    peeled, seeded, and
    chopped
1 bay leaf
1 teaspoon salt
1 teaspoon ground red
    pepper or crushed red
    pepper flakes
½ cup white wine

Cut the giblets into small pieces; set aside.

In a medium skillet, heat the olive oil and add the onion, tomatoes, and bay leaf. When the tomatoes have cooked down to a purée, add the salt and red pepper.

Stir in the giblets and cook for 2 minutes. Add the wine and simmer until the liquid is almost gone and the giblets are tender. Serve with toasted bread rounds or crackers.

Creamy Shrimp Turnovers

Rissóis Angolano
Makes about 60 turnovers

rissóis *are served in most Portuguese-speaking countries. In Portugal, we find them served as snacks in cafés; while in Brazil they are very popular at St. John's Day festivals; and in Mozambique and Goa, they are served at parties and with drinks at bars. I learned to prepare these tasty creamy turnovers from a dear friend, Sara dos Santos, while living in Luanda, Angola, in 1978–1979. The recipe may seem a bit complicated, but it is well worth the effort. Invite a friend to share the preparation with you.*

FILLING:

- 1½ pounds medium raw shrimp with shells
- 2 cups boiling water
- 2 teaspoons salt
- 2 tablespoons butter
- 1 tablespoon olive oil
- 1 medium onion, chopped
- 1 small tomato, finely chopped
- 4 cloves garlic, minced
- 1 tablespoon chopped fresh parsley
- 1½ teaspoons lemon juice
- 1 teaspoon hot sauce

FOR THE FILLING: In a large pot, cover the shrimp with the 2 cups boiling water. Add the salt, bring to a slow boil, and simmer for 2 to 3 minutes, or until the shrimp turn pink. Remove the shrimp and reserve the cooking liquid. Shell the shrimp and chop coarsely. Heat the butter and olive oil in a large skillet. Add the onion and sauté until soft. Add the tomato, garlic, parsley, lemon juice, hot sauce, and salt to taste. Cook for 5 to 10 minutes, or until soft. Stir in the shrimp.

FOR THE WHITE SAUCE: Melt the butter in a small saucepan. Add the flour and cook for 1 to 2 minutes, forming a roux. Remove from the heat and slowly add the milk and ¼ cup of the shrimp water to the roux, using a wire whisk to stir. Return to the heat and bring to a boil; reduce the heat and simmer gently for 5 to 6 minutes, or until slightly thickened, stirring occasionally. Whisk the egg yolks into the pan slowly, stirring continuously for 1 minute. Add the sauce to the shrimp mixture. Taste and adjust the seasonings if necessary. Set aside to cool.

WHITE SAUCE:

2 tablespoons butter

2 tablespoons all-purpose flour

½ cup milk

¼ cup cooking liquid from shrimp

2 egg yolks

PASTRY DOUGH:

2 cups milk

3 tablespoons butter

1 teaspoon salt

4½ cups all-purpose flour

ASSEMBLY:

1 egg, beaten

1 cup bread crumbs

Vegetable oil for frying

FOR THE PASTRY DOUGH: Bring 2 cups water, the milk, butter, and salt to a boil. Remove from the heat and slowly add 4 cups of the flour, a little at a time. Return to the heat, reduce to medium, and stir with a wooden spoon until the dough comes away from the sides of the pan, about 5 minutes. Cool until you can handle it. Knead the remaining ½ cup of the flour into the dough. Roll out on a lightly floured board to one-eighth-inch thickness.

ASSEMBLY: Cut 3-inch circles from the dough and place 1 teaspoon of the shrimp mixture on half of each circle. Brush the edges with beaten egg. Fold and seal each pastry round, dip in beaten egg, then in the bread crumbs. Place the turnovers on a baking sheet and continue to make half-moon rissóis until all the dough is used. Pour the vegetable oil into a medium-size pan to a depth of two inches. Heat it over medium-high heat to 365 degrees F on a deep-frying thermometer. Fry the pastries until golden brown. Drain the *rissóis* on paper towels. Serve at room temperature.

NOTE: Uncooked, these turnovers can be frozen for up to 3 months. Freeze before frying and deep-fry while frozen, just before serving. Or, when ready to serve, remove from the freezer, spread out on a lightly greased baking sheet, and bake at 325 degrees F for 15 to 20 minutes or until hot.

Island Rice

t he island in the bay of the city of Luanda is now connected to the mainland by a landfill. Many of the city's residents flock to the "island" on weekends to enjoy the beautiful beaches. The Hotel Presidente *there serves a wonderful Sunday brunch and then snacks all day long. This recipe is my adaptation of one that I have enjoyed at brunch on the many occasions when my family and I have spent the day at the beach.*

½ cup olive oil
1 large onion, chopped
2 cloves garlic, minced
4 tomatoes, peeled, seeded, and chopped
2 red chili peppers, seeded and minced
1 sprig parsley, minced
1 sprig mint, minced
2 whole cloves
1 bay leaf
2 teaspoons salt
1 quart fish broth, hot
¼ cup white wine
1 cup uncooked white rice
2 pounds grouper
½ cup fresh cilantro, minced
2 tablespoons butter, cut into small bits

h eat the olive oil in a large skillet over medium heat; add the onion and garlic and cook until the onion is translucent. Add the tomatoes, chili peppers, parsley, mint, cloves, bay leaf, and 1 teaspoon of the salt. Simmer until the tomatoes are tender, about 15 minutes. Add the hot fish broth and the wine. As soon as the broth comes to a boil, add the rice; cover, reduce heat, and cook for 10 minutes.

Cut the grouper into serving pieces; sprinkle them with the remaining 1 teaspoon salt, and place on top of the rice. Cover and cook another 10 minutes. Before removing from the heat, sprinkle the top with cilantro and bits of butter. Serve hot.

Rice with Seafood

Arroz de Mariscos
6 to 8 servings

ngola's coastal waters abound with shellfish. There are lobsters, crayfish, shrimp, and crabs, and mollusks such as cockles, oysters, clams, and barnacles. Many of these shellfish are similar to those found in the ocean off the coast of Portugal. Little wonder that the Portuguese settlers so enjoyed the local cuisine. In Portugal, this dish is known as Arroz de Lagostins e Camarões, which translates as "Rice with Crayfish and Shrimp." In Cape Verde there is a similar dish called Arroz de Cabidela de Marisco, meaning "Rice and Shellfish Stew," that is very popular on the leeward island of São Vicente. And in Goa, the dish is called Arroz Refogado, or "Stewed Rice." In Angola the gindungo pepper is used, which is similar to the piripiri hot pepper of Mozambique. The rice should be moist and piquant. This regional dish is also considered to be indispensable at students' end-of-term parties.

2 pounds medium shrimp
   with shells and heads
4 small lobsters, lobster
   tails, or 1 pound
   langoustines
2 pounds clams or cockles
¾ cup olive oil
1 large onion, minced
4 cloves garlic, minced
1 medium green pepper,
   seeded and cut into
   thin strips
2 medium tomatoes, peeled,
   seeded, and chopped
1 bay leaf
4 red chili peppers, minced
1 teaspoon salt
2 cups uncooked white rice

lace the shrimp and lobsters in a large pot; cover with water and bring to a boil. Cook for 5 minutes, and then remove the seafood, saving the water. Peel the shrimp, remove the meat from the lobsters, and return the shells to the water along with the shrimp heads. Bring the liquid to a boil and cook for 10 minutes. Set aside. Slice the lobster meat into 1-inch slices. Wash and shuck the clams, remove the meat, saving the juice, and set aside. Strain the juice from the clams and save.

Place the oil, onion, and garlic in a large pot over medium heat and cook until the onion is translucent. Add the bell pepper, tomatoes, and bay leaf and simmer until the tomatoes form a sauce, about 20 minutes. Add the chili peppers and the salt. Mix the clam juice with enough of the water from the boiled shells to make 4 cups and add to the skillet. Bring to a boil and add the rice. Stir, cover, and cook for 15 minutes or until the rice is tender. Add the seafood, mix well, and heat on low for 3 minutes, just to warm the seafood. Serve hot.

Cuisine of Angola | 63

Rice Soup

Sopa de Arroz
4 servings

This is an Angolan adaptation of the traditional canja, *which is a soup enjoyed throughout the Portuguese-speaking world. Most* canjas *are made with chicken, but in Angola beef is used. This soup is especially popular in the capital of Luanda and its environs.*

1 pound stew beef
8 ounces beef bones
1 medium onion, minced
1 cup uncooked white rice
½ cup fresh chopped mint
    leaves
Salt to taste

Cut the stew beef into 1-inch cubes. Wash the beef bones and place the beef cubes and the bones in a large pot. Add 8 cups of water, bring to a boil, reduce the heat to a simmer, and cook until the beef is tender, about 30 minutes.

Remove the bones and return any meat on the bones to the pot. Add the onion, rice, mint and salt. Cover and simmer for 20 minutes, or until the rice is tender. Divide between 4 soup bowls and serve.

Hangover Soup

Muzongue com Pirão
4 to 6 servings

t his soup is said to cure hangovers and, therefore, is usually served the day after a large party when one has had too much to eat and drink. Serve with Manioc Purées (page 69).

SOUP:
2 medium onions, chopped
3 tomatoes, peeled, seeded and chopped
½ cup palm oil
1 teaspoon salt
1 pound sweet potatoes, peeled and cubed
1 teaspoon ground red pepper
2 pounds white fish fillets, such as snapper, cod, tilapia, or haddock
8 ounces boned smoked fish
1 pound spinach, cooked

PIRÃO:
4 cups fish broth or water
1½ cups manioc flour (see sources, page 355)

FOR THE SOUP: Heat 8 cups of water in a large pot with the onions, tomatoes, palm oil, and salt. Bring to a boil. Mix the sweet potatoes with the red pepper and add to the pot. Cut the fish into 1-inch wide strips and add to the pot. Reduce the heat and simmer until the fish is opaque and the potatoes are tender.

FOR THE PIRÃO: Heat the fish broth in a pot to boiling. Slowly add the manioc flour, whisking continually to prevent lumps from forming. Cook until the manioc thickens, about 2 minutes.

Place the soup in bowls and add a large spoonful of pirão. You can either add the spinach to the soup during the last minute of cooking or serve it on the side.

Collards in Peanut Sauce

Couves Cozidos com Oleo-de-Palma e Amendoim
4 to 6 servings

this is a traditional dish of the Kimbundu people from the region around the capital city of Luanda. To make a complete meal, I add one pound of chopped shrimp ten minutes before the dish is ready. This dish is also sometimes made with fresh mushrooms instead of collards. In this variation, the peanuts are sautéed in oil with red pepper flakes and salt for five minutes before the water is added. Cooking time is also reduced to fifteen minutes for the mushrooms. Serve this mushroom variation with fish or meat and white rice.

1 pound collard greens
1 cup raw, unsalted
   peanuts
1 tablespoon red pepper
   flakes
1 teaspoon salt
3 tablespoons palm oil
   (see note)

remove the collard stems. Wash the leaves and stack them on a cutting board. Cut into 1-inch squares and set aside.

Grind the peanuts in a food processor or meat grinder until they resemble a powder. Place the ground peanuts in a medium pot and add 4 cups of water. Bring the water to a boil, adding the pepper flakes and salt. Add the collards to the peanut mixture and simmer for 30 minutes or until the collards are tender. Add the palm oil, mix well, and simmer another 25 minutes. Serve with grilled fish or meat and white rice.

NOTE: If you are concerned about cholesterol, you may substitute vegetable oil for half or one-third of the palm oil.

Banana Ragout with Bean Purée

Guisado de Puré de Feijão com Bananas
4 to 6 servings

t his is a dish of the Kimbundu people of Angola. In the Kimbundu *language the dish is called* kitande. *It is usually served with Manioc Purée (page 69). Some cooks omit the bananas and add* chouriço *(smoked sausage) to the bean purée. This dish is also served with roasted or boiled sweet potatoes or cooked manioc.*

2 cups dried navy or Great
    Northern beans,
    washed and sorted
2 teaspoons salt
¼ cup palm oil
¼ cup vegetable oil
1 medium onion, minced
6 ripe bananas, peeled and
    sliced
2 cups manioc meal, finely
    ground and toasted

r efrigerate the beans overnight in cold water to cover.

The following day, remove the beans from the water, place in a towel, and rub to remove the skins. When all the skins are removed place the beans in a pot and cover with cold water. Cook the beans for 2 hours, or until they are soft. Season with salt and add the palm oil. Simmer the beans until they become a purée, another 20 minutes.

In a frying pan, heat the vegetable oil and sauté the onion until golden. Add the beans.

Serve with sliced bananas and manioc meal on the side. Each diner should sprinkle manioc meal over the bean mixture.

Corn Pudding

Canjica

4 side-dish servings

this dish is also found in Brazil, where it is served on St. John's Day. But in Brazil, canjica is a dessert and calls for coconut, coconut milk, sugar, and cinnamon and is served cold (see Brazilian Corn Pudding, page 131). In Angola, white beans are added to the corn along with palm oil and the canjica is served as a side dish with meats.

2 cups dried Great
    Northern beans,
    washed and sorted
4 ears corn
¼ cup palm oil
1 teaspoon salt

refrigerate the beans overnight in cold water to cover plus about 4 inches.

The following day, drain the beans and place in a large saucepan. Cover them with about 8 cups of fresh cold water. Cook for 1 hour, uncovered.

Cut the kernels from the ears of corn; add the corn to the beans and cook for another 30 minutes, or until the beans are tender.

Drain any water left in the pot and add the palm oil to the beans. Season with salt and stir to mix well. Return to the heat and simmer for 2 more minutes. Serve with roasted meats or poultry.

Manioc Purées

Funji and Pirão

these purées are served with stews, soups, or any meat, fish, or poultry dish that has a little sauce or liquid to make the purée. They go particularly well with Hangover Soup (page 65), Fish Ragout (page 74), and Angolan-Style Chicken (page 75).

FUNJI:

4 cups chicken or beef
    broth (see note)
1 cup finely ground corn-
    meal or manioc flour

PIRÃO:

1 pound fish heads,
    or 4 cups fish stock
1 cup manioc flour

FOR THE FUNJI: Bring the broth to a boil. Slowly pour the cornmeal or manioc flour into the boiling broth, stirring with a whisk to avoid lumps. Continue stirring for 3 minutes, or until the purée is the consistency of cooked cereal.

NOTE: Use chicken broth for chicken dishes and beef broth or water for meat dishes.

FOR THE PIRÃO: Cook the fish heads in 6 cups water for 15 minutes. Remove 4 cups of the liquid, strain, and place in another pot. Bring to a boil and pour the manioc flour into the liquid stirring constantly with a whisk to avoid lumps. Cook the purée for about 5 minutes, or until the purée is the consistency of cooked cereal. Serve with fish or seafood stews.

Fish Stew

Caldeirada de Peixe

4 to 6 servings

t his recipe of Portuguese origin calls for a large whole fish like grouper, halibut, cod, or salmon cut into steaks. Fillets are not thick enough and will fall apart with cooking.

2 pounds thick fish steaks
1 teaspoon salt
1 pound white potatoes,
    thickly sliced
2 green bell peppers,
    sliced horizontally
1 tomato, peeled and
    seeded
2 onions, thinly sliced
1 bay leaf
1 cup olive oil
2 red chili peppers, crushed
    in a mortar and pestle
Cooked white rice

p lace the fish steaks on a baking sheet. Sprinkle them with the salt on both sides. Set aside for 10 minutes.

In a large deep skillet, layer the potatoes, bell peppers, tomato, fish, onions, and bay leaf. Pour the olive oil and 1 cup of water over the ingredients. Sprinkle with the crushed red peppers and cook over low heat until the vegetables are tender, about 20 minutes. Add water as necessary so that the dish doesn't dry out. Serve on a large deep platter with white rice on the side.

Shellfish in Hot Sauce

Mariscos Cozidos com Gindungo
4 servings

t he Angolan coastal waters abound with shellfish and the locals have used them to create many wonderful dishes. This dish calls for lobster, shrimp, oysters, and clams. The secret for preparing a mouthwatering meal is to use seawater or dried seaweed. In the cooking broth, the red peppers bring out the flavor and the lard makes the seafood flesh tender and succulent.

4 quarts seawater, or
   4 sheets dried seaweed
2 tablespoons lard or
   margarine
3 red chili peppers, minced,
   or 3 tablespoons red
   pepper flakes
4 lobsters (1½ pounds
   each) or lobster tails
8 prawns or jumbo shrimp
   with shells
8 oysters in their shells,
   well-scrubbed
8 clams in their shells,
   well-scrubbed

i n a large pot heat the seawater, or use 4 quarts tap water with dried seaweed. Bring to a boil and add the lard and chili peppers. Return to a boil and add the seafood.

Remove the shrimp, oysters, and clams after 5 minutes. Continue cooking the lobsters for another 5 to 7 minutes. If the lobsters are very large, cook for a total of 20 minutes or until bright red.

Discard any clams or oysters that do not open. Divide the seafood among 4 plates and serve with a bowl of hot sauce (page 141) for dipping.

Squid Sautéed with Potatoes

Lulas Guisadas com Batatas
2 servings

S quid as well as cuttlefish are mollusks that are greatly appreciated by the Angolans. This recipe is delicious and easy to prepare.

1 pound baby squid sacs,
   cleaned
2 tomatoes, minced
1 onion, diced
½ cup peanut oil
2 teaspoons paprika
1 teaspoon salt
1 bay leaf
1 pound white potatoes,
   diced

C ut the squid sacs into 1-inch pieces and place in a pan with the tomatoes and onion over medium heat. Add the peanut oil, paprika, salt, and bay leaf. Simmer until the squid is almost tender, about 30 minutes.

Add 1 cup of water and the potatoes. Stirring occasionally, cook until the potatoes are tender, another 10 minutes. Serve the squid in the same pan in which it was prepared.

Sea Bass with Vegetables

Goraz Cozido com Verduras

4 to 6 servings

during the year we lived in Luanda, 1978–1979, my dear friend Sara Maria dos Santos prepared this dish for my family on many occasions. This dish is quick, healthy, and delicious. You may substitute any white fish for the sea bass, but I would suggest grouper, red snapper, or halibut.

4 garlic cloves, minced
2 teaspoons salt
1 teaspoon lemon juice
2 pounds sea bass steaks
4 medium white potatoes, quartered
4 medium carrots, peeled and quartered
1 medium cabbage, peeled and quartered
1 chicken bouillon cube
1 medium onion, thinly sliced
½ cup olive oil, warmed

place the garlic and 1 teaspoon of the salt in a mortar. Crush the garlic well with the pestle, then add the lemon juice and mix well. Rub the fish with this mixture and set aside.

Place the potatoes, carrots, and cabbage in a large pot with water to barely cover. Add the remaining 1 teaspoon salt and bring to a boil. Add the bouillon cube, reduce the heat, and simmer uncovered for 15 minutes.

Place the fish on top of the vegetables, layer onion slices over the fish, and cover. Simmer until the fish is tender, about 10 minutes.

Remove the fish and place it in the center of a serving dish. Surround the fish with the drained vegetables and drizzle with warm olive oil. Serve immediately.

Fish Ragout

Muamba de Peixe
4 servings

this is a marvelous blend of fish and okra. In 1979, I first sampled this dish in the mansion of the governor of the district of Moçamides in southern Angola. We were treated to a four-course meal, and one of the dishes was Muamba de Peixe. Since then, this dish is one that I have prepared many times for family and friends.

⅔ cup palm oil,
  or ⅓ cup palm oil and
  ⅓ cup vegetable oil
2 onions, chopped
4 garlic cloves, chopped
1 pound okra, trimmed and
  halved
12 ounces butternut
  squash, peeled and
  cubed
8 ounces white potatoes,
  peeled and cubed
2 tomatoes, seeded and
  chopped
Salt and black pepper to
  taste
2 pounds white fish steaks
1 teaspoon red pepper
  flakes

heat the palm oil in a large pan. Add the onions and garlic and stir until the onions are translucent. Add the okra, squash, potatoes, tomatoes, and 1 cup of water. Reduce the heat, cover, and simmer for 15 minutes.

Salt and pepper the fish and place in the pan with the vegetables. Sprinkle the red pepper flakes over all and add 2 cups of water so that the vegetables will not stick. Cover, and simmer stirring occasionally, being careful not to break up the fish. When the fish is cooked through, about 10 minutes, serve with Manioc Purée (page 69) or buttered rice.

Angolan-Style Chicken

Muamba de Galinha

4 to 6 servings

muamba *is a dish found in many of the cuisines of southwest Africa, specifically the countries of Angola, Namibia, and western South Africa. The main ingredients are chicken, okra, pumpkin, onions, and palm oil. Palm oil is made from the red fruit of the African palm tree. There are some cooks who also add white potatoes to this dish.*

4 pounds boneless chicken thighs
2 large onions, minced
¾ cup vegetable oil
2 large cloves garlic, chopped
1 bay leaf
½ to ¾ cup palm oil, or half palm oil and half vegetable oil
4 fresh chili peppers (*gindungo*), chopped and seeded
1 pound pumpkin or butternut squash, peeled and cubed
1 pound okra, trimmed and cut in half
3 tablespoons lemon juice
1 teaspoon salt

Cut the chicken thighs in half and place them in a large pot with the onions, vegetable oil, garlic, and bay leaf over medium heat. Stir to mix the ingredients well. Cook for 20 minutes, or until the chicken is tender and the vegetables have formed a sauce, adding a little water from time to time to keep the dish from drying out.

Add the palm oil, peppers, pumpkin, okra, lemon juice, and salt. Cook over low heat for 15 minutes to allow seasonings to permeate the sauce. Serve hot in a large serving dish accompanied by Manioc Purée (page 69).

Grilled Chicken

Churrasco
2 servings

this method of grilling chicken is very popular in most of the Portuguese-speaking world. Portugal and Brazil have many churrascarias, *restaurants where grilled chicken is featured.* Mozambique has its Frango à Cafreal, *and Brazil has its* Churrasco *and* Galeto. *In Angola, restaurants serve the* churrasco *with French fries and a green salad. Naturally, the meal would not be complete without a glass of good Portuguese wine. I first tasted this grilled chicken at a seaside restaurant in Luanda in 1979 and it has been a favorite ever since.*

1 whole frying chicken
    (3 to 4 pounds)
3 chili peppers, chopped
1 teaspoon salt
½ cup (1 stick) butter,
    melted

heat charcoal in a grill until it turns white, or preheat gas grill to high heat.

Split the chicken in half through the breast bone but do not cut through the back. Lay the chicken flat and set aside.

Mash the peppers and salt in a mortar until the mixture resembles a paste. Add the peppers to the melted butter and mix well. With a pastry brush, brush the butter mixture on all sides of the chicken.

Place the chicken over the hot coals. Baste occasionally with the butter mixture, turning frequently until the chicken is golden on both sides, about 20 minutes. Place the chicken on a platter and serve with French fries and a salad.

NOTE: The best way to eat this chicken is to pick it up with your hands. This is the accepted method even in the best restaurants.

Grilled Pork Loin Chops

Lombinhos de Porco Grelhados
2 servings

i n days of old, indigenous Angolans living in the central highlands hunted wild boar and antelope in the forest. They cooked the meat, which they rubbed with gindungo butter, over coals. Today, the preferred meat is pork. It is still grilled over coals in the customary way but is usually purchased at the local butcher shop or supermarket.

2 pork loin steaks, or
   4 pork loin chops
1 tablespoon olive oil
1 teaspoon salt
¼ teaspoon ground black
   pepper
2 tablespoons butter,
   softened
1 teaspoon ground red
   pepper

h eat the charcoal in a grill until it turns white, or preheat a gas grill to high heat.

Rub the pork loin steaks with the olive oil and sprinkle with salt and pepper. Refrigerate for 2 hours.

Meanwhile, mix the butter and ground red pepper together to form a paste (see note). Brush the steaks with the butter and place them on the grill for about 5 minutes. Brush the other side of the steaks and turn them over to grill on the other side. Continue brushing and turning until done to the desired temperature. Serve immediately.

NOTE: What makes this dish distinctive is, of course, the hot red pepper and butter paste. You can substitute Tabasco or any other hot sauce mixed with either butter or olive oil.

Goat-Meat Stew

Caldeirada de Cabrito
10 to 12 servings

1 small goat (4 to 5 months old), cut into serving pieces, or 8 pounds goat meat, cubed

Boiling water to cover goat meat

¾ cup vegetable oil

2 pounds onions, thinly sliced

6 pounds white potatoes, peeled and sliced

4 pounds tomatoes, peeled, seeded, and thinly sliced

6 green bell peppers, seeded, and sliced into strips

Salt and black pepper to taste

2 tablespoons red pepper flakes

½ cup chopped fresh parsley leaves

½ cup chopped fresh cilantro leaves

2 bay leaves

2 cups port or sweet red wine

1 cup cognac

in 1978, my family and I spent the year traveling in three of the Portuguese-speaking countries of Africa. In Luanda, Angola, I was able to celebrate my birthday with this traditional dish. Our host made this wonderful stew and it was truly a memorable meal. I was fortunate to spend another birthday in Luanda in 1992, and experienced the same wonderful meal, this time made by our dear friend Sara dos Santos. This is her recipe and every time I prepare it I am reminded of those wonderful times we spent in Luanda and the wonderful dishes she taught me to prepare.

Wash the pieces of goat meat well and place in a large pot of boiling water. Return the pot to a boil and remove the goat meat. Set aside.

In a large skillet, heat the oil and sauté the onions until limp. In a large stew pot, layer one-third each of the onions, potatoes, goat meat, tomatoes, and bell peppers. Sprinkle with salt, pepper, and the red pepper flakes. Continue layering until all the ingredients are used.

Sprinkle the parsley and cilantro over the ingredients. Add the bay leaves and cover with the wine, 2 cups water, and the cognac. Cover tightly and cook over low heat for 30 to 40 minutes, or until the goat meat is tender. Do not remove the cover and do not stir. Just shake the pan occasionally to prevent sticking. This will keep the potatoes from breaking up. Serve hot with white rice.

Stewed Beef

Carne Guisada
4 servings

this stew should have enough broth to be able to make *Manioc Purée* (page 69). Serve it in the pan in which it was prepared or, if you prefer, in individual bowls.

¼ cup vegetable oil
1¾ pounds stew beef, cut into cubes
2 tomatoes, peeled and chopped
1 medium onion, chopped
4 ounces okra, trimmed and cut into 1-inch pieces
1 pound pumpkin, peeled and cubed
1 teaspoon salt
½ cup palm oil
2 tablespoons manioc flour (see Sources, page 355)

In a large pot, heat the oil and sauté the beef cubes, turning until lightly browned on all sides. Add the tomatoes, onion, and 1 cup of water and cook covered, over medium-low heat, until the beef is tender, about 1½ hours.

Add the okra, pumpkin, and salt and cook another 15 minutes. Pour the palm oil over the stew and mix well. Add the manioc flour to thicken the broth and cook for 5 minutes more. Serve hot with Manioc Purée (page 69) on the side.

Vinaigrette Sauce

Molho Cru

Makes about 3 cups

molho cru *literally means "raw sauce" (i.e., not cooked). This sauce is usually served with grilled meats, fish, and shellfish. It will keep for weeks, covered tightly, in the refrigerator.*

1½ cups fresh parsley leaves
1 cup chopped green
   onions
½ cup white vinegar
4 cloves garlic
2 teaspoons ground cumin
½ teaspoon salt

Combine all ingredients in a food processor and grind to a paste. Chill.

Serve on the side with grilled meat, fish, or shellfish.

Peanut Dessert

Doce de Amendoim
Makes about 12 pieces

this dessert, along with a coconut candy, is very popular in *Muxiluanda, a suburb of Luanda. In the past this dessert was made with brown sugar, but today it is made with white sugar. There are some cooks who like to add cinnamon, but this recipe is the most traditional, and even today, the most popular. Doce de Amendoim is very similar to the Brazilian Peanut Brittle (page 135), another example of the Portuguese taking foods and culinary ideas to other lands.*

1 cup raw unsalted peanuts
1 cup sugar

preheat the oven to 300 degrees F. Place the peanuts on a baking sheet and roast them in the oven for about 15 minutes, or until they are lightly toasted, turning to roast evenly. Remove and let cool.

Meanwhile, cook the sugar and ¼ cup water in a small pot until the mixture reaches the syrup stage (230 degrees F, or when a little syrup is removed with a skimmer, a fine layer is formed that can be moved about easily).

At this point, pour the mixture into a metal bowl and sprinkle the peanuts over the syrup. Mix well so that the peanuts and sugar form a ball. When the mixture cools enough to handle, separate it into 12 pieces with a wet knife. Let pieces cool completely and place in a container with an airtight lid.

Angolan Coconut Candy

Cocada Angolana
Makes 10 to 12

this dessert is also very popular in the northeast of Brazil and is sold by Baianas *(women wearing white lace dresses who are members of the Afro-Brazilian religious sect, known as* Condomblé*) on street corners as well as in bakeries. In Angola it is made in one solid piece and is sprinkled with cinnamon.* Cocada *is very popular at parties and on religious holidays.*

4 cups sugar
2 whole cloves
4 cups grated unsweetened coconut
1½ cups milk
2 tablespoons ground cinnamon

heat 4 cups of water, the sugar, and cloves in a large pot over medium heat and cook to the soft ball stage (236 degrees F or when the syrup is dropped from a spoon it forms a thread with a little ball or pearl on the end).

Remove the cloves and add the grated coconut. Cook until the coconut is tender, about 5 minutes. Add the milk and bring to a boil. Pour into a deep dish and chill.

When ready to serve, sprinkle with the cinnamon and scoop into serving dishes.

Passion Fruit Cake

Bolo de Maracujá
10 to 12 servings

this dessert is a favorite of Laura Cardosa, wife of Boaventura Cardoso, writer and ex-ambassador of Angola to Italy. My husband and I were invited to a lunch at their home in Rome and were treated to a typical Angolan meal where we had the opportunity to taste this wonderful dessert.

5 eggs, separated
4 tablespoons butter, softened
2 cups sugar
2 cups all-purpose flour
1 cup cornstarch
1 tablespoon baking powder
1 cup fresh passion fruit pulp, seeds removed

heat the oven to 350 degrees F. Butter and flour a tube cake pan.

Beat the egg yolks, butter, and sugar until creamy. Add the flour, cornstarch, and baking powder and mix well. Beat the egg whites until stiff and fold them into the batter. Add the passion fruit pulp and mix well.

Pour the batter into the cake pan and bake for about 25 minutes or until a toothpick inserted into the center of one side comes out clean. Cool on a rack. When cool, turn out on a serving plate.

NOTE: This cake can be served with whipped cream or ice cream. I have served it drizzled with sweet passion fruit glaze and topped with sliced almonds.

Baked Bananas

Bananas Assadas
6 to 8 servings

banana *desserts are very popular throughout the Portuguese-speaking world. This dessert is easy to prepare and delicious.*

6 medium green bananas
3 tablespoons butter,
   softened
1 teaspoon ground
   cinnamon
½ cup honey

preheat the oven to 400 degrees F. Peel the bananas and place them in a single layer in a baking dish. Brush the bananas with the butter and sprinkle with the cinnamon. Bake in the oven for 10 minutes. Place on serving dishes and drizzle with the honey. Serve warm.

BLACK-EYED PEA SALAD, PAGE 12
WITH CODFISH CROQUETTES, PAGE 9 (PORTUGAL)

**COLLARD GREEN SOUP
WITH SPICY CHEESE WAFERS,
PAGE 22 (PORTUGAL)**

ANGOLAN-STYLE CHICKEN, PAGE 75 (ANGOLA)

GOLDEN DESSERT, PAGE 129 (BRAZIL)

CHOCOLATE BONBONS, PAGE 133 (BRAZIL)

PRAWNS WITH HOT SAUCE, PAGE 141 (CAPE VERDE)

COCONUT PUDDING, PAGE 190 (EAST TIMOR)

GOAN RICE, PAGE 204 (GOA)

GUINEAN FISH STEW, PAGE 229 (GUINEA-BISSAU)

CHICKEN TURNOVERS WITH MANGO CHUTNEY, PAGE 290 (MOZAMBIQUE)

CUISINE OF
Brazil

traditional Brazilian cuisine is basically a combination of the cultural and cooking heritage of three groups: the indigenous peoples, whose cuisine forms the roots of Brazilian cuisine; the Portuguese, who arrived in the sixteenth century and account for European, Moorish, and Asian influences; and the Africans, who introduced some basic ingredients and culinary usages. Each of these groups has left a definitive mark on present-day Brazilian cuisine.

Brazil is divided into five geographic regions, each of whose cuisine reflects the historical ethnic origins of its early inhabitants. In the northern regions the Indian, Portuguese, and African influences are most evident. In the southern regions we find the cuisine strongly influenced by the Italian, German, Polish, and Japanese immigrants who arrived in the nineteenth and twentieth centuries. These immigrants brought food traditions that often enhanced established regional cuisines.

With respect to the three early groups (indigenous, Portuguese, and Africans), we begin with Brazil's earliest inhabitants. The Tupi were the first aboriginal people to interact with the Portuguese, who arrived in the early 1500s. The Portuguese learned from the natives how to incorporate the many foods found there into their own diet and to cultivate new agricultural products. One of these, the manioc tuber, produced many by-products. First, there is the flour made from the tuber after it is peeled, grated, hung to dry, and then roasted. The result is a coarse meal known as *farinha de mandioca*, which is as basic to the diet of Brazilians today as it was to the Tupi Indians before the arrival of the Portuguese. This meal or flour was made into sun-dried cakes called *carimã*, a favorite children's snack, and a porridge called *mingau*. A crispy lacy snack called *beiju* was also made from the flour of the root that we know as tapioca. Tapioca, a by-product of manioc, results when the starch of the manioc root is heated, causing the starch grains to pop open and clump together, forming small granules.

Other food crops grown by the Indians were sweet potatoes, squash, beans, peanuts, gourds, and peppers. Native fruits consumed were papaya, guava, cashew apples (*cajú*), and bananas. The seeds from the *guaraná*, tree were ground into a powder to make a caffeine-rich beverage which was valued as a stimulant and for its reputedly aphrodisiac effect. The rivers abounded with fish, and what the Indians did not consume fresh they salted and dried. The most consumed fish was the *pirarucu* and it was prepared by either boiling or wrapping it in banana leaves and roasting it over coals. Another fish consumed by the Indians was the manatee (*peixe boi*). Turtle meat and eggs were also eaten.

The Portuguese also played a central role in the establishment of what is known as traditional Brazilian cuisine. Because of their contacts with the Spanish, the 800 years that they were occupied by the Moors, and their early presence in sub-Saharan Africa, the Portuguese gained an early knowledge of cookery and the uses of products that they carried from trading posts and the areas they eventually colonized. Most important were the Azores, Madeira, and the Cape Verde archipelago, the latter having served as an entrepôt for foods, customs, and culinary habits. By the 1800s, mills were in operation in Brazil that produced various types of sugar, molasses, and alcoholic beverages, as well as by-products that were used to feed cattle and other farm animals that the Portuguese brought to Brazil. Catholic nuns who emigrated continued their tradition of making puddings, cakes, and egg-based desserts.

Early in Brazil's history, mining was introduced in the southern region and often food had to be imported to feed the miners. Some of the foodstuffs that were brought in were ham, sausage, olive oil, cheese, vinegar, and wine; new eating habits were created and cookery took on a different form. Portuguese farmers also introduced the cultivation of such crops as rice and coffee, which was introduced in the sixteenth century. By the end of the eighteenth century there were coffee plantations as far south as São Paulo.

The African contribution to Brazilian cuisine is probably the most recognizable. In the late sixteenth century, the Portuguese introduced sugarcane, which they brought from Southeast Asia, to the northeast region of Brazil. The first sugar plantation was established in the state of Pernambuco. This opened the way for more plantations, which brought more settlers to the region. These settlers brought African slaves to work the plantations and with them came new culinary customs and eating habits. The cuisine that began to take shape was known as *comida de azeite* (food with oil), referring to the palm oil that is still an important ingredient in the food of the northeast. The African palm tree that produces the red fruit from which the oil is made was brought to Brazil from Africa in the early part of the seventeenth century and was planted throughout the northeast. This red oil, known as *dendem* or *dendê*, extracted from the pulp of the fruit, gives the Afro-Brazilian food a unique flavor and color.

Palm oil was not the only African contribution. Even though hot peppers are of pre-Colombian-American origin, they were taken to Africa in the sixteenth century by colonizers, and returned to the northeast of Brazil with African slaves in the seventeenth century. By the beginning of the eighteenth century, many African dishes had entered into the Brazilian cuisine and were sold by slaves on street corners in the city of Salvador, Bahia. Many female vendors sold foods of Nigerian (Yoruba) origin, especially *acarajé* (black-eyed pea fritters), *abará* (baked black-eyed pea cakes in banana leaves), *caruru* (shrimp and okra stew), *vatapá* (shrimp and bread pudding), coconut candy, and other desserts. Today, many of these foods are still sold on street corners by women who are members of the Afro-Brazilian religious sect known as *Condomblé*. They dress in the traditional white lace blouse and skirt, headdress, and gold and bead necklaces worn by members of the sect.

Slave cooks often prepared Portuguese menus, but substituted African ingredients, used palm oil instead of olive oil, and invented a variety of porridge dishes using yams and bananas. This markedly African cuisine is not only present in the daily fare of Brazilians today, but also at folk celebrations and festivals, and at lunches and dinners to celebrate birthdays, anniversaries, and other special occasions. Many restaurants serve this food and advertise it as "typical." This cuisine is not confined to the state of Bahia, but has spread throughout the country as a cuisine that is served for special occasions.

Brazil's contribution to world cuisine is considerable. Portuguese mariners took Amerindian, African, and Asian agricultural products to many parts of the world. From Brazil they took chocolate, avocados, peppers, potatoes, tomatoes, manioc, and guaraná. They also took the sweet potato from its native South America to Africa. From Africa, the sweet potato spread to Europe, North America, and Asia. Another fascinating example is that of the peanut. As noted in this book's introduction, this legume, native to South America, traveled in the cargo of Portuguese merchant ships to Africa before coming to the United States with slaves.

The introduction also relates the history of okra in Brazil (see pages 2–3), elsewhere in the Americas, as well as in Angola and São Tomé and Príncipe.

The recipes in this chapter include the foods native to Brazil and those that colonizers, slaves, and immigrants brought to this land. All of these resulted in what is known today as traditional Brazilian cuisine.

Shrimp Pastries

Empadas de Camarão
Makes about 24 pastries

i t is said that Brazilian gourmands have been known to swim across Guanabara Bay from Rio to Niteroi (a distance of about five miles) to sample a better empada. These tasty little pies are so much a part of Brazilian cuisine that you find them served everywhere, in taverns or botequims, as they are called there. They are easy to prepare with a food processor. Serve with a dry white wine or Rum Drink (page 136).

SHRIMP MARINADE:
4 large cloves garlic,
    minced
3 tablespoons lemon juice
1 teaspoon salt
¼ teaspoon black pepper
8 ounces small raw shrimp,
    peeled and chopped

PASTRY DOUGH:
2 cups all-purpose flour
1 teaspoon salt
1 cup (2 sticks) butter or
    margarine, softened
1 egg yolk

FOR THE SHRIMP MARINADE: Mix the garlic, lemon juice, salt, and pepper together in a medium bowl. Stir in the shrimp and set aside while you prepare the dough.

FOR THE PASTRY DOUGH: Pour the flour into a medium bowl; add the salt and mix well. Add 3 tablespoons of water, the butter, and egg yolk. Stir until a soft dough forms. Turn out onto a lightly floured board and knead the dough until well mixed. Set aside for 1 hour, covered.

FILLING:

2 medium, ripe tomatoes, peeled and quartered

2 medium onions, peeled and quartered

½ green bell pepper, quartered and seeded

¼ cup fresh parsley leaves

2 cloves garlic, peeled

3 tablespoons olive oil

½ cup pitted black olives, quartered

1 tablespoon tomato paste

½ teaspoon Tabasco sauce, or other hot sauce

1 teaspoon flour

1 egg yolk, beaten

FOR THE FILLING: In a food processor or by hand, mince the tomatoes, onions, bell pepper, parsley, and garlic. Heat the olive oil in a 10-inch skillet. Add the vegetable mixture and stir well. Add the shrimp mixture and olives. Simmer for 10 minutes. In a small bowl, mix ¼ cup water with the tomato paste and Tabasco sauce. Pour the sauce over the shrimp mixture and stir well. Thicken with the flour, stirring until blended. Remove from the heat and let cool for about 20 minutes.

ASSEMBLY: Preheat the oven to 450 degrees F. Roll out the dough on a floured surface to about ⅛ inch thick. Using a 4-inch round cookie cutter, cut out 48 rounds and line 24 muffin tins with the circles of dough (the muffin tins should be 1 inch deep). Fill each with about 2 tablespoons of the shrimp mixture. Top with another round of pastry; pinch the sides together and brush the tops with the egg yolk. Bake for 20 minutes, or until golden. Cool on racks for 5 minutes before eating. Serve warm or at room temperature.

Rice and Sardine Croquettes

Bolinhos de Arroz com Sardinhas
Makes about 30

*t*his is one of the savory appetizers that are so popular at Brazilian get-togethers. The combination of rice and sardines may seem a bit unusual to the American palate, but it makes for a delicious appetizer. In São Tomé, an island off the west coast of Africa and a former Portuguese colony, manioc is used in this recipe instead of rice. In Portugal, fish is added to the dough, and is then deep fried. In Mozambique, chopped shrimp are substituted for the sardines.

2 cups cold Brazilian Rice (page 110)
3 cans (4⅜-ounce) boneless, skinless sardines, drained and mashed
½ cup freshly grated Parmesan cheese (see note)
2 eggs, beaten
Salt and black pepper to taste

COATING:
2 eggs, beaten
1 cup dry bread crumbs
Vegetable oil for frying

*m*ix the rice with the sardines, cheese, and eggs until well incorporated. Place in a medium pot and cook over low heat, stirring constantly, until the mixture holds its shape. Stir in salt and pepper to taste and set aside to cool.

Shape the sardine mixture into 2-inch balls or croquette shapes, dip into the beaten eggs, and then roll in the bread crumbs. Pour the oil into a medium-size pan to a depth of two inches and heat over medium-high heat to 365 degrees F on a deep-frying thermometer. Fry the croquettes a few at a time until golden brown. Drain on paper towels and serve at room temperature with toothpicks.

NOTE: Substitute white cheddar or Asiago for the Parmesan for a sharper cheese taste.

Black-Eyed Pea Fritters

Acarajé
Makes about 60

i tasted my first acarajé in 1960 in Salvador, Bahia, Brazil. Near the Praça da Sé, a bus depot, I noticed a woman seated at a makeshift stand at a curb selling little fried cakes. Because of the wonderful aroma I decided to buy one and responded yes to her question "com pimenta?" ("with hot sauce?"). It turned out to be a black-eyed pea cake, fried in red palm oil, cut open and filled with sautéed dried shrimp and hot pepper sauce. Delicious!

5 cups dried black-eyed
    peas, washed and sorted
½ cup dried shrimp, soft-
    ened in warm water
2 large onions
2 cloves garlic
2 teaspoons salt
Palm oil for frying
Acarajé Sauce (page 92)

refrigerate the black-eyed peas overnight in cold water to cover.

The next day rub the peas with the palms of your hands to loosen the skins and then pull them off, or place the peas in a folded napkin and lightly press with a rolling pin. Discard the skins.

Drain the shrimp and reserve the liquid.

Put the peeled peas through a meat grinder or in a food processor with the onions, drained shrimp, and garlic. If using a meat grinder use a fine blade. After processing, add the salt and mix the ingredients well. Beat with a wooden spoon or mixer until fluffy. Add a little of the shrimp water if the mixture is too dry.

Pour the palm oil into a deep iron or heavy skillet to a depth of two inches. Heat over medium-high heat to 365 degrees F on a deep-frying thermometer. Drop the batter by spoonfuls into the hot oil and fry until they float and are golden. Drain on paper towels. Make a slit on one side of each fritter and put in a spoonful of the Acarajé Sauce or *Vatapá* (page 114). Serve hot or at room temperature.

Acarajé Sauce

Molho de Acarajé
Makes about 3 cups

1 cup dried shrimp, soft-
    ened in warm water
1 medium onion, chopped
2 dried chili peppers,
    or 2 tablespoons red
    pepper flakes
2 cloves garlic
1 teaspoon salt
½ cup palm oil
1 cup small raw peeled
    shrimp, coarsely
    chopped

drain the shrimp. Place the onion, dried shrimp, chili peppers, garlic, and salt in a blender and purée.

Heat the palm oil in a frying pan, add the fresh shrimp and cook for about 2 minutes, stirring occasionally. Add the purée, mix well and simmer for 3 minutes to heat through. Remove from the heat and cool.

NOTE: This sauce can be served with Black-Eyed Pea Fritters (page 91), Rice Hausa-Style (page 108), Chicken Bahian-Style (page 120), and Shrimp and Bread Pudding (page 114).

Chicken Pastries

Empadinhas de Galinha
Makes 2 dozen

i n Portugal, empadinhas *were made with lamb and spices intro-duced by the Moors, but when brought to Brazil they were adapted to the ingredients available locally and have become a staple of* Brazilian cuisine. Empadinhas *and pastries fit into the category of* sal-gado, *which literally means "salty," but includes any appetizer or fin-ger food served with drinks before a meal.* Empadinha *dough uses shortening and eggs and is always baked, while* pastel *dough is simi-lar to pie pastry and can be baked or fried. Serve these pastries as part of a buffet with other finger foods. The filling should be prepared one day in advance so the flavors can meld.*

MARINADE:
1 medium onion, chopped
¼ cup white vinegar
¼ cup chopped fresh
    parsley
¼ cup olive oil
3 tablespoons lemon juice
2 cloves garlic
4 fresh mint leaves
1 teaspoon dried savory
1 teaspoon salt
1 teaspoon coriander seeds
½ teaspoon black pepper

FILLING:
6 boneless skinless chicken
    thighs
1 tablespoon butter or
    margarine
¼ cup tomato sauce
2 tablespoons cornstarch
3 cups whole milk
2 egg yolks, lightly beaten

FOR THE MARINADE: Blend all the ingredients in a blender or food processor until a purée forms. Set aside.

FOR THE FILLING: Remove any fat from the chicken and place the chicken in a non-reactive bowl. Pour ½ cup of the marinade over the chicken. Cover and refrigerate overnight, turning occasionally.

The following day, melt the butter in a large skillet over medium-high heat and quickly brown the chicken on all sides. Cover, reduce the heat, and cook for 15 minutes, turning once. Add the remain-ing marinade and continue cooking for 5 minutes. Add the tomato sauce and ⅓ cup water. Mix well and cook until the chicken is opaque, about 5 more minutes. Remove the chicken from the sauce and let cool. Shred the chicken and set aside.

Mix the cornstarch with ⅓ cup of the milk and add it to the sauce in the skillet. Stir until smooth.

(CONTINUED)

Heat the sauce over low heat until it begins to thicken, slowly add the remaining 2⅔ cups milk, stirring continuously, until the sauce is smooth. Remove the skillet from the heat. Beat the egg yolks with 2 tablespoons of the warm sauce. Pour the egg yolk mixture into the skillet over low heat. Cook the mixture, stirring occasionally, for about 5 minutes to further thicken it. Add the chicken, mix well, and taste for seasonings.

PASTRY:

2½ cups all-purpose flour
¼ cup (½ stick) butter
¼ cup lard or shortening
½ teaspoon salt
3 egg yolks
¼ cup whole milk

12 black olives
3 eggs, hard-boiled and
    quartered
1 egg, lightly beaten

FOR THE PASTRY: Pour the flour into a large bowl. Melt the butter and lard together and add them to the flour, mixing until crumbly. In another bowl, combine the salt and 1 tablespoon of water. Add the egg yolks to the salt water one at a time. Fold the egg mixture into the flour and add the milk. Mix well and shape into a ball. Cover and set aside to rest for 1 hour.

ASSEMBLY: Preheat the oven to 350 degrees F and grease 12 muffin tins. Uncover the pastry and roll out on a floured board as thinly as possible, about ⅛ inch thick. Cut 12 rounds about 1-inch larger than the muffin tins. Press the pastry rounds into the tins and up the sides. Fill the tins three-quarters full with the filling. Top each cup with an olive and a piece of hard-boiled egg. Cut 12 more rounds of dough ½ inch larger than the diameter of the top of the muffin tins. Press each one on top of a cup; press the edges together to seal with the tines of a fork dipped in water. Brush each pastry top with the beaten egg. Bake for 20 to 30 minutes or until golden. Cool, and serve as part of an appetizer buffet or as a light lunch with a green salad.

Beef Croquettes

Bolinhos de Carne
Makes 20 to 25 croquettes

i n the years when most households had cooks, it took approximately three hours to prepare beef croquettes and they were reserved for parties and special festive occasions. Today, because many women work, help is expensive, and these croquettes are time consuming, housewives are purchasing them already prepared at delis and supermarkets. This particular recipe uses ground beef, and because it doesn't call for stuffing, is less time consuming. The end result is still delicious.

⅛ cup vegetable oil
1½ pounds ground beef
   (see note)
¼ cup grated onion
1 large tomato, peeled,
   seeded, and minced
2 cloves garlic, minced
Salt and black pepper
2 tablespoons chopped
   fresh parsley
1 medium potato, peeled,
   cooked, and mashed
¼ cup all-purpose flour

COATING:

2 eggs, lightly beaten
2 teaspoons milk
2 cups all-purpose flour

Vegetable oil for frying

i n a large nonstick frying pan, heat the vegetable oil on medium-high and sauté the ground beef, onion, tomato and garlic, stirring until the beef is cooked through and the onions are translucent. Mix in salt and pepper to taste and the parsley. Lower the heat to a simmer and add the mashed potato and ¼ cup flour, stirring constantly until the mixture comes away from the sides of the pan. Remove from the heat and set aside to cool.

FOR THE COATING: Beat the eggs with the milk in a shallow bowl. Place the 2 cups flour in another shallow bowl. Pour the oil into a deep iron or heavy skillet to a depth of three inches. Heat it over medium-high heat to 365 degrees F on a deep-frying thermometer. Using 2 tablespoons for each piece, form the beef mixture into egg shapes (croquettes) until all is used. Roll the croquettes first in the egg mixture and then in the flour. Fry the croquettes in the oil until golden. Drain on paper towels. Serve at room temperature.

NOTE: These croquettes can also be made with leftover roast beef. In that case, grind the meat in a meat grinder then proceed with the recipe. Ground chicken also works well in this recipe.

Hearts of Palm Pastries

Pastéis de Palmito
Makes 60 pastries

t his vegetarian appetizer is enjoyed by all Paulistas, the people of São Paulo. The pastries are served along with the typical plate of beans and rice in the finest restaurants. One can also find them in open-air markets, fried on the spot for hungry shoppers.

FILLING:
2 tablespoons butter
½ cup minced onion
1 can (7¼-ounce) hearts of
    palm, drained and
    chopped
1 tablespoon flour
1 cup whole milk
1 teaspoon salt
¼ teaspoon black pepper
10 pitted black olives,
    chopped

DOUGH:
5 cups all-purpose flour
5 tablespoons light brandy
1 tablespoon salt
1½ teaspoons sugar

Vegetable oil for frying

FOR THE FILLING: Melt the butter in a medium saucepan over medium heat. Add the onion and stir frequently until lightly golden. Stir in the palm hearts and cook for another 5 minutes. Meanwhile, dissolve the flour in the milk and add it to the palm heart mixture, stirring constantly to keep lumps from forming. Cook until the filling thickens, and then remove it from the heat. Season the filling with the salt and black pepper, stir in the olives, and set aside.

FOR THE DOUGH: Pour the flour into a large bowl. Make a well in the center and add the brandy, salt, and sugar. Mix well. Add 1½ cups of water, a little at a time, mixing well after each addition, until the dough comes together in a ball. Place the dough on a floured surface and knead until smooth. Roll the dough ¼ inch thick and cut into 3-inch circles.

PASTRIES: Place a teaspoon of filling in the center of each circle. Dampen the edges with water and fold over to form a half circle. Press the edges together with the tines of a fork. Repeat until all the circles are used. Pour the oil into a deep iron or heavy skillet to a depth of two inches. Heat it over medium-high heat to 365 degrees F on a deep-frying thermometer. Fry the pastries a few at a time until golden brown on both sides, about 3 minutes total. Remove and drain on paper towels. Serve warm or at room temperature.

Afro-Brazilian Warm Okra Salad

Salada de Quiabo
4 to 6 servings

*i*n the northeast of Brazil, okra is a very popular vegetable. As I said in my introduction, okra was brought to Brazil by slaves from the west coast of Africa and is a principal ingredient in many of the dishes associated with the Afro-Brazilian religious sects (Condomblé and Macumba). This dish is often served with grilled fish.

2½ pounds fresh okra
1 teaspoon salt

VINAIGRETTE:
2 onions, finely chopped
¾ cup olive oil
¼ cup red wine vinegar
6 cloves garlic
2 teaspoons Dijon mustard
¾ teaspoon salt
½ teaspoon Tabasco
Black pepper to taste

*r*emove the tops and tails of the okra and cut the pods into ¼-inch slices. Put in a large pot, pour enough water over them to cover, and bring to a boil with the salt. Cover, reduce the heat, and cook for 5 minutes. Drain the okra and place in a large bowl.

Blend the ingredients for the vinaigrette in a blender until smooth and pour over the okra while it is still warm. Mix well and serve at room temperature.

Rice Salad

Salada de Arroz
4 servings

*r*ice salads are as popular in Brazil as they are in the rest of the
Portuguese-speaking world. Each country or territory uses
slightly different ingredients. This particular salad can be made
with white or Brazilian Rice.

2 cups cold, cooked white
rice or Brazilian Rice
(page 110)
1 Granny Smith apple,
peeled, cored, and cut
into julienne strips
1 cup cooked peas
½ avocado, peeled and
chopped
1 tablespoon chopped
pimiento
2 tablespoons olive oil
1 tablespoon lemon juice
1 tablespoon white vinegar
1 teaspoon Dijon mustard
1 teaspoon salt
¼ teaspoon black pepper

GARNISH:
½ head lettuce, shredded
3 hard-boiled eggs
8 ounces medium shrimp,
cooked (optional)

*p*lace the rice in a large bowl. Add the apple,
peas, avocado, and pimiento. In a smaller bowl,
mix together the olive oil, lemon juice, vinegar, mustard, salt, and pepper. Add this dressing to the rice
and vegetables, mix well, and pack into an oiled tube
mold. Chill at least 2 hours.

Arrange the lettuce on a platter and un-mold the rice
on top. Decorate the platter with sliced hard-boiled
eggs, and shrimp, if desired.

NOTE: Cooked and chilled beets, cut julienne can
also be used as a garnish. For a vegetarian dish, eliminate the shrimp.

Baked Crabmeat Omelet

Frigideira de Siri

6 servings

i n Brazil, the name frigideira or fritada *is given to any dish with chopped or minced ingredients covered with beaten eggs and baked in the oven. The most popular of these dishes are made with shrimp, codfish, crabmeat, fish, or* lingüiça. *In Mozambique, a similar dish, Shrimp and Carrot Pudding (page 307), is baked in a form pan.* Frigideiras *are common throughout the Portuguese-speaking world.*

1 can (14-ounce) unsweet-
  ened coconut milk
2 thick slices day-old
  peasant bread
1 pound crabmeat
2 medium onions, chopped
3 tablespoons lemon juice
2 large cloves garlic,
  crushed with
  1 teaspoon salt
1 teaspoon salt
¼ teaspoon black pepper
2 tablespoons olive oil
2 chayotes, peeled and
  chopped
2 medium tomatoes, peeled,
  seeded, and chopped
1 tablespoon chopped
  fresh parsley
6 eggs, separated
Shortening or butter to
  grease pan

GARNISH:

6 green bell pepper rings
6 tomato slices, centers
  removed
6 slices stuffed green olives

p our the coconut milk into a bowl, add the slices of bread, and let stand for ½ hour. Preheat the oven to 400 degrees F.

In a large bowl mix the crabmeat, onions, lemon juice, garlic, salt, and pepper. Heat the olive oil in a skillet over medium heat, add the crab mixture, and sauté 2 minutes. Add the chayotes, tomatoes, and parsley. Stir, lower the heat, and simmer until all the liquid has evaporated. Stir the bread and coconut milk into the crab mixture, remove from the heat and let cool. Grind the mixture in a food processor or meat grinder.

Beat the egg whites until stiff. Beat the yolks and fold into the egg whites. Add salt and pepper to taste. Grease a 10-inch deep-dish pie pan and pour in a layer of the egg mixture to cover the bottom of the dish. Mix ¼ cup of the eggs with the crabmeat and spoon the crab mixture over the egg layer. Top with the rest of the eggs. Decorate the top with the pepper rings. Place 1 tomato slice inside each pepper ring and an olive slice in the center of each tomato slice. Bake until the top is golden, about 20 minutes. Cool 10 minutes. Serve hot.

Ground Beef Pie

Frigideira de Carne
6 to 8 servings

*t*his pie is one of the dishes usually served for a Sunday brunch or a Bahian buffet. For lunch or a light supper, serve with a green salad.

2 pounds stew beef
2 tablespoons white vinegar
2 cloves garlic, chopped
1 teaspoon salt
2 slices smoked bacon
  (optional)
1 tablespoon lard or
  shortening
1 large onion, minced
2 chayotes, peeled and
  chopped
4 medium tomatoes, peeled
  and chopped
6 eggs, separated
1 tablespoon vegetable oil

GARNISH:
6 slices tomato
6 slices green bell pepper
6 slices onion

*t*rim the fat from the beef and cut the meat into 1-inch cubes. Sprinkle the vinegar over the meat. Place the garlic and salt in a mortar and pound to a paste. Mix the garlic with the beef and set aside for 30 minutes.

Cut the bacon into ½-inch pieces and fry in the lard in a large frying pan until crisp. Add the onion and cook until lightly golden. Add the beef, chayotes, and tomatoes. Cover and cook over medium heat until the beef is lightly browned, about 5 minutes. Remove from the heat and cool. Put the meat mixture through the coarse disk of a meat grinder or pulse in a food processor; set aside.

Preheat the oven to 375 degrees F. Beat the egg whites to stiff peaks; beat the yolks and fold them into the whites. Fold ¼ cup egg into the meat mixture to moisten. Brush the bottom and sides of a 10-inch deep glass or ceramic pie dish with the vegetable oil. Pour in ½ cup of beaten eggs and spread over the bottom. Top with the meat mixture and cover the meat with the remaining beaten eggs. Bake for 20 minutes, or until golden. Remove from the oven and decorate with the tomato slices, green pepper slices, and onion slices. Return the pie to the oven for an additional 5 minutes to cook the vegetables. Serve warm.

Elegant Soup

Sopa Delicada
4 to 6 servings

portuguese Jews who fled to Brazil during the Inquisition brought their tradition of potato dumpling soup. This version is one that has undergone some modifications over the centuries, including the addition of ham.

2 quarts beef stock
1 large carrot, peeled and chopped
½ cup chopped parsley
2 pounds (3 or 4 medium) Yukon potatoes, with skins on
2 teaspoons salt
½ cup grated Parmesan cheese
3 eggs, separated
3 tablespoons ground ham or turkey ham
2 tablespoons butter
¼ teaspoon ground nutmeg
1 cup all-purpose flour
Vegetable oil for frying

pour the stock into a large pot. Add the carrot and parsley and boil for 10 minutes.

Wash the potatoes and cook in a separate medium pot with cold water and 1 teaspoon of the salt for 20 minutes. When the potatoes are tender, peel and push them through a strainer or ricer, or mash them. While still warm, add ¼ cup of the cheese, the egg yolks, ground ham, butter, nutmeg, and remaining 1 teaspoon salt. Mix well.

Make little balls the size of walnuts from the potato mixture, roll them in flour one at a time, and place on a baking sheet until all the mixture is used. Pour the oil into a deep iron or heavy skillet to a depth of two inches. Heat it over medium-high heat to 365 degrees F on a deep-frying thermometer. Fry the balls a few at a time until golden brown. Remove from the oil and place on a rack or absorbent paper.

Remove the carrots and parsley from the stock and bring the stock to a boil. Add the potato dumplings, reduce the heat, and simmer for 3 to 5 minutes. Pour the soup into a tureen and sprinkle with the remaining Parmesan cheese. Serve immediately.

Brazilian Bean Stew

Feijoada à Brasileira
18 to 20 servings

f eijoada, *the national dish of Brazil, was created in the slave quarters of Bahia, and is enjoyed throughout the country. In the northeast* feijoada *is made with brown beans and in the south, particularly in Rio de Janeiro, black beans are the norm.* Feijoada *is a dish known throughout the Portuguese-speaking world and it is very probable that the Portuguese were responsible for taking this dish from Brazil to their colonies and territories. In Cape Verde there is Bean Stew, Cape Verdean-Style (page 150), in Timor there is East Timor Bean Stew (page 178), and in Mozambique there is Mozambican Bean Stew (page 297). Each is a variation of the original. Portugal's northwestern province, Trás-os-Montes, has a version that is made with kidney beans, pig's ears, pig's snout, pig's feet, sausage, salt pork, and ham. This stew is popular for lunch on Ash Wednesday, when the first smoked meat of the year is eaten. In Brazil* feijoada *is traditionally eaten for lunch on Saturdays, special occasions, and at large parties. It should be prepared a day or two before serving. This will give the flavors a chance to meld and give you a chance to prepare the accompaniments and side dishes for the* feijoada. *Even though this is a time-consuming dish, the culinary experience is well worth the time spent preparing it.*

THE DAY BEFORE SERVING: Refrigerate the beans overnight in cold water to cover. Refrigerate the dried beef and *paio* overnight in separate pans of cold water. Wash the pork loin, pat dry, and place in an ovenproof glass dish. Sprinkle the pork with salt, pepper, and garlic powder to taste. Pour the wine over the pork, add the bay leaf and garlic slices, and arrange the sliced onion over and around the pork. Cover the pork and place in the refrigerator to marinate overnight.

THE FOLLOWING DAY: Prick the fresh sausages with a fork and set aside. Parboil the paio and smoked sausages and set aside. Drain the beans, cover with fresh cold water, and cook over medium heat, covered, for about 2½ hours, adding water as needed to keep the beans covered. Add the sausages and paio to the beans after the beans have cooked for 1½ hours. After the beans have cooked for 2 hours, cut the dried beef into 1-inch cubes and add

8 cups dried black beans, washed and sorted
1 pound Brazilian dried beef or beef jerky
1 pound *paio* or Canadian bacon
6 pounds pork loin roast
Salt, black pepper, and garlic powder to taste
2 cups white wine
1 bay leaf
4 cloves garlic, sliced
1 medium onion, sliced
2 pounds fresh pork sausages
2 pounds smoked or Portuguese sausages
1 tablespoon shortening
2 large onions, chopped
1 large tomato, chopped
4 garlic cloves, minced
1 tablespoon chopped fresh parsley
2 tablespoons red pepper flakes
Orange slices as a garnish

to the beans. Taste the bean liquid for seasonings and adjust.

While the beans are cooking, preheat the oven to 350 degrees F. Remove the pork loin from the refrigerator, place in the oven, and roast, covered, for 1 hour. Remove the cover and continue roasting until the meat browns slightly, about a half hour more, basting occasionally.

About a half hour before serving, melt the shortening in a large pan and gently sauté the onions, tomato, garlic, parsley, and red pepper until the onions are soft. Add about 1 cup of the beans to the vegetables and mash with a wooden spoon. Pour about 2 cups of the beans liquor over the mixture and simmer until the mixture thickens. Return the mixture to the pot of beans. Simmer until thoroughly blended, about 10 minutes. Taste the beans and correct the seasonings.

To serve, remove the meats from the beans and pour the beans into a large chafing dish or soup tureen. Place the pork loin in the center of a large platter and slice thinly. Slice the fresh sausages into ½-inch pieces and place on one side of the pork loin. Slice the paio and the dried beef and place on the platter. Serve with orange wedges, Toasted Manioc Meal with Palm Oil (page 107), Brazilian Rice (page 110), Collard Greens, Minas Gerais-Style (page 105), Hot Pepper and Lemon Sauce (page 124), and Rum Drink (page 136).

Brazilian-Style Succotash

Pudim de Milho e Feijão
8 servings

i n the sixteenth and seventeenth centuries, this dish was very popular with the entire Brazilian population and was served at most festive occasions. When invited to dine with their Catholic friends, many secret Jews expressed a preference for this dish over others that contained pork. By doing this they were able to honor their religious dietary restrictions and avoid eating prohibited foods without drawing attention to their religion.

1 package (10-ounce)
   frozen lima beans
1 package (10-ounce)
   frozen corn
3 eggs, lightly beaten
3 tablespoons all-purpose
   flour
1 tablespoon sugar
1 teaspoon salt
1 teaspoon black pepper
¼ teaspoon ground nutmeg
¼ cup (½ stick) butter
1 small onion, minced
½ green bell pepper,
   minced
2 cups half-and-half

p reheat the oven to 325 degrees F. Grease a 2-quart ovenproof casserole.

Combine the lima beans, corn, and eggs in a medium bowl. In another bowl, combine the flour, sugar, salt, pepper, and nutmeg.

Melt the butter in a medium pot and sauté the onion and bell pepper until soft. Add the flour mixture to the onion mixture and stir well. Stir in the half-and-half and add the vegetable mixture. Pour into the prepared casserole.

Place the casserole in a larger pan of hot water to a depth of 1-inch, to form a bain-marie. Bake for 1 hour, or until a toothpick inserted in the center comes out clean. Serve at room temperature with beef or pork.

Collard Greens, Minas Gerais-Style

Couve à Mineira

8 to 10 servings

these collard greens usually accompany the famous Brazilian national dish Feijoada à Brasileira *(page 102)*. *Even though this particular recipe is from the state of Minas Gerais, the method of preparing the greens is appreciated throughout Brazil. It is generally made with* couve galega, *a type of cabbage grown in Portugal and similar to our collard greens. The Portuguese took these greens to Brazil, Angola, Cape Verde, and Guinea-Bissau.*

4 pounds collard greens
3 tablespoons olive oil
1 medium onion, finely
    chopped
2 large cloves garlic,
    minced
1 teaspoon salt
½ teaspoon black pepper
1 teaspoon red pepper
    flakes

remove the stalks and veins from the leaves of the collards. Stack the leaves one on top of the other and roll up tightly like a cigar. Cut the roll into ⅛-inch slices and set aside.

Heat 2 quarts of water to boiling with 1 tablespoon of the olive oil. Add the collard greens and cook uncovered, for about 5 minutes to wilt them; drain and set aside. Heat the remaining 2 tablespoons olive oil in a large frying pan and sauté the onion and garlic until the onion is translucent. Season the greens with salt and pepper. Add the greens and the red pepper flakes to the onions and sauté for 10 minutes, stirring occasionally, or until the greens are tender.

NOTE: Do not cover the greens while cooking or they will lose their bright green color.

Spicy Greens

Efó
8 servings

efó, *a word of African origin, refers to a type of leafy green. In Bahia* efó *is prepared with a variety of greens—the most popular being the leaves of* lingua de vaca *and* taioba. *Since these are not available outside of Brazil, you can substitute spinach. In the Comdomblé religion, all of the gods and goddesses* (Orixás) *love to eat* efó *with the exception of* Oxalá *who detests spicy food. Bahians and other northeasterners consider this dish one of the examples of their Afro-Brazilian cuisine. In Bahia,* efó *is prepared and served in a clay pot. It is accompanied by Bahian-style Shrimp and Okra (page 113), and Hot Pepper and Lemon Sauce (page 124).*

1½ cups dried shrimp
1½ cups (12 ounces) roasted, unsalted peanuts
1 cup (8 ounces) roasted unsalted cashews
1 onion, quartered
4 cloves garlic
2 tablespoons chopped fresh cilantro
⅓ cup palm oil, or half palm oil and half vegetable oil
2 pounds spinach, stemmed, chopped, and blanched
½ cup coconut milk
1 tablespoon red pepper flakes

Soak the dried shrimp in warm water for 20 minutes to soften. Drain the shrimp and place in a meat grinder or food processor along with the peanuts, cashews, onion, garlic, and cilantro and grind all to a pulp. Set aside.

Heat the palm oil in a large pot and sauté the ground shrimp and nut mixture for 5 minutes over medium heat. Add the spinach, coconut milk, red pepper, salt, and pepper. Lower the heat to a simmer and cook, stirring occasionally, until the mixture is almost dry. Just before serving, pour a little more palm oil over the dish. Serve with white rice and manioc flour. (The manioc flour is sprinkled over the greens.)

Toasted Manioc Meal with Palm Oil

Farofa de Azeite-de-dendem
10 servings

*f*rying in palm oil is one of the many ways to prepare this meal. It can also be cooked with water, broth, or butter. Some variations call for the addition of pumpkin, bacon, egg, or sausage. Serve this dish with Brazilian Bean Stew (page 102) or Chicken Bahian-Style (page 120).

2 cups manioc meal
¼ cup palm oil, or half palm oil and half vegetable oil
1 large onion, minced
2 hard-boiled eggs, chopped (optional)
¼ cup chopped black olives (optional)

*h*eat a large skillet over medium heat and add the manioc meal. Stir constantly until the manioc meal is lightly toasted. Remove from the heat and pour into a bowl.

Add the palm oil to the skillet, heat over medium heat. Add the onion and sauté until it is translucent. Pour the manioc into the skillet and stir to coat completely. Serve hot or at room temperature. The *farofa* may be garnished with hard-boiled eggs or olives.

NOTE: To serve with fish or shellfish, add 4 ounces of chopped dried or fresh shrimp to the pan with the onion, and sauté until both are golden. If using dried shrimp, soak in warm water for 20 minutes before adding to the pan.

Rice, Hausa-Style

Arroz-de-Hauça
8 to 10 servings

arroz-de Hauça *is one of the favorite dishes of Brazilian novelist Jorge Amado. In fact, in many of his novels he depicts characters enjoying this dish of African origin (the Hausa people are from northern Nigeria). In the early sixties, when I lived in Bahia, I was privileged to spend many Sunday afternoons at his home with his wife, Zelia Gattas, and other friends. One Sunday after a party at Jorge and Zelia's home, we were served some leftover* arroz-de-hauça. *The dish was made by a cook who was called in because it is her specialty and is a bit complicated to make. What she prepared was a delicious dish and I have followed her recipe to a "T." Remember to soak the dried beef overnight to remove excess salt so that it is ready for cooking the following day.*

RICE:
1 large onion, minced
3 cloves garlic, minced
¼ cup olive oil
4½ cups uncooked white rice
8 cups boiling water
1 cup coconut milk
Butter for the mold

DRIED BEEF:
2 pounds dried beef (*carne seca*)
1 large onion, thinly sliced
2 tablespoons olive oil
2 tablespoons palm oil, or half palm oil and half vegetable oil
1 cup coconut milk

FOR THE RICE: Place onion and garlic in a large pot with the olive oil over medium heat. Sauté until the onion is translucent. Add the rice and 8 cups of boiling water; stir, cover, reduce the heat to a simmer, and cook for 15 minutes. Add the coconut milk and continue cooking for 10 minutes or until the rice is tender. Remove the rice from the heat and pour into a buttered 2-quart ring form pan. Set aside.

FOR THE BEEF: Cut the dried beef into small cubes and simmer in water to cover for 20 minutes. Drain. In a large pan over medium heat, sauté the onion in the olive and palm oils until translucent. Add the dried beef, and when the beef has browned, add the coconut milk and continue to cook until the liquid has evaporated. Set aside.

Cuisines of Portuguese Encounters

SHRIMP:

1 tablespoon olive oil
2 tablespoons palm oil, or
    half palm oil and half
    vegetable oil
1 large onion, minced
1 cup dried shrimp, soaked
    in warm water to
    soften
1 cup coconut milk

SAUCE:

1 large onion, minced
1 large tomato, peeled and
    seeded
½ cup dried shrimp, soaked
    in warm water to soften
2 tablespoons olive oil
2 tablespoons palm oil, or
    half palm oil and half
    vegetable oil
1 tablespoon red pepper
    flakes
1 tablespoon lemon juice

FOR THE SHRIMP: Heat the olive and palm oils in a small skillet over medium heat and sauté the onion until it is translucent. Add the dried shrimp and the coconut milk and cook until the shrimp is soft, about 10 minutes. Set aside.

FOR THE SAUCE: Place the onion in a food processor along with the tomato and dried shrimp. Pulse until the mixture resembles a purée. In a medium skillet, heat the olive and palm oils and add the mixture from the food processor, the red pepper flakes, and lemon juice. Simmer the mixture for 10 minutes. Set aside.

TO SERVE: Invert the rice mold onto a platter. Place the shrimp in the center of the mold and surround the mold with the beef. Serve the sauce on the side.

Mountain Rice

Arroz da Serra
6 to 8 servings

*t*his rice dish is from the sertão or "backlands" of the southern Brazilian state of São Paulo. Influenced by the Tupi-Guarani, it is now a part of Brazil's national cuisine.

2 cups uncooked white rice
1 pound ground beef
6 medium green bananas
1 tablespoon vegetable oil
8 ounces fresh goat
   cheese, sliced

*b*ring 4 cups of water to a boil. Add the rice, stir, cover, reduce the heat, and simmer for 20 minutes or until tender. Meanwhile, in a large frying pan, sauté the beef until the meat looses its pink color. Set aside. Peel the bananas and cut into ½-inch slices. In the same frying pan, heat the oil and brown the bananas quickly on both sides. Remove and drain on absorbent paper.

Preheat the oven to 350 degrees F. Butter a 2-quart ovenproof casserole and layer half of each ingredient, beginning with rice, then ground beef, slices of cheese, and banana slices. Place a second layer of each ingredient over the first. Bake the rice for 15 minutes, or until the cheese is melted. Serve warm.

Brazilian Rice

Arroz Brasileiro
6 to 8 servings

2 tablespoons olive oil,
   lard, bacon fat, or margarine (not butter)
2 cups long-grain rice
2 medium onions, diced
5 cups boiling water
1 teaspoon salt
1 medium tomato, finely
   chopped

*h*eat the olive oil in a medium skillet. Add the rice and onions and sauté, stirring with a wooden spoon until the onions are golden and the rice is lightly browned, about 10 minutes. Stir in the tomato. Remove from the heat.

Pour the boiling water slowly over the rice mixture to avoid splattering. Stir and return to the heat and bring to a boil. When the mixture boils, cover the pan and lower the heat. Simmer for 25 minutes or until all water is absorbed. Remove from the heat, uncover, and let steam evaporate.

Bahian Fish Ragout

Moqueca de Peixe

4 to 6 servings

he word moqueca *probably comes from the Tupi-Guarani word* pokeka, *although the dish itself is of African origin. It was originally a ragout of fish cooked in palm oil with peppers, then wrapped in banana leaves, and roasted over hot coals. Today this classic dish is usually cooked without the banana leaves, on top of the stove.*

2½ pounds firm white fish fillets, such as grouper, halibut or cod
1 small tomato, chopped
1 small onion
1 cup fresh cilantro
4 cloves garlic
1 teaspoon red pepper flakes
1 teaspoon salt
¼ teaspoon peppercorns
3 tablespoons lemon juice
1 large onion, thinly sliced
2 medium tomatoes, thinly sliced
1 cup unsweetened coconut milk
½ cup palm oil or vegetable oil

Wipe the fish fillets dry, cut them into serving pieces and put in a shallow glass casserole. In a food processor, purée the chopped tomato, small onion, cilantro, garlic, red pepper flakes, salt, and peppercorns. Add the lemon juice and mix well. Pour the mixture over the fish and marinate for 2 hours, turning occasionally.

Place the fish fillets in a large skillet. Top the fish with the onion and tomato slices. Pour the coconut milk and palm oil over the vegetables; cook covered over medium heat until the fish and vegetables are tender (about 6 minutes). Serve with Manioc Purée (page 69).

Holy Week Pie

Torta de Semana Santa
4 to 6 servings

in Victoria, Brazil, many continue to observe Holy Week as they did years ago by serving this delicious dish in their homes. Also known as Torta Capixaba, *it was traditionally eaten only for supper on Good Friday, but today it is served at lunch as well and also for supper on Holy Saturday and Easter Sunday. This pie is traditionally prepared in an earthenware casserole and can be served either hot or cold.*

1 pound salt cod
3 cloves garlic, minced
2 teaspoons salt
½ cup vegetable oil
2 large onions, minced
1 jalapeño pepper, minced
4 large tomatoes, peeled
   and chopped
¼ cup chopped fresh parsley
¼ cup chopped fresh cilantro
1 pound shucked fresh
   oysters, in their juice
1 dozen shucked fresh
   clams, in their juice
1 pound small raw shrimp,
   cleaned and deveined
1 pound lobster meat
1 pound crabmeat
¼ cup lemon juice
6 hearts of palm
½ teaspoon black pepper
12 large eggs

GARNISH:
1 large onion, thinly sliced
4 hard-boiled eggs, sliced
   crosswise
½ cup sliced black olives

Soak the salt cod in cold water to cover for 24 hours in the refrigerator, changing the water frequently. Pound the garlic and 1 teaspoon of the salt together in a mortar and pestle until they resemble a paste; set aside. Heat the vegetable oil in a large skillet over medium heat and sauté the onions and jalapeño until soft. Add the garlic paste, tomatoes, parsley, and cilantro, stirring to blend the vegetables together. Cover and simmer for 10 minutes.

Preheat the oven to 375 degrees F. Drain the clams and oysters, reserving all juices; set aside. Drain the salt cod, and add the salt cod, oysters, clams, shrimp, lobster meat, and crabmeat to the vegetables and continue to simmer until the fish and seafood are just cooked. Remove the skillet from the heat, stir in the lemon juice, cover, and let stand until cool, about 15 minutes.

Stir in reserved juices from the clams and oysters, the hearts of palm, and black pepper. Pour the mixture into a large 3-quart buttered shallow casserole. Beat the eggs with the remaining 1 teaspoon salt and pour over the mixture. Decorate the top with the onion slices, place the egg slices inside the onion slices and the olives around the onions. Bake for 20 minutes, or until a toothpick inserted comes out clean. Cut the torte into wedges and serve warm.

Bahian-Style Shrimp and Okra

Caruru

6 to 8 servings

i n the city of Salvador, Bahia, this okra-based dish figures impor-
tantly in Afro-Brazilian religious ceremonies where it is known as
amalá, a dish preferred by Shango, the majestic Yoruba African god
of fire and lightning. In September, caruru is also the main dish served
during the festivities in honor of Cosme and Damien, the twin saints of
Bahian Afro-Catholic tradition. This old and unique festival, known as
"caruru of Cosme and Damien" is observed by families with twins. The
head of the household invites friends to enjoy a caruru in honor of the
family's twins and to venerate Cosme and Damien.

1 pound dried shrimp
1 pound fish fillets, such as
    cod, grouper, or any
    firm white fish
3 tablespoons lemon juice
2 teaspoons salt
½ cup raw unsalted peanuts
2 medium onions, chopped
6 large cloves garlic
¼ cup palm oil, or half
    palm oil and half
    vegetable oil
2 pounds okra, trimmed
    and thinly sliced
1 pound medium raw
    shrimp with shells,
    boiled in salted water,
    then peeled

p reheat the oven to 350 degrees F. Soak the dried
shrimp in warm water to cover for 20 minutes,
then drain. Wash the fish fillets in cold water and pat
dry with paper towels. Place the fillets in a shallow
dish, and sprinkle with the lemon juice and 1 teaspoon of salt. Let marinate for 30 minutes. Spread
the peanuts on a baking sheet and toast in the oven
for about 10 minutes, or until lightly browned.

Using the smallest disk of a meat grinder or food
processor, grind the dried shrimp, peanuts, onions,
and garlic to a purée. Heat the palm oil in a large,
deep skillet and sauté the peanut mixture over
medium heat, stirring constantly, for about 5 minutes. Lower the heat, add the okra and season with
the remaining salt. Cook for about 20 minutes, stirring occasionally, adding more water if necessary.
Break the fish into small pieces and add with the
fresh shrimp to the mixture. Mix well and simmer for
10 minutes until the mixture comes away from the
sides of the pan. Serve with white rice.

Shrimp and Bread Pudding

Vatapá
10 to 12 servings

during colonial times, vatapá *was one of the best-loved Afro-Brazilian dishes. Today,* vatapá *retains its popularity in Bahia where it is served on many ceremonial occasions.* Vatapá *appears on the menu of most restaurants featuring Bahian cuisine. To quote Manuel Querino, a Bahian scholar: "The palate is more appreciative than the senses. Music may go in one ear and out the other. The vision of a beautiful picture soon disappears from a short memory. But the remembrance of a good* vatapá *is eternal."*

I had the pleasure of eating vatapá *a number of times during celebrations in Salvador. Waldeloir Rego, my good friend and leading authority on Candomblé, believes that what is reproduced here is the most authentic* vatapá *recipe. Remember, as Dorival Cayimi, the great Bahian vocalist, advises in his classic folk song* "vatapá," *"Não parar de mexê-ô/ Que é para não embolar," which means "Keep on stirring/so it doesn't get lumpy!"*

FISH MARINADE:
3 tablespoons lemon juice
2 cloves garlic, crushed
1 teaspoon salt
¼ teaspoon black pepper

1 pound grouper or other
   white fish fillets

mix together the fish marinade ingredients and pour over the fish fillets. Let marinate for 2 hours.

Preheat the oven to 375 degrees F. Place the cashews and peanuts on a baking sheet and toast for about 10 minutes, shaking occasionally, until they are lightly golden.

Using a meat grinder or food processor, grind the onions and garlic to a purée and place them in a large bowl. Soak the dried shrimp in hot water to cover for 10 minutes; drain. Grind the dried shrimp and add them to the onions. Grind the cashews and peanuts and add to the bowl with the onions.

PUDDING:

1 cup raw unsalted cashews
1 cup raw unsalted peanuts
2 large onions, coarsely
    chopped
4 large cloves garlic
8 ounces dried shrimp
1 large loaf (1½ pounds)
    plain white bread
1 pound medium raw
    shrimp, with shells
¾ cup palm oil, or half palm
    oil and half vegetable oil
1 can (14-ounce) unsweet-
    ened coconut milk (see
    note)

Remove the crust from the bread and break into large pieces. Soak the bread in cold water for 5 minutes. Squeeze the water from the bread pieces and put them through the grinder. Set aside.

Place the raw shrimp, fish, and marinade in a large pot with water to cover. Bring to a boil and cook until the shrimp just turn pink. Remove the shrimp and fish from the pot and save the water. Peel the shrimp and set aside. Flake the fish and set aside.

Heat the palm oil in an 8-quart pot. Add the onion-nut mixture. Using a wooden spoon, stir the mixture continuously for 5 minutes. Add the ground bread and mix well. Pour in half of the coconut milk and 1 cup of the water from the shrimp and fish pot; stir well. Pour in the remaining coconut milk, the flaked fish, and the shrimp. Cook for another 15 minutes, stirring occasionally until the mixture thickens. The finished dish should be a thick, orange purée that can be eaten with a fork.

NOTE: The original recipe calls for whole coconuts to produce coconut milk. I now use canned coconut milk because it is quicker and doesn't change the taste.

Shrimp Couscous

Cuscuz de Camarão à Paulista
8 servings

O f North African origin, couscous, a dish made with steamed semolina, has changed its appearance in its travels around the world. It was brought to Portugal by the Moors and later traveled to Brazil via Africa. In the Brazilian northeast, couscous is a dessert made with tapioca, rice or corn, coconut, and sugar, and served like a cake. In the south, in São Paulo, couscous is a savory seafood dish. This recipe is from São Paulo.

COUSCOUS:
4 cups white corn flour (see note)
1 tablespoon manioc meal
1 teaspoon salt
½ cup (1 stick) butter

SHRIMP:
8 ounces large raw shrimp
1 pound medium raw shrimp
2 tablespoons lemon juice
1 teaspoon salt
½ teaspoon black pepper
½ cup (1 stick) butter or vegetable oil
⅓ cup grated onion
2 tablespoons chopped fresh parsley
1 cup tomato sauce
1 teaspoon red pepper flakes

Preheat the oven to 350 degrees F.

FOR THE COUSCOUS: Mix together the corn flour and manioc meal and place on a baking sheet with sides. Bake for 5 minutes, stirring once every minute so that the flours toast evenly. Heat the salt and 1 cup water to boiling; remove the flours from the oven and sprinkle them with the boiling water. Mix well with a fork and return to the oven for another 2 minutes. The mixture will be a little lumpy. Add the butter and mix well.

FOR THE SHRIMP: Peel, clean, and dry both sizes of shrimp. Place the shrimp in a large bowl and add the lemon juice, salt, and pepper. Marinate the shrimp for 1 hour.

Heat the butter in a large skillet and add the onion and parsley. Sauté the mixture for 3 minutes and add the shrimp; cook for an additional 2 minutes. Add the tomato sauce and red pepper flakes, cover, reduce the heat to a simmer, and cook until the shrimp are opaque. Remove the large shrimp and save to decorate the couscous. Add the corn flour mixture to the remaining shrimp and mix well.

ASSEMBLY:

3 tomatoes, peeled and
chopped
3 hard-boiled eggs, sliced
½ cup pitted black olives
1 can (4 ounce) sardines in
tomato sauce, cut in
half
2 hearts of palm, sliced ½
inch wide
1 green bell pepper, sliced
1 large collard green leaf
or a white cloth napkin

FOR THE ASSEMBLY: In a couscousière (couscous cooker) or a large sieve, arrange layers of the tomatoes, eggs, olives, and sardine halves on the bottom and up the sides in a decorative manner. Add a layer of the couscous mixture and the hearts of palm and pepper slices. Press some of the large shrimp into the couscous mixture. Continue to form layers with the ingredients until all are used. Cover the couscous with the collard green leaf or a large white napkin and steam over boiling water until the mixture is cooked and dry, about 30 minutes. The leaf will be cooked or the napkin will be completely wet. Remove and let cool for 30 minutes. Unmold the couscous onto a serving platter and serve with a green salad.

NOTE: The original recipe calls for corn flour, which is found in Latin American and Mexican markets, but finely ground cornmeal makes a good substitute.

Shrimp with Manioc Purée

Bobó de Camarão
6 to 8 side-dish servings

t he term bobó *derives from a West African word which means "a mixture of ingredients." There are various ways to prepare a bobó. It can be made with breadfruit, beans, or manioc. When it is linked with an ingredient like shrimp, it takes on the ingredient's name. In Angola there is a shrimp dish called* ipété *and the ingredients are exactly the same as this* bobó *dish. Originally this dish was served simply with white rice. Today, many Bahians serve* bobó *as a side dish with grilled fish, chicken, or fresh shrimp.*

4 pounds medium raw
  shrimp
6 tablespoons lemon juice
1 teaspoon salt
½ teaspoon black pepper
1 large onion
1 bay leaf
1 cup fresh cilantro
½ cup parsley
2 pounds manioc root,
  peeled and grated
2 cans (14-ounce) coconut
  milk
4 tablespoons palm oil, or
  half palm oil and half
  vegetable oil
1 large onion, minced
4 cloves garlic, crushed
1 pound tomatoes, peeled
  and seeded
1 large green bell pepper,
  seeded, and minced
1 cup chopped Brazil nuts

p eel and clean the shrimp, saving the shells. Season the shrimp with the lemon juice, salt, and pepper.

Place the shrimp shells in a large pot. Add the onion, bay leaf, half the cilantro, and half the parsley. Cover with water and bring to a boil. Reduce the heat and simmer until the liquid is reduced by half. Strain the liquid and set aside.

Place the grated manioc root in a pot with 1 cup of the shrimp liquid and 1 can of the coconut milk. Cover and cook over medium heat until the manioc is almost a purée, about 20 minutes. Set aside.

Heat 2 tablespoons of the palm oil in a large skillet. Add the shrimp and sauté, stirring continually, until the shrimp is just pink. Remove the shrimp from the pan and keep warm.

Add the minced onion and garlic to the pan and cook until the onion is golden. Add the tomatoes and green pepper and cook for 3 minutes.

Add the manioc with its liquid and cook over low heat until the tomatoes and peppers are soft. Add the other can of coconut milk and the rest of the shrimp liquid to the vegetables and cook until the vegetables are tender.

Add the Brazil nuts, the rest of the cilantro and parsley, the shrimp, and the remaining 2 tablespoons palm oil. Simmer for 3 minutes. Serve with white rice.

NOTE: Some cooks add dried shrimp to the dish. To do that, soak 1 cup of dried shrimp in warm water. Drain and grind or process to a powder. Add to the pan with the onion and garlic and continue with the rest of the recipe.

Chicken Bahian-Style

Xinxim de Galinha

4 to 6 serving

X inxim de Galinha *is another special Afro-Brazilian dish from the state of Bahia. This dish has gained national fame and is served at parties and festivals throughout Brazil, but nowhere is it prepared like it is in Bahia. I had my first taste of* xinxim *in 1961, in the city of Salvador, Bahia, at the home of my dear friend Norma Sampaio. Later that same year, I attended a Condomblé ceremony at the cult house of the famous priestess Olga de Alaqueta. There I had another opportunity to enjoy this dish of Nigerian origin. I was also able to observe Condomblé devotees prepare this succulent food of the gods. This recipe is very similar to the one prepared at Olga's. Instead of a whole chicken, I use a combination of breasts and thighs. Serve with Brazilian Rice (page 110), or Toasted Manioc Meal with Palm Oil (page 107), and a chilled Bouzy or Cabernet Sauvignon.*

1 chicken (3 to 4 pounds), cut into 8 pieces, or 8 breast halves or thighs
1 teaspoon salt
6 cloves garlic, chopped
3 tablespoons lemon juice
1 medium onion, chopped
1 cup dried shrimp, softened in warm water, then drained
1 cup unsalted roasted peanuts
1 cup palm oil, or half palm oil and half vegetable oil

W ash the chicken pieces and dry well. Pound the salt and 3 of the garlic cloves into a paste in a mortar with pestle. Add the lemon juice, mix well, and rub the mixture into the chicken pieces.

In a meat grinder or food processor, grind the onion, 3 garlic cloves, dried shrimp, and peanuts. Heat the palm oil in a large skillet. Add the ground ingredients and simmer for 5 minutes, stirring occasionally.

Add the chicken and a little water, mix well, and cook for 30 minutes, or until the chicken is cooked through, stirring occasionally and adding water when necessary so that the sauce doesn't dry out.

Sephardic Hash

Picadinho
8 to 10 servings

i n the sixteenth century, many Sephardic Jews left the Iberian Peninsula to settle in Brazil. Once in Brazil, Sephardic cuisine underwent modifications due to the influence of the new ingredients and the food cultures of the local Indians and slaves of African origin. Thus, even though in Portugal the traditional Sephardic precursor of picadinho (picado de vaca) had olives and eggs as chief ingredients, in the northern Brazilian state of Bahia it is made with okra and chayote. Palm oil took the place of vegetable oil, and because the juices of the chayote and okra sufficed, cooks usually added no broth. In southern Brazil, in the state of Rio Grande do Sul, Sephardic cooks added raisins and manioc flour to the meat mixture. The Brazilian version of the recipe that appears here, unlike the Portuguese original, calls for tomatoes and green peppers.

2 pounds round steak
2 tablespoons vegetable oil
1 large onion, chopped
4 cloves garlic, minced
2 green bell peppers,
    seeded and chopped
2 large tomatoes, peeled
    and chopped
2 teaspoons salt
½ teaspoon black pepper
1 teaspoon dried oregano
2 tablespoons flour
2 cups beef broth
2 cups uncooked white rice
5 hard-boiled eggs,
    chopped
1 cup stuffed green olives

t rim all the fat from the steak and cut it into ¼-inch squares or mince it in a food processor (do not grind).

Heat the vegetable oil in a large pot and sauté the onion and garlic until soft. Add the bell peppers and sauté 1 minute more. Add the chopped meat, stir well, and continue sautéing until the meat loses its pink color but is not browned. Add the tomatoes, 1 teaspoon of salt, the pepper, and oregano. Sprinkle the flour over the meat mixture, and cook stirring for 1 minute. Add the broth, mix well, then cover and simmer for 30 minutes, or until the sauce thickens.

In another medium pot heat 4 cups of water and the remaining 1 teaspoon salt to boiling. Add the rice; stir, cover, and simmer for 20 minutes or until tender. Place the rice in the center of a large, deep platter. Pour the meat over the rice and garnish with the hard-boiled eggs and olives.

Meat and Vegetable Stew

Cozido Baiano
14 to 16 servings

C ozido *is Brazil's answer to Portugal's boiled dinner. The variety of meats and vegetables make this dish a very tasty meal. Begin preparing it a day in advance of serving so that the chicken and meats can marinate overnight. Serve this dish with Hot Pepper and Lemon Sauce (page 124).*

MARINADE:

4 cloves garlic
2 teaspoons salt
3 onions, chopped
1 cup white vinegar
½ cup chopped fresh
    parsley leaves
¼ cup chopped fresh
    cilantro leaves
3 bay leaves, crushed
1 teaspoon coriander
    seeds, crushed

FOR MARINADE: Crush the garlic and salt in a mortar and place the mixture in a bowl with the onions, vinegar, parsley, cilantro, and bay leaves. Crush the coriander seeds and add to the mixture. Place the chicken thighs in one large bowl and the beef and chuck roasts in another. Divide the marinade between the two bowls and rub into the meats. Let marinate overnight in the refrigerator.

STEW: The following morning, remove the chicken and beef from the marinades. Heat 2 tablespoons of the shortening in a large saucepan and brown the chicken on all sides. In another large saucepan, heat the remaining 2 tablespoons shortening and brown the roasts. When the chicken and roasts are brown, add 2 cups of water to each pot, cover, and simmer for 1 hour.

Put the meats and liquid together in a large deep 6-quart pot. Add the tomatoes, onions, ham bone, and enough water to cover, and simmer until the meats are tender. Add the smoked pork sausages, manioc root, pork loin, fresh pork sausages, whole sweet potatoes, whole white potatoes, cabbage, turnips, and string beans. Add enough water to cover the vegetables and season with salt.

STEW:

4 pounds chicken thighs
3 pounds beef rump roast
3 pounds lean chuck roast
4 tablespoons lard or
   shortening
4 large tomatoes, chopped
3 medium onions
1 ham bone with meat
3 pounds smoked pork
   sausages
3 pounds manioc root
2 pounds pork loin
2 pounds fresh pork
   sausages
6 sweet potatoes
9 medium white potatoes
1 large head cabbage,
   quartered
6 medium white turnips
2 pounds string beans,
   ends trimmed
Salt to taste
3 pounds butternut squash,
   peeled and cut into
   3-inch cubes
2 pounds fresh okra,
   trimmed
10 plantains, peeled
Manioc flour

Cover the pot and simmer over low heat. Remove the vegetables from the pot as they become tender and keep them warm. When all the vegetables have been removed, add the squash, okra, and plantains and continue simmering. Again remove each vegetable as it becomes tender.

To serve, place the chicken pieces in the center of a large platter. Slice the beef and arrange the slices around the chicken. Arrange half of the vegetables around the meats. Keep warm. Slice the pork loin and place in the center of another large platter. Arrange the remaining vegetables around the pork loin. Cut the sausages into 1-inch pieces and place around the vegetables. Keep warm.

Place 2 cups of the broth in a small pot. Add ¼ cup mashed sweet potatoes to the broth, bring to a boil and pour the broth over the vegetables and meats. With the remaining broth, make a Manioc Purée (page 69). Use 1 cup manioc flour for each 2 cups of broth. Serve the purée on a separate platter.

NOTE: The number of meats and vegetables can be reduced to suit your taste.

Hot Pepper and Lemon Sauce

Molho de Pimenta e Limão
Makes 1½ cups

this sauce is served as an accompaniment to almost every dish served in Bahia, whether beef, pork, poultry, fish, or shellfish. It is always prepared with malagueta *peppers. The green, unripe peppers are preferred. When they turn red they are less acid, less oily, and less piquant.*

8 to 10 green malagueta peppers, 1 to 2 inches long
1 cup fresh parsley
1 cup fresh cilantro
3 tablespoons lemon juice
1 teaspoon salt
2 onions, sliced paper thin

Cut the peppers in half lengthwise and remove the seeds.

Place the peppers, parsley, cilantro, lemon juice, and salt in a mortar and pound to a purée. (A food processor can also be used.) Put the onion slices in a dish and pour the sauce on top.

NOTE: I occasionally mix 2 tablespoons of olive oil with the purée before pouring it over the onions, which results in a smoother and tastier sauce.

Brazilian Sauce

Molho Brasileiro
Makes about 1 cup

This sauce is usually served as a side dish to moisten roasted or grilled beef, pork, chicken, or fish that is dry. It is also used to enhance lettuce salad.

1 small onion, thinly sliced
1 tomato, thinly sliced
1 cup fresh chopped
    cilantro
½ cup vegetable oil
2 tablespoons vinegar
Salt and black pepper to
    taste

Place the onions in a bowl. Pour boiling water over the onions and let stand for 1 minute.

Drain the onions and let cool. Mix the onions with the remaining ingredients and serve.

NOTE: Scalding the onions for 1 minute removes the acid and makes them more digestible.

Minas Cheese Rolls

Pãezinhos de Queijo
Makes 2 dozen

*t*he city of Minas Gerais is known for these little cheese rolls made with goat cheese. They are popular as a snack or served with meals. You can substitute Parmesan for the goat cheese without altering the taste.

1 cup whole milk
½ cup (1 stick) butter, melted
1 tablespoon salt
4 cups tapioca flour (see note)
5 eggs
2 cups crumbled fresh goat cheese

*p*reheat the oven to 375 degrees F and lightly grease a baking sheet.

In a medium saucepan heat 1 cup of water, the milk, butter, and salt over medium heat until hot, but not boiling. Place the flour in a large bowl and pour in the hot liquid. Mix well and let cool for 20 minutes.

Beat the eggs one at a time into the batter, and then add the cheese. Mix well. Form the dough into balls the size of walnuts. Place on the prepared baking sheet. Make a slit on top of each roll with a sharp knife. Bake the rolls for about 20 minutes, or until lightly golden. Serve warm.

NOTE: Tapioca flour can be found in most supermarkets and health food stores.

Rolled Stuffed Bread

Pão Enrolado
Makes 1 loaf

i n August of 1999, while in São Paulo visiting with our old friends
Antônio and Isabel Carelli, their daughter, Fabiana, baked a loaf of
this incomparable bread for us. It is perfect as part of a buffet table
or as a light lunch with a green salad.

3 tablespoons baking
  powder, or 3 cubes
  (3 ounces total) fresh
  yeast
1 cup warm milk
2 cups all-purpose flour
½ cup vegetable oil
2 teaspoons sugar
1 teaspoon salt
8 ounces ham or smoked
  sausage, thinly sliced
2 medium tomatoes, thinly
  sliced
2 cups grated mozzarella
  cheese
¼ cup chopped fresh
  oregano

d issolve the baking powder or yeast in warm
milk. Place the flour in a large bowl and add the
oil, sugar, salt, and milk mixture. Mix the ingredients
and knead to form dough.

Roll out the dough into a 9 x 11-inch rectangle.
Arrange a layer of ham on top of the dough, leaving a 1-inch border all around. Top the meat with
slices of tomato. Sprinkle the tomatoes with the
grated cheese and oregano. Roll up the dough,
beginning with a longer side. Place it on a buttered
baking sheet and let rise in a warm place for 60
minutes.

Heat the oven to 400 degrees F and bake the bread
for 30 minutes, or until golden. Serve warm, cut into
1-inch slices.

Beer Rolls

Pãezinhos de Cerveja
Makes 40 rolls

hese little rolls are also very popular in Portugal and the rest of the Portuguese-speaking world. This recipe makes enough for a party buffet. Great for mini sandwiches! Begin preparation the day before serving.

1 package (¼ ounce) yeast
½ cup warm milk
2 tablespoons sugar
7 to 8 cups all-purpose
    flour
1 cup beer, at room
    temperature
1 tablespoon salt
4 eggs, separated
½ cup (1 stick) butter,
    melted, plus additional
    for brushing

issolve the yeast in the warm milk. Let the yeast sit for 5 minutes. Add 1 tablespoon of the sugar, 2 cups of the flour, the beer, and salt. Mix well, cover, and let sit in a draft-free place overnight.

The following day, beat the egg whites into stiff peaks; set aside. To the beer mixture, add 2 more cups of flour and the egg yolks, one at a time, 1 more tablespoon of sugar, and the butter. Beat well. Slowly add 2 more cups of flour, kneading after each addition. Fold in the egg whites. Knead in enough of the remaining 1 to 2 cups of flour until the dough is smooth and elastic. Place in a warm place and let rise until double in size, about 1 hour.

Preheat the oven to 375 degrees F. Tear off pieces of the dough the size of golf balls and shape into rolls. Place on greased baking sheets, cover, and let rise for 20 minutes.

Brush the rolls with melted butter and bake for about 20 minutes, or until golden. Let cool on racks and serve at room temperature.

Golden Dessert

Quindim
Makes 1 dozen

legend has it that Portuguese nuns, who were well-known for their tasty egg custards, brought this recipe with them to Brazil. Coconut, which is not native to Portugal, was added later by African slaves. Quindim *is a very sweet dessert that was popular during slavery times in the masters' houses of the sugar plantations in the north of Brazil. These dessert cakes were served at family dinners and elaborate parties. Baked in small individual pastry tins, or muffin tins, they are then inverted and served in little silver paper cups for a festive touch. As the* quindim *cooks, the coconut rises to the top and forms a light brown crust. When inverted, the coconut is on the bottom and the yolks form a golden dome on top. This recipe can be doubled and baked in an angel food cake mold or a Bundt pan. It is then called a* quindão, *which means "big cake."*

1 cup extra-fine sugar
¼ cup (½ stick) butter or
    margarine, softened
9 egg yolks
1 whole egg
1 cup freshly grated
    coconut (or frozen fresh
    unsweetened coconut)
Melted butter or margarine
    for tins
Sugar for dusting tins

preheat the oven to 350 degrees F.

Place the sugar and butter in a medium bowl. Beat the mixture until fluffy. Add the egg yolks and the whole egg, one at a time, mixing well after each addition. Fold in the coconut and mix well without beating.

Brush 12 muffin tins with the melted butter and dust with sugar. Fill the tins almost to the top with the custard. Place the muffin tin in a baking pan. Pour hot water into the pan to a depth of 1 inch making a bain-marie. Bake the quindims for about 35 minutes, or until they are firm and slightly golden.

Cool for 10 minutes on a rack. Remove from the tins and place coconut side down in silver paper cups or on a serving dish, and chill overnight or for at least 4 hours.

Corn Flour and Prune Cake

Bolo de Fuba de Milho com Ameixa Preta
10 to 12 servings

this cake was well-known in the city of Salvador, Bahia, at Condomblé celebrations. Waldoleir Rego, an esteemed friend and an expert on Bahian and Condomblé food culture, first prepared this dessert for me in the early sixties. The preparation time is shortened by using canned coconut milk, but the outcome is the same—moist and delicious.

4 eggs, separated
1 cup (2 sticks) butter, softened
2½ cups sugar
2 cups finely ground cornmeal
1 cup all-purpose flour
1 cup coconut milk
⅔ cup chopped prunes
3 tablespoons grated Parmesan cheese
1 teaspoon salt
1 teaspoon grated lemon peel
1 teaspoon ground cinnamon
¼ teaspoon ground cloves
1 tablespoon baking powder
½ cup milk

preheat the oven to 400 degrees F. Beat the egg whites until soft peaks form; set aside.

In a large bowl, beat the egg yolks, butter, and sugar until creamy. Continue beating while adding the cornmeal, flour, coconut milk, prunes, cheese, salt, grated lemon peel, cinnamon, and cloves. Fold in the egg whites. Dissolve the baking powder in the milk and stir into the batter.

Butter a 2-quart mold and dust it with flour. Pour the batter into the mold and bake for 10 minutes. Reduce the heat to 350 degrees F and continue baking for 30 to 35 minutes, or until a wooden skewer inserted in the center comes out clean. Cool on a rack for 10 minutes. Remove the cake from the pan and cool completely before placing on a serving dish.

Corn Pudding

Canjica de Milho Verde
6 to 8 servings

i n Bahia, canjica *is served as part of St. John's Day festivities on June 24th. St John's is also the day for the feast of maize, or corn, so there are many dishes made with corn to celebrate the occasion.* Canjica *is made from fresh corn kernels, coconut milk, cinnamon, and sugar. In northern Brazil, where it is called* mungunzá, *it is made with hominy and roasted peanuts. In São Paulo and Minas Gerais, as well as Bahia,* canjica *is made with freshly grated corn and called* chá-de-burro, *which translates as "donkey's tea."*

8 ears fresh corn
1 can (14-ounce) coconut
   milk
5 tablespoons sugar
1 tablespoon butter
¼ teaspoon salt
Ground cinnamon

With a sharp knife, cut the kernels from each cob into a medium bowl. With the dull side of the knife, scrape the milk and pulp from the cobs into the bowl. Place the corn in a blender or food processor. Add 1 cup of the coconut milk and grind to a smooth paste. Strain through a coarse strainer into a medium pot, using the back of a wooden spoon to press the paste through the strainer.

Add the sugar, butter, salt, and remaining coconut milk. Cook over low heat, stirring constantly, until the mixture thickens. When the mixture is thick enough to coat the back of the spoon, remove it from the heat and cool.

Pour the mixture into a 10-inch serving dish and refrigerate. Before serving, place a doily on the pudding and sprinkle cinnamon over the top. Remove the doily and serve.

Dreams

i *first tasted this wonderful sweet in Bahia in 1960, and it remains one of my favorites. Sonhos are served both in Brazil and Portugal during the Christmas holidays and for weddings and anniversaries. Sprinkle the cooled sonhos with powdered sugar or with Sweet Syrup (page 53) for a beautiful presentation.*

1 cup all-purpose flour
2 teaspoons baking powder
¼ teaspoon salt
1 can (14-ounce) sweet-
    ened condensed milk
2 tablespoons butter
2 eggs, separated
¼ cup (1½ ounces)
    chopped Brazil nuts
¼ cup whole milk

p reheat the oven to 400 degrees F. Grease miniature muffin tins.

Sift the flour, baking powder, and salt into a small bowl. Heat the condensed milk with the butter in a medium pot. When the mixture is hot, add the dry ingredients all at once, stirring rapidly. Reduce the heat to low, cook for 5 minutes, stirring constantly. Cool the mixture for 5 minutes.

Beat the egg whites until stiff peaks form. Beat the egg yolks, and fold in the whites. Add the nuts, milk, and condensed milk mixture. Spoon the batter into the prepared tins, filling three-fourths full. Bake for 8 minutes. Reduce the heat to 300 degrees F and bake for another 8 minutes or until a toothpick comes out clean. Remove from tins and cool on a wire rack.

Chocolate Bonbons

Brigadeiros
Makes about 20 balls

t hese chocolate sweets were named after Brigadier Eduardo
Gomes, a famous Brazilian air force commander in the 1940s,
who was a chocoholic. They are very popular at birthday parties
and other festive occasions.

1 can (14-ounce) sweet-
ened condensed milk
¼ cup unsweetened cocoa
powder
1 tablespoon butter
¼ teaspoon salt
1 cup chocolate sprinkles

i n a medium pan, combine the milk and cocoa
powder. Cook over low heat stirring constantly
with a wooden spoon, until the mixture pulls away
from the sides of the pan, about 20 minutes. Add the
butter and salt and mix thoroughly before removing
the mixture from the heat.

When the mixture is cool, rub your hands with butter or spray with a butter spray and shape the mixture into little balls about one inch in diameter. Roll
the balls in the chocolate sprinkles and place in mini
silver or paper cupcake forms. Store the bonbons in
the refrigerator until ready to serve.

NOTE: This recipe can be doubled or even tripled for
parties.

Mother-in-Law's Eyes

Olhos de Sogra
Makes about 1 dozen

*t*his dessert is one of the many examples of Brazilian culinary humor. In Brazil there are several desserts with imaginative and funny names. The coconut filling adds a sweet taste to the tart prune.

1 pound pitted prunes
(choose large ones of
the best quality)
1 cup sugar
1 cup grated unsweetened
coconut, lightly packed
2 egg yolks, beaten
Whole cloves for garnish
Confectioners' sugar for
rolling

Slice open the pitted prunes and form them into the shape of boats.

Place the sugar and 1 cup of water in a saucepan over low heat. Add the grated coconut and egg yolks. Cook slowly, stirring from time to time, until the mixture thickens, about 10 minutes. Remove from the heat and cool slightly.

Stuff each prune with the coconut mixture, using a small spoon. Let the filling cover the top of each prune. Place 1 clove in the center of each prune, forming the pupil of the eye. Roll the boat-shaped prunes in the powdered sugar and place on a serving tray. Serve with coffee.

Brazilian Peanut Brittle

Pê-de-moleque

Makes 50 pieces

moleque *comes from the Kimbundu* muleke, *which in Angola means "lad" or "boy." In modern Brazilian-Portuguese, the word took on a pejorative meaning. Today in Brazil,* moleque *means "urchin" or "brat" and is used without regard to color or race. But the name of the dessert derives from its original meaning when it designated a black boy. The Portuguese* pê *translates as "foot." Thus, the literal translation of the dessert is "black boy's foot." In contemporary Brazilian, the term is thought of humorously as "street urchin's foot."*

Butter for greasing
1 can (14-ounce) sweetened condensed milk
1 cup sugar
1 cup milk
1 cup roasted unsalted peanuts, without skins

butter a marble surface or baking sheet and a rolling pin.

Pour the condensed milk, sugar, and milk into a deep, medium pot and mix well. Heat the mixture over medium heat, stirring constantly, until it pulls away from the sides of the pan, about 10 minutes.

Add the peanuts; mix well, and remove from the heat. Beat the mixture with a wooden spoon until it looks opaque.

Pour the mixture onto the buttered surface and roll with the buttered rolling pin to about ½ inch thickness. Cut into squares or triangles while still warm. Cool and store in airtight containers.

Demitasse Coffee

Cafezinho
2 servings

brazilians take their cafezinho *in demitasse cups half filled with sugar. It has been estimated that the average adult drinks between ten and fifteen cups a day!*

4 tablespoons Brazilian
coffee beans, freshly
ground
2 tablespoons sugar

heat 1½ cups of cold water just to boiling; remove from the heat and stir in the coffee grounds. Let stand for 1½ minutes, then stir again. Pour the liquid through a cloth strainer or cheesecloth directly into demitasse cups. Add 1 tablespoon of sugar to each cup and stir.

Rum Drink

Caipirinha
Makes 4 drinks

caipirinha *is Brazil's signature cocktail. The drink originated in sugarcane-growing regions. Cachaça, caipirinha's chief ingredient is in fact, alcohol distilled from sugarcane juice. Cachaça is not easily available outside of Brazil, but check your local liquor store as some are importing it. White rum is a good substitute even though it's distilled from molasses.*

2 fresh limes
2 tablespoons sugar
1 cup *cachaça* or white
rum
1 cup crushed ice

peel the rinds from the limes and chop; squeeze the juice from the limes. In a medium bowl, combine chopped lime rinds, freshly squeezed lime juice, and sugar. Add the *cachaça*, and mix well. Pour the mixture into a shaker with the crushed ice. Strain into 6 oz. whiskey glasses and serve.

Paulista Rum Drink

Batida
Makes 2 drinks

t he literal translation of batida is "beaten," but this drink is not beaten, it is stirred. Like caipirinha (page 136), it is a slightly pungent drink made with cachaça, a rum made not from molasses, but the juice squeezed from sugarcane. It is sometimes known as a Batida Paulista. Many Brazilians would say that a Brazilian Bean Stew (page 102) would not be complete without a batida.

3 ounces *cachaça* or white rum
1½ ounces lemon juice
2 teaspoons sugar
2 ice cubes, crushed

p lace all the ingredients in a cocktail shaker and shake well. Pour into glasses and serve immediately.

VARIATIONS:

COFFEE BATIDA: In a cocktail shaker put 1½ ounces *cachaça* or rum; 1 teaspoon sugar; ¼ cup strong cold coffee; 1 egg white, strained; and cracked ice. Shake well.

PINEAPPLE BATIDA: In a cocktail shaker put 1½ ounces pineapple juice; 1 teaspoon sugar; 4 teaspoons lemon juice; 3 ounces white rum or *cachaça*; and cracked ice. Shake well.

COCONUT MILK BATIDA: In a cocktail shaker put 1 cup coconut milk; 1 cup cow's milk; ½ cup gin; ½ cup *cachaça* or white rum; and sugar to taste. Shake well; add 1 crushed ice cube before serving.

CUISINE OF
Cape Verde

the Cape Verde Islands are located in the mid-Atlantic Ocean, some 387 miles off the Guinea Coast of West Africa. The archipelago consists of ten islands and five islets, divided into the windward (Barlavento) and leeward (Sotovento) groups. The six islands in the Barlavento group are Santo Antão, São Vicente, Santa Luzia, São Nicolau, Sal, and Boa Vista. The islands in the Sotovento group are Maio, Santiago, Fogo, and Brava. All but Santa Luzia are inhabited.

The Cape Verde archipelago was uninhabited until 1456, when Diogo Gomes sailed from Portugal and landed on the archipelago on his way around the southern tip of Africa to the Far East. In 1462, Portuguese settlers arrived on the island of Santiago and founded Ribeira Grande (now called Cidade Velha, "Old City")—the first European city in the tropics. In the sixteenth century, African slaves were brought to the islands to work on plantations established by Portuguese settlers. As a result, many Cape Verdeans are of mixed African and Portuguese origin. In fact, the Cape Verdean archipelago emerged as the first and most tolerant Creole society of the ancient overseas empire of Portugal and, probably, of the whole world. In this context, the term "Creole" signifies a racial, linguistic, social, cultural, and culinary hybridity.

Because of their location on the sea lanes between Africa and the Americas, the Cape Verde Islands became a major intermediary trade center for both slaves and crops and other food products. The slaves from the west coast of Africa brought with them their knowledge of the preparation of tropical foods. From Europe, Asia, and the Americas, the Portuguese introduced to Cape Verde agricultural products such as corn, sugarcane, and manioc root, along with domestic animals such as cattle and swine. Cape Verde served as an *entrepôt* during the slave traffic, when slave ships, not only from Portugal but also from Spain, England, France, and Holland, made port in these islands before sailing for the New World. The Europeans took advantage of these Cape Verdean stopovers, often to take on crew members and slaves for the long voyage across the Atlantic. Slaves were usually fed a dish made of corn, meat or fish, bacon, vegetables, and beans, which evolved into Cape Verde's national dish, and became known as *cachupa*. This dish probably reflects the fact that of all the territories and colonies of the ancient Portuguese empire, it was in Cape Verde, during slavery, that the Creole elite emerged. These Cape Verdeans, the majority of whom were *metiços* (people of mixed race), formed an upper class, many of whom served as bureaucrats and public functionaries in the socio-economic colonial structure. It was in

Cape Verde that the first secondary school and the first seminary were established in Portuguese Africa. During the nineteenth century, the Cape Verdean intellectuals, both black and *metiço*, gave impetus to the Creole culture, this being a culture "made at home." This hybridity very well applies to Cape Verde's national cuisine. Since as early as the sixteenth century, Cape Verdeans have also emigrated in large numbers. One thus finds Cape Verdean dishes in Portugal, Brazil, Holland, Italy, and the United States, especially in southern New England.

The Cape Verdean diet is made up of many diverse products, including corn, beans, sweet potatoes, manioc, and various meats usually garnished with vegetables. Cape Verde, with its seas rich in fish and seafood, offers many local specialties whose preparation goes from easy to somewhat complex. The fish most appreciated are tuna, swordfish, and grouper, while barnacles, octopus, shrimp, and lobster are among the favored seafood. Chicken, Guinea hen, pork, and turtle are the most preferred meats.

Prawns with Hot Sauce

Gambas com Piripiri
4 servings

prawns are plentiful in the Cape Verde Islands and a favorite any time of day. This dish is usually served with plenty of local beer. Prawns with hot sauce are also very popular in other Portuguese-speaking countries, such as Mozambique, Angola, Guinea-Bissau, and Brazil.

1 teaspoon salt
3 pounds raw prawns or jumbo shrimp
½ cup (1 stick) melted butter
1 tablespoon ground red pepper

bring 2 quarts of water to a boil with the salt. Drop the prawns into the boiling water. When the water returns to a boil, remove the prawns and plunge them into ice water.

When the prawns have cooled, drain, peel, and sauté them in the butter mixed with red pepper for two minutes. Serve with Hot Sauce and beer.

NOTE: Prawns can also be grilled and served as a main dish.

Hot Sauce

Piripiri

4 whole hot chili peppers
1 teaspoon salt
5 garlic cloves
Juice of 2 lemons
    (6 tablespoons)
1 cup olive oil or butter

Wash chili peppers, remove stems, slice in half, and remove the seeds. Cut peppers into small pieces and place in a food processor. Add the salt, garlic, lemon juice, and olive oil. Place in a small pot and heat on low for 5 minutes. Mix well and place in serving dish.

Pastry with the Devil Inside

Pastel com o Diabo Dentro
Makes about 24 pastries

he "devil" in this appetizer is the hot pepper used in the filling. The combination of sweet potato, cornmeal, and tuna may seem unusual or strange, but just one bite will convince you otherwise. "Delicious" will be your response. Be sure to use fresh tuna, if available, because the hot pepper marinade is better able to permeate the raw fish and give it a spicy flavor. Double the recipe if you are planning a party. These pastries are also good with a green salad for a light lunch.

DOUGH:

2 large (about 2½ pounds) sweet potatoes, unpeeled
2 cups finely ground or regular yellow cornmeal (see note)

FOR THE DOUGH: Wash the potatoes and place them in a large pot with water to cover. Bring the water to a boil, reduce the heat, and simmer until the potatoes are tender, about 30 minutes. When the potatoes are done, remove them from the pot, cool, and save the water. Peel the potatoes, cut them into cubes, and mash until all the lumps disappear. With a wooden spoon, stir in the cornmeal, ½ cup at a time. Continue to add the cornmeal until the mixture forms a soft dough. If the dough becomes too dry, add a teaspoon or two of the water from the boiled potatoes. Roll the dough into a ball, cover with a damp cloth, and refrigerate while you prepare the filling.

FOR THE FILLING: Place the tuna in a small bowl. Add the garlic, red pepper flakes, vinegar, and salt and mix well. Marinate the tuna for 30 minutes. Heat the 2 tablespoons vegetable oil in a medium frying pan. Add the onion and sauté until it is soft and translucent. Add the tomato and tomato paste, mix well, and simmer for 5 minutes, or until the tomato is soft. Stir

FILLING:

1 pound fresh tuna, chopped
　　fine by hand, or 2 cans
　　(6-ounce) water-packed
　　tuna, drained
3 large cloves garlic,
　　minced
1 to 2 tablespoons red
　　pepper flakes, or
　　2 red chili peppers,
　　finely chopped
1 tablespoon white vinegar
1 teaspoon salt
2 tablespoons vegetable oil
1 medium yellow onion,
　　coarsely chopped
1 large tomato, finely
　　chopped
2 teaspoons tomato paste

Vegetable oil for frying

in the tuna mixture and cook over low heat for about 5 minutes (or if using canned tuna, until the mixture is heated through). Add some of the water from the potatoes as needed, so that the mixture remains moist. Remove from the heat and cool.

PASTRIES: Remove the dough from the refrigerator. Spread a sheet of plastic wrap on the counter. Place 1 heaping tablespoon of dough, about the size of a golf ball, in the center of the plastic wrap. Press with the heel of your hand to form a circle 3 to 4 inches in diameter. Place a tablespoon of filling in the center of the dough. Using the piece of plastic, fold one half of the dough over the other half, to form a half circle. Pull back the plastic and press the edges to seal. Repeat with the remaining dough and filling.

Pour the oil into a deep fry pan or heavy skillet to a depth of two inches. Heat it over medium-high heat until a test piece of dough sizzles. Fry the pastries, 4 at a time, until golden, about 1 minute on each side. Drain on paper towels and serve warm or at room temperature.

NOTE: I have made this recipe with both finely ground (*harina*) and regular cornmeal. The regular cornmeal gives the dough a coarser texture and the harina, a lighter texture. Both are very tasty.

Manioc Tart with Beef Filling

Empadão de Puré de Mandioca com Carne
8 servings

*t*his delicious tart, which has a crust and coating made from manioc purée, comes originally from the leeward island of Santiago. Today, the tart has transcended its island of origin and is popular throughout the islands as well as in other countries of the Portuguese-speaking world. In Brazil a variation of this tart is called Ground Beef Pie (page 100). Instead of manioc, Brazilian cooks often use a layer of omelet as a bottom crust and cover the meat mixture with beaten egg that puffs when baked.

MANIOC:

2 pounds manioc root
1 teaspoon salt
½ cup warm milk
1 egg
1 tablespoon butter or
    margarine

FILLING:

¼ cup vegetable oil
1 medium onion, minced
1½ pounds lean ground
    beef
2 medium tomatoes,
    chopped
2 cloves garlic, minced
1½ teaspoons red pepper
    flakes
1 bay leaf

FOR THE MANIOC: Peel the manioc root, wash, and cut it into cubes. Be sure to remove the hard core in the center. Place the manioc in a medium pot with the salt and add water to cover. Simmer for 20 to 25 minutes or until tender. Drain and mash. Add the milk, egg, and butter. Mix well until the manioc resembles mashed potatoes. Set aside.

FOR THE FILLING: Heat the oil in a large skillet and sauté the onion until translucent. Add the beef, tomatoes, garlic, pepper flakes, and bay leaf. Reduce the heat and simmer for 15 minutes, adding a little water if necessary until the filling is just moist.

SAUCE:

¼ cup vegetable oil
2 medium onions, thinly
    sliced
1 large tomato, chopped
¼ cup chopped fresh
    parsley
2 cloves garlic, minced
1 teaspoon red pepper
    flakes

1 egg yolk, beaten

FOR THE SAUCE: Heat the oil in a skillet until hot but not steaming. Add the onions, tomato, parsley, garlic, and pepper flakes. Reduce the heat and simmer for about 15 minutes. Keep warm.

Preheat the oven to 350 degrees F. In a 2-quart casserole, place half of the manioc purée and spread it to all corners. Top with all of the beef filling and complete with the rest of the manioc purée. Brush the top with the egg yolk. Bake about 25 minutes or until the top is golden. Cool for about 10 minutes before slicing. Serve hot with the tomato sauce on the side.

Avocado Stuffed with Dates

Abacate com Tamaras
8 servings

*t*his is a very popular salad on the windward island of São Vicente. Some cooks add lobster or shrimp to make it a complete meal for lunch or a light supper. It goes well with a chilled glass of white Dão wine.

4 ripe avocados
½ cup finely chopped dates
¼ cup port wine
1 tablespoon sugar
Crushed ice

Cut the avocados lengthwise in half and remove the seeds. Carefully remove the pulp with a spoon, so as not to tear or puncture the shells. Reserve the shells.

Place the pulp in a large bowl and mash with a fork until it has a smooth consistency. Add the dates, port, and sugar. Mix well. Stuff the shells with the avocado mixture, cover with plastic wrap and chill at least 2 hours. Serve the filled avocado halves over crushed ice.

Guinea Hen Salad from São Nicolau

Galinha do Mato em Salada

4 to 6 servings

this salad comes from the windward island of São Nicolau in the Cape Verde archipelago, where Guinea hens are very common. However, a stewing chicken can be substituted. This salad is great for dinner on a warm day.

1 Guinea hen or stewing chicken (about 5 pounds)
1 tablespoon salt
1 medium onion, halved
1 cup fresh parsley
1 bay leaf
1 teaspoon red pepper flakes
2 pounds white potatoes
1 pound manioc root
1 pound green bananas
½ teaspoon ground red pepper
½ cup olive oil
Salt and black pepper to taste

Wash the hen or chicken and cut it into 8 pieces. Soak it for 20 minutes in water to cover mixed with the salt. Remove the chicken from the water and place it in a large pot with the onion, parsley, bay leaf, and red pepper flakes. Add enough water to cover, bring to a boil, and simmer for 2 hours, or until tender.

Meanwhile, peel the potatoes and the manioc root, place them in a medium pot, cover with water, and cook for 20 minutes, or until tender. Remove and set aside. Cook the bananas, whole and unpeeled, in boiling water for 3 minutes.

Remove the chicken from the water, cool, and cut into bite-size pieces, removing the skin and bones. Place the chicken in a large bowl. Cut the potatoes and manioc into 2-inch pieces, being sure to remove the core from the center of the manioc. Add the potatoes and manioc to the chicken. Peel the bananas and cut into 1-inch slices and add to the salad. Mix the ground red pepper with the olive oil, pour over the salad, season with salt and pepper to taste. Toss the salad and serve at room temperature.

Night-Vigil Chicken Soup

Sopa Noite Guarda-Cabeça
8 to 10 servings

night-Vigil Chicken Soup gets its name from the mothers of new-borns drinking the soup to keep up their energy while they stand vigil all night. Now why are they standing vigil? Well, legend has it that on the seventh day after an infant's birth, the umbilical cord usually falls off. And if the umbilical cord has not been kept clean, demons might come to suck the blood from the child's navel. So the custom is for family members to sit up all night making music and singing to scare away the demons.

Many of the first Portuguese to settle in Cape Verde were either Sephardic Jews or New Christians (converts from Judaism). It is possible that this dish evolved from the traditional Jewish chicken soup that was made with dumplings made from rice and finely chopped breast meat. This soup is also said to cure hangovers and certain ailments.

1 chicken (3 pounds), cut into 8 pieces
2 tablespoons salt
2 cloves garlic, peeled and chopped
½ bay leaf, crumbled
1 tablespoon vegetable oil
1 medium onion, thinly sliced
1 pound Yukon potatoes, peeled and cubed
1 pound manioc root, peeled and cubed
½ cup uncooked white rice
1 medium tomato, peeled and cubed
¼ cup fresh mint leaves

Soak the chicken parts in cold water with 1 tablespoon of the salt for 20 minutes. Remove the chicken, pat dry with paper towels, and rub with a mixture of the remaining 1 tablespoon salt, the garlic, and bay leaf.

Heat the oil in a large soup pot and sauté the onion. When the onion becomes translucent, add the chicken pieces and sauté for 3 minutes, stirring occasionally, or until the chicken is lightly browned.

Add 3 quarts of water to the pot and bring to a boil. Add the potatoes, manioc, and rice to the chicken. Stir well and then add the tomato. Cover, reduce the heat, and simmer for 35 minutes, or until the chicken is tender. Serve in a soup tureen. Place a few mint leaves in each soup bowl and invite guests to serve themselves.

Shrimp Soup from the Island of Santo Antão

Caldo de Camarão da Ilha de Santo Antão
6 servings

i *n this recipe the vegetables are cooked to a purée, which gives the dish an appearance of a cream soup.*

4 pounds medium raw
    shrimp, with heads and
    tails
¼ cup olive oil
1 onion, thinly sliced
2 pounds ripe tomatoes,
    peeled and chopped
2 pounds manioc root,
    peeled and chopped
2 pounds white potatoes,
    peeled and chopped
1 pound green bananas,
    peeled and sliced
2 cloves garlic
Salt to taste
Malagueta pepper to taste

r inse the shrimp and cook them in salted water to cover for 5 minutes, or until just pink. Peel the shrimp and save the heads along with the water they were cooked in.

In a large pot, place the olive oil and onion and sauté until the onion is light golden. Add the shrimp and fry lightly in the onion mixture.

With a mortar and pestle, pound the shrimp heads and return them to the cooking water. Strain the broth into the pot with the shrimp and add the tomatoes, manioc root, potatoes, bananas, and garlic. If needed, add more water to cover the vegetables. Cover the pot and cook on low heat until the vegetables become a purée, about 20 minutes. When ready, season with salt and malagueta pepper to taste. Serve immediately.

Bean Stew, Cape Verdean-Style

Cachupa Rica
8 to 10 servings

C achupa *is to Cape Verde what* paella *is to Spain,* feijoada *is to Brazil, and* bouillabaisse *is to France.* Cachupa *began as poor folk's fare. In a large pot, peasant women would combine left-overs such as beans, bananas, green vegetables, and occasionally a couple of pieces of goat meat. The resulting concoction slowly gained acceptance among the privileged classes, and as it grew in popularity a deluxe* cachupa *evolved with chicken, several types of sausages, and a variety of vegetables and legumes. Today it is Cape Verde's national dish, and many of the islands' best restaurants feature* Cachupa Rica, *a rich* cachupa, *for Sunday brunch.* Cachupa *is a must for celebrations.*

On a visit to Cape Verde in 1978, I first sampled this dish at the home of my good friend, Dinah Custódio. One of the pieces of advice she gave me was to prepare the dish a day or two before serving; this permits the flavors to meld nicely.

2 cups dried hominy
1 cup small dried fava beans, washed and sorted
1 cup dried Great Northern beans, washed and sorted
1 pound fresh pork sausage (*linguiça*)
1 pound smoked pork sausage (*chouriço*)

(CONTINUED)

P lace the hominy, fava beans, and Great Northern beans in separate pots, add cold water to cover each, and refrigerate overnight.

The following day, drain the hominy and Great Northern beans and place them together in a large pot with cold water to cover. Remove the outer skin of the favas by rubbing them between your hands (this should be easy since they have soaked), and add them to the pot with the hominy. Bring to a boil, reduce the heat, and simmer for 1 hour. Add the whole sausages to the mixture and simmer for 1 more hour, or until the beans are tender.

Season the chicken with the salt and red pepper and set aside. In a large pan, heat the vegetable oil. Add the onions and garlic and sauté until the onions are translucent. Add the tomatoes and simmer for 5 minutes.

1 chicken (3 pounds), cut up, or chicken thighs
2 teaspoons salt
1 teaspoon red pepper flakes
½ cup vegetable oil
2 large onions, thinly sliced
5 cloves garlic, chopped
2 pounds firm tomatoes, quartered
1 medium head cabbage
4 ounces salt pork, sliced (optional)
2 pounds sweet potatoes, peeled and cubed
2 pounds manioc root, peeled and cubed
2 pounds pumpkin, peeled and cubed
2 pounds plantains or green bananas, peeled and sliced 1-inch thick

Remove half of the tomato-onion mixture and place it in a large pot with the chicken pieces. Stir until the chicken is coated with the sauce. Add 2 cups of water and simmer until the chicken is tender, approximately 30 minutes, adding more water as necessary to keep a little sauce in the pot.

Cut the cabbage into eighths and remove the core. Add the cabbage to the pan with the remaining tomato-onion sauce; mix well. In another large pot, cook the sliced salt pork until the fat renders out. Pour off all but 1 tablespoon of the fat. Add the sweet potatoes, manioc, and pumpkin. Add the cabbage mixture to the vegetables and enough water to barely cover. Simmer until the vegetables are tender, 25 to 30 minutes, adding more water to cover if the mixture begins to thicken. Add the plantains during the last 5 minutes of cooking.

To serve, remove the sausages from the beans and cut them into 1-inch pieces. Return the sausages to the bean pot. Place the beans in a soup tureen or a large, deep dish. Serve the vegetables on a large platter, and the chicken separately in a deep, covered dish.

Vegetable Ragout

Guisado de São Nicolau
4 to 6 servings

*t*his vegetable ragout is very popular on the island of São Nicolau. It is made with local vegetables and is easy to prepare. You can substitute sweet potatoes for the yams, butternut squash for the pumpkin, and vegetable shortening for the lard without significantly altering the desired taste of the dish.

2 tablespoons lard or shortening
1 tablespoon vegetable oil
2 large onions, thinly sliced
2 large firm tomatoes
2 cloves garlic, minced
½ teaspoon red pepper flakes
1½ pounds Yukon potatoes, peeled and cubed
1½ pounds manioc, peeled and cubed
1½ pounds yams or sweet potatoes, peeled and cubed
1 pound pumpkin or butternut squash, peeled and cubed
6 green bananas, peeled and sliced 2-inch thick
¼ cup minced fresh parsley

*h*eat the lard and vegetable oil in a skillet and sauté the onions until they are golden.

Process the tomatoes in a food processor. Add the tomatoes, garlic, and pepper flakes to the onions. Add the potatoes, manioc, yams, pumpkin, and bananas to the onion mixture and cover with water. Bring to boil, reduce the heat to a simmer, and cook for 20 minutes, or until the vegetables are tender.

Sprinkle with the parsley. Serve with rice, alone, or as a side dish with meats.

Vegetable Stew

Djagacida
4 to 6 side-dish servings

One is able to savor **djagacida** *on all of the islands of the Cape Verdean archipelago, but particularly on the island of Brava. On Brava, the main ingredients are slices of pumpkin, cornmeal, and favas. On the island of Maio, the main ingredients are peas and cornmeal. This recipe is from the island of Brava.*

1 large onion, chopped
2 ounces salt pork, sliced
1 tablespoon lard or
    shortening
2 cups chopped pumpkin
    or butternut squash
2 garlic cloves, minced
1 bay leaf
2 collard green leaves,
    stems removed
1 cup dried fava beans,
    cooked in water for 1
    hour and drained
2 cups corn flour, or finely
    ground cornmeal (see
    note)
Salt to taste
4 slices bacon, fried crisp

Place the onion, slices of salt pork, and lard in a large pot and cook over medium heat until the onion is translucent.

Add the pumpkin, garlic, and bay leaf. Cover the mixture with one of the collard green leaves. Spread the cooked fava beans over the leaf and cover the beans with the corn flour and enough water to cover the flour. Season with salt, cover with the other collard leaf, and bring to a boil. Lower the heat and simmer until the flour is cooked, about 5 minutes. Remove the leaves, arrange on a platter, and decorate with the crisp bacon.

NOTE: The original recipe calls for corn flour, which is found in Latin American and Mexican markets, but finely ground cornmeal is a good substitute.

Cornmeal Purée

Xerém-de-Festa
8 to 10 side-dish servings

felix Monteiro, an eminent Cape Verdean ethnologist, observed that grinding cornmeal with a mortar and pestle is a simple household chore that can become spectacular when accompanied by rhythmic work songs. Women sing these songs particularly when preparing cornmeal for such occasions as the celebration of Saint Sebastian's and Saint John's holidays as well as for wedding feasts. Normally, an older woman distributes the kernels of corn to the individual mortars. This matriarch then leads the women in song as they wield their pestles, while others clap hands or play tambourines. At each mortar there are three women or girls who pound the corn to the beat of the tambourines. For every three hits of the pestle, there is a beat of the tambourine, accompanied by the hand clapping. When the last of the cornmeal is retrieved from the mortars, the ceremony comes to an end.

On the island of Santiago, coconut milk is used for the purée instead of water. The cream used is called manteiga da terra, literally meaning "butter from the land." It is made from goat's-milk cream that has been allowed to ferment, which gives it a unique smell. Some cooks even add sausages, pork, barnacles, or hot peppers to the corn.

4 cups fresh corn kernels
1 teaspoon salt
1 bay leaf
¼ cup whipped cream

place the corn in a food processor and pulse off and on for about 30 seconds, or until the kernels are almost a purée. Bring 8 cups of water to a boil with the salt and bay leaf. Add the corn, reduce the heat, and simmer uncovered until the mixture is thick, about 20 minutes. When ready to serve, remove the bay leaf and fold in the whipped cream.

Fava Bean Rice

Arroz de Favona

6 to 8 servings

favas are very popular in the Algarve, Portugal's southernmost province. There they are cooked in water, drained, and sautéed with bacon and blood sausages, seasoned with mint, and served in a casserole. In other parts of the country, favas are cooked in water, flavored with coriander and mint, but not drained. Both blood and pork sausages are added and served with lettuce seasoned with onion, coriander, olive oil, and vinegar. This recipe is a Cape Verdean version of the Portuguese original. Begin preparing the dish a day in advance as the beans must be soaked overnight.

1½ cups dried fava beans, washed and sorted

1 large onion, thinly sliced

¼ cup vegetable oil

2 medium tomatoes, chopped

1 teaspoon salt

1 pound *chouriço* (smoked pork sausages), thinly sliced

2 cups uncooked white rice

refrigerate the fava beans overnight in cold water to cover. The following day, drain the beans, peel off the outer shells, cover the beans with fresh water and cook for 1 hour, or until tender. Drain.

Place the onion in a large skillet with the vegetable oil. Sauté the onion until translucent, then add the chopped tomatoes, 4 cups of water, salt, and drained fava beans. Bring to a boil and add the sausage and rice. Cover, reduce the heat, and simmer for 25 minutes or until the rice is tender. Serve with Tuna Steaks (page 157) and cooked manioc.

NOTE: For a spicy dish, add 1 tablespoon red pepper flakes when you add the water.

Rice with Tuna

Arroz de Atum

6 to 8 servings

t he waters off the Cape Verde islands abound with tuna. There is a large tuna-canning factory on the island of Sal and you can even purchase two-pound and four-pound cans of tuna in supermarkets. Fresh tuna is also very plentiful and much appreciated. This is a popular risotto-like dish from the island of Santiago.

¼ cup olive oil

1 large onion, chopped

2 tomatoes, peeled, seeded, and chopped

2 green bell peppers, seeded and chopped

1 tablespoon red pepper flakes

1 can (8-ounce) oil-packed tuna, or 8 ounces fresh tuna, cut into small pieces

2 cups uncooked white rice

4 hard-boiled eggs, sliced (optional)

½ cup chopped fresh parsley

h eat the olive oil in a large pot. Sauté the onion until it is lightly golden. Add the tomatoes, green peppers, and red pepper flakes. Bring to a boil and add the tuna and the oil in the can. Reduce the heat and simmer for 5 minutes.

Add 4 cups of water, bring to a boil, and add the rice. Return the liquid to a boil, reduce the heat, cover, and simmer for 20 minutes, or until the rice is tender and moist.

Serve the rice on a deep platter. Decorate with the hard-boiled eggs (if using) and sprinkle with the parsley.

Tuna Steaks

Bifes de Atum
4 to 6 servings

this dish is simple to prepare and very popular among the locals on the island of Santiago. Serve with boiled manioc or white potatoes, fried cornmeal, or Fava Bean Rice (page 155).

¼ cup vegetable oil
1 large onion, sliced
2 ripe tomatoes, chopped
¼ cup white wine
1 tablespoon lard
1 bay leaf
2 pounds (4 to 6) tuna
  steaks
2 teaspoons red pepper
  flakes
1 teaspoon salt
½ cup fresh cilantro leaves

heat the vegetable oil in a large skillet. Add the onion and cook until translucent. Add the chopped tomatoes, white wine, lard, and bay leaf.

Place the tuna steaks in a large deep skillet. Top the tuna with the onion mixture, crushed red peppers, and salt. Simmer over medium heat until the steaks are cooked through. Sprinkle the steaks with the cilantro leaves.

Fish Stew with Coconut Milk

Caldo de Peixe com Leite de Coco
8 to 10 servings

this fish stew is often served for lunch on Sundays or for special occasions. Even though it is served throughout the island of Santiago, it is best known in the "Old City" (Cidade Velha).

3 ripe tomatoes, chopped
2 onions, thinly sliced
½ cup olive oil
½ cup vegetable oil
1 cup fresh cilantro leaves
2 cloves garlic, chopped
1 teaspoon chopped
    malagueta or chili pepper
1 bay leaf
2 pounds Yukon potatoes,
    peeled and cubed
2 pounds sweet potatoes,
    peeled and cubed
1 pound green bananas,
    peeled and sliced 1
    inch thick
1 pound manioc root,
    peeled and cubed
1 pound yams, peeled and
    cubed
1 pound pumpkin or
    butternut squash,
    peeled and cubed
2 cups coconut milk
4 pounds fish steaks
    (grouper or halibut)
Salt to taste

in a large clay or 4-quart aluminum pot, place the tomatoes, onions, olive oil, vegetable oil, cilantro, garlic, hot peppers, and bay leaf and sauté the mixture for 3 minutes.

Add the potatoes, sweet potatoes, bananas, manioc root, yams, and pumpkin. Pour the coconut milk over the vegetables, stir well, and bring to a boil. Reduce the heat and cook for 10 minutes.

Place the fish steaks on top of the vegetables, cover the pot, and simmer, shaking the pot occasionally, until the fish is cooked through, about 20 minutes. Season the dish with salt. Serve immediately, accompanied by Manioc Purée (page 69).

Grilled Lobster

Lagosta Grelhada

2 servings

i n 1978, during a stay of four months in Cape Verde on the island of Santiago, I tasted this dish at the home of dear friends Dinah and Osvaldo Osório. Since lobster is a crustacean plentiful throughout the islands, it is much appreciated by the Cape Verdeans, who especially enjoy it prepared in this manner. This dish goes well with white rice and a green salad.

2 lobsters (1½ pounds
   each)
Boiling water
6 tablespoons lemon juice
2 bay leaves, crumbled
½ cup (1 stick) butter
   melted
2 tablespoons chopped
   fresh parsley

h eat charcoal in a grill, until it turns white hot, or preheat a gas grill to high level.

Plunge the lobsters into boiling salted water to blanch (about 2 minutes). Remove them from the water and cut in half down the middle. Remove the intestines and gills and season with half of the lemon juice and the bay leaves.

Place the lobsters on the grill, shell side down, and grill until they turn a bright red. Serve with the melted butter seasoned with the remaining lemon juice and parsley. This dish goes well with white rice and a green salad.

Chicken with Vegetables

Molho de São Nicolau
10 to 12 servings

i*n standard Portuguese,* molho *means a "sauce" or "gravy." But on the island of São Nicolau,* molho *is a Creole word for a "tradition-al dish." On that Cape Verdean island, no wedding reception would be complete without* molho *on the menu. The combination of chicken with bananas, manioc, yams, pumpkin, and hot peppers is simply marvelous.*

2 teaspoons salt

3 cloves garlic, minced

4 malagueta or red chili peppers, seeded and chopped

2 chickens (7 to 8 pounds total), cut into serving pieces (see note)

2 tablespoons lard or shortening

2 large onions, thinly sliced

2 large ripe tomatoes

6 green bananas, peeled and sliced 1 inch thick

1½ pounds manioc root, peeled and cubed

1½ pounds yams, peeled and cubed

1 pound pumpkin or butternut squash, peeled and cubed

½ cup chopped fresh cilantro

p lace 1 teaspoon of the salt, the garlic, and peppers in a mortar and mash to a purée. Rub the chicken pieces with the purée and set aside.

In a large pot, heat the lard and sauté the onions until lightly golden. Add the chicken pieces. Cut the tomatoes into eighths and pulse them in a food processor for 5 seconds. Add the tomatoes and 3 quarts of water to the pot. Bring to a boil. Reduce the heat and simmer for 30 minutes, covered.

In a medium pot over medium heat, cover the bananas with water and the remaining 1 teaspoon salt and cook until soft, about 5 minutes. After the chicken has simmered for 30 minutes, add the drained bananas, manioc, yams, and pumpkin to the pot. Continue simmering for another 30 minutes, uncovered, or until the vegetables are tender. Taste for seasonings. To serve, pour the chicken and vegetables into a large deep platter and sprinkle with the chopped cilantro.

NOTE: This dish can also be prepared with pork or goat meat (*carneiro*).

Pork Roast with Vegetables

Gigoti

4 servings

*g*igoti *comes from the volcanic island of Fogo. It is traditionally prepared for weddings and is always accompanied by a cornmeal purée made from dried kernels of corn that are pounded into a thick pulp in large mortars. (See Cornmeal Purée, page 154.)*

2 pound pork roast with
    some fat
½ cup white vinegar
½ cup white wine
1 large clove garlic,
    smashed
1 teaspoon salt
2 tablespoons lard or
    shortening
1 large onion, thinly sliced
1 bay leaf
2 pounds collard greens
1 pound manioc root,
    peeled and cut into
    ½-inch slices

*t*he day before serving, cut the pork into cubes and place in a non-metallic bowl. Season with the vinegar, white wine, garlic, and salt; cover and refrigerate overnight.

The following day, heat the lard in a skillet and sauté the onion until golden. Add the bay leaf and marinated pork. Cover and cook on low heat for 30 minutes.

Remove the tough stems from the greens and cut the leaves into small pieces. Add the collards and the manioc slices to the pork and continue cooking until the manioc is tender, about 15 more minutes.

Turtle Steaks

Bifes de Tartaruga
4 servings

I n Cape Verde, particularly on the island of Santiago, turtle meat is much appreciated in soups and stews as well as cut into steaks. This recipe for turtle steaks is very delicious. Even though turtle meat is not available everywhere, I thought it important to include the recipe as an example of the cuisine on this island.

1 pound turtle steaks
2 cloves garlic, smashed
2 or 3 malagueta peppers
1 tablespoon white wine
Salt to taste
1 bay leaf, crumbled
2 tablespoons butter
1 onion, minced

Season the turtle steaks with the garlic, malagueta peppers, white wine, salt, and bay leaf. Let marinate for 1 hour.

In a large frying pan, heat the butter and sauté the onion until almost golden. Raise the heat to high and add the turtle steaks with the marinade. Fry quickly until golden on both sides. Cover the pan, reduce the heat, and cook until the sauce has thickened, about 10 minutes. Serve with white rice and cooked manioc root.

Preserved Mangos

Conserva de Manga

Makes about 5 cups

*t*hese preserved mangos are a delicious side dish for grilled fish or chicken.

1 teaspoon salt
3 to 4 unripe mangos,
   peeled and diced
1 cup vegetable oil
⅛ cup white vinegar
1 tablespoon red pepper
   flakes
1 tablespoon grated fresh
   ginger

*h*eat 2 cups of water with the salt to boiling. Add the diced mangos and return to a boil. When the water returns to a full boil, remove the mangos with a slotted spoon and transfer them to a glass bowl.

Add the oil, vinegar, pepper flakes, and ginger to the mangos. Stir until they are covered completely. Spoon the mixture into a glass jar and pour any remaining liquid over the top. Cover and chill for 2 to 3 days before eating. Serve as a preserve or a condiment with grilled fish or chicken.

Honey Cake

Bolo de Mel
6 to 8 servings

his cake is as popular on the island of Santo Antão in Cape Verde as it is on the Portuguese island of Madeira. In Madeira, molasses is used instead of honey, and it results in a very dark cake that is the texture of a soft cookie. Whether in Cape Verde or the Madeira Islands, this cake is a favorite at Christmastime.

1 cup honey
3 tablespoons unsalted
    butter, softened
2 eggs, separated
2 cups all-purpose flour
1 tablespoon baking powder
1 teaspoon grated lemon
    peel
1 cup ground almonds

preheat the oven to 350 degrees F.

Combine the honey and butter and beat until well incorporated. Add the egg yolks one at a time, incorporating well.

Mix the flour and baking powder together and add the lemon peel. Beat the egg whites into peaks. Fold the flour and the egg whites into the honey mixture, alternating each. Fold in the ground almonds.

Butter a 10-inch round cake pan. Pour the batter into the pan and bake for 1 hour, or until a toothpick comes out clean. Cool for 30 minutes before slicing.

Cuisines of Portuguese Encounters

Pineapple Kisses

Beijinhos de Ananás
Makes about 40 kisses

t his dessert comes from the windward island of Santo Antão. Both pineapples and coconut palms are native to the island.

2 large pineapples
1 coconut, grated, or 3
   cups frozen, fresh,
   unsweetened coconut
   meat
3½ cups sugar, plus
   additional for rolling
About 40 whole cloves

p eel and core the pineapples and cut into 1-inch cubes. Grind the cubes in a meat grinder with a small hole disk or in a food processor to a purée. Save all the juice.

Place the ground pineapple and juice in a large pot. Add the grated coconut meat and sugar and cook over medium heat, stirring constantly with a wooden spoon, until the mixture pulls away from the sides of the pan, about 10 minutes. Let the mixture cool for about 20 minutes.

Form mixture into 1½-inch balls. Roll the balls in sugar and place a clove in the center of each. To serve, place the balls in paper cups or curly aluminum paper.

Cape Verdean Corn Bread

Broa Cabo Verdeana
Makes 2 dozen rolls or 1 loaf

bread made from corn is present in almost all of the countries and territories where Portuguese is spoken. In Cape Verde on the island of Santo Antão, bananas and honey are added to the dough, which gives a special flavor to this bread of Portuguese origin.

½ cup sugar
1 tablespoon butter
6 ripe bananas, mashed
1 cup honey
1 cup milk
2 eggs
2 cups fine cornmeal
2 cups all-purpose flour
1 teaspoon baking soda
1 teaspoon ground cloves
1 teaspoon ground cinnamon
1 teaspoon fennel seeds
1 teaspoon ground nutmeg

preheat the oven to 375 degrees F.

In a large bowl, beat the sugar and butter until light. Add the bananas, honey, milk and eggs, mixing well after each addition.

In another bowl, mix the cornmeal, flour, baking soda, cloves, cinnamon, fennel seeds, and nutmeg. Mix the dry ingredients into the banana mixture until a dough forms. Knead lightly.

Form the dough into balls the size of golf balls or into oval shapes. Butter a baking sheet and dust it with flour. Bake the rolls for about 30 minutes, or until golden brown. Serve hot.

Banana Liqueur

Licor de Banana
Makes 1 quart

t his recipe takes about 7 weeks to prepare and uses only the banana peels. Use the banana flesh to make Banana Fritters (page 224) or Dreams (page 132).

12 ripe bananas
4 cups light brandy
    (*aguardente*), or
    white rum
8 cups sugar

p eel the bananas. Place the peels in a large jar with the *aguardente*. Cover and store for 10 days in a dark place.

After 10 days, place the sugar in a pot and cover with ½ cup of water. Bring the sugar to a boil and continue cooking until the mixture is syrup, that is, when a little syrup is removed with a skimmer and a fine layer forms that can be moved around easily, about 10 minutes.

Mix the syrup with the liqueur. Strain the mixture and pour it into a quart bottle. Cork it; place the bottle on its side, and let it age about 6 weeks before tasting.

Coconut Milk Drink

Refresco de Côco
Makes 4 glasses

this drink is often prepared as a treat for children along with a
snack after school, but young and old alike enjoy it.

2 cups unsweetened
coconut milk
2 cups milk
3 tablespoons sugar
1 banana, cut into 1-inch
rounds
¼ cup ground cinnamon

blend the coconut milk and milk in a blender. Add
the sugar and blend for 5 seconds. Pour into a
container and chill.

When ready to serve, pour into glasses and decorate
with slices of banana rolled in the cinnamon.

CUISINE OF
East Timor

t he island of East Timor is located in the Sonda Archipelago, north of Australia. A dispute between the Portuguese and the Dutch, which began at the beginning of the seventeenth century, lasted until the island was divided in half. The western part was claimed by the Dutch and the eastern part, including the islands of Ataúro, Jaku, and the enclave of Oé-kussi, became part of the Portuguese overseas provinces. In 1975, it became the territory of East Timor, and was taken over by Indonesia. This territory finally gained its independence in May 2002, after 450 years of foreign occupation.

The Timorense culture is rich and diversified, and the cuisine is a combination of the various influences from years of occupation and colonization. There are dishes that are typically Timorense, and others that are obviously influenced by the Portuguese, Chinese, Arabs, and Indians.

The Luso-Timorense families introduced new ingredients for such favorite dishes as salt cod, sardines, and various fruits that arrived every six months by ship from Portugal. The ability of the Timorense to communicate in Portuguese facilitated the introduction of traditional Portuguese dishes, from *feijoada* to *caldo verde*, *Caldeirada* to roast suckling pig, and even *açordas*, into the Timor diet. This all came about when Portuguese priests and missionaries arrived and wanted to enjoy the food of their native land. The Portuguese gastronomic influence was very strong and the Timorense cuisine is richer for it.

The Chinese settled in Timor in the middle of the eighteenth century. They were a closed community in terms of family, culture, and religion, even though a few converted to Catholicism. Many of them settled in the city of Díli and ran the commerce. Their gastronomic contribution was second only to that of the Portuguese. They loved to give parties and invite the local Timorense, and because of their guests, served the meals with knives, forks, and spoons instead of chopsticks. *Chau min*, a dish that the Timorense later adopted as their own, differs from the *chau min* known in Asia. Other dishes that have been adapted from Chinese culture are *Arroz Chau Chau* (page 177), and *Peixe Cozido a Vapor* (page 181).

The Indians who settled in Timor were, for the most part, of Goan origin, many of whom married native Timorense. Naturally, this intermarriage influenced, to some extent, the culinary habits of some sectors of the population. And the new dishes that came with these settlers were eventually accepted by the local population. Soon there was not a festival in Timor where one did not sample a few Indian dishes, like a curry, a *sarapatel*, and a duck *chacooti*. These dishes continue to be prepared by Timorense families and descendents of Goans and are enjoyed at festivals, weddings, birthdays, and other special events.

Timorense cuisine today is, without a doubt, an expression that is creative and alive. Some traditional foods are prepared in hollowed-out bamboo branches (*nos*), wrapped in banana, palm, or coconut leaf sacks, and cooked over vapor in clay pots. Other foods are cooked, roasted, or grilled over coals. The fundamental ingredients in the Timorense diet are rice and corn. Corn is roasted or ground and cooked and mixed with greens. Rice is boiled in water or cooked in coconut milk, or in bamboo branches.

The meats most utilized in Timorense cooking are buffalo, pork, veal, goat, and chicken—these animals being domesticated at home, from the hunt, or bought at the market. The meat is usually cut into pieces and put on sticks and grilled over coals. The buffalo and the pig have been the animals selected for ritual ceremonies and prized by families as the chosen meat for wedding ceremonies. The buffalo is also used as a work animal in the fields.

Timor, surrounded by the ocean, is rich in fish and seafood. The fish most enjoyed by the locals are grouper, red mullet, cuttlefish, sardines, needle fish, eel, and sawfish. Harpoons and nets are used to catch many of the fish. Shrimp, crab, and octopus are some of the seafood also enjoyed.

Seasonings most often used in Timorense cooking are tamarind, marjoram, mint, saffron, ginger, piripiri peppers, lemon, and salt. Preserves are divided into three categories: sweet, sour, and hot, and are called *budos*. The *budo* is served as an accompaniment to the main dish, and is eaten in small portions from the edge of the plate with the rest of the food. Preserves are made from lemons, tomatoes, papaya, cucumber, manga, and piripiri peppers, among others. Vegetables and legumes consumed are beans, manioc, sweet potatoes, yams, sago from the sago palm, corn, and rice. Fruits enjoyed are the mango, banana, guava, avocado, coconut, tamarind, fig, lemon, breadfruit, java plum, and pomegranate.

After Timor was invaded many Timorense fled to Portugal, Macao, and Australia. The result of this acculturation and the adaptation of the Timorense community in these foreign lands resulted in their cuisine becoming a part of those societies. Timorense who eventually returned to their home island also incorporated into their traditional cuisines culinary customs and foods from those lands in which they had sought refuge.

Steamed Meat Dumplings

Seu-Mai

Makes about 2 dozen

every Portuguese-speaking country or territory has its own version of a meat pastry, be it an empada, pastel, rissole, or chamuça. These steamed dumplings are Timor's version.

PASTRY:
2½ cups all-purpose flour
2 eggs

FILLING:
4 tablespoons vegetable oil
1 small onion, minced
8 ounces ground beef
6 large mushroom caps, coarsely chopped
1 dried squid, or other dried fish, chopped (½ cup)
2 tablespoons soy sauce
1 tablespoon fish sauce
1 teaspoon salt
¼ teaspoon black pepper

FOR THE PASTRY: Pour the flour into a bowl and add the eggs. Mix well until a dough forms. If the dough is too firm, add a few drops of water. Roll out the dough on a floured surface to ⅛ inch thick. Cut the dough into 3-inch squares and set aside, covered.

FOR THE FILLING: Heat the oil in a large skillet and add the onion. Sauté the onion until golden and then add the meat and mushrooms. Mix well and add all the other ingredients. Stir well to combine and set aside.

DUMPLINGS: Take 1 square of the dough and place 1 teaspoon of filling in the center. Bring all the sides together, squeezing the filling up so that it shows in the center. Place a toothpick in the center of the meat. Steam the dumplings in a colander over boiling water about 20 minutes, or until the filling is set. Serve warm or at room temperature.

Manioc Pastries

Pastéis de Mandioca
Makes about 2 dozen

Pastries made with manioc dough are also much appreciated in Mozambique, Portugal, São Tomé and Príncipe, and Brazil. In São Tomé and Príncipe, these pastries are made with sardines. In Brazil, they are filled with ground meat, dried beef, shrimp, or cheese and are called Bolinhos (page 95). In Portugal, fish is added to dough made with eggs; and in Mozambique, the filling is shrimp instead of sardines. This Timorense version is filled with dried cod. Be sure to begin the preparation the day before serving because the cod has to soak overnight.

1 pound salt cod, peeled and cubed
2 pounds manioc root, peeled and cubed
1 onion, finely chopped
½ cup manioc flour
2 eggs
2 tablespoons chopped fresh parsley
1 teaspoon salt
½ teaspoon black pepper
Vegetable oil for frying

Soak the salt cod in cold water to cover for 24 hours in the refrigerator, changing the water frequently. Drain; remove the skin and bones. Place the cod in a bowl and cover with boiling water. Cover the bowl and let sit for 20 minutes. Drain.

Cook the manioc in water to cover until tender, about 20 minutes. Strain the manioc and add it to a bowl with the onion, manioc flour, eggs, parsley, and cod fish. Mix well and incorporate the salt and pepper. Remove 1 tablespoon of dough and form it into a ball or egg shape. Repeat with the remaining dough.

Pour the oil into a deep frying pan or heavy skillet to a depth of two inches. Heat it over medium-high heat to 365 degrees F on a deep-frying thermometer. Fry the pastries, a few at a time, in the hot oil until golden. Remove and place on paper towels to drain. Serve hot or at room temperature.

Skewered Goat Meat with Peanut Sauce

Sassate com Molho
Makes about 24

i n East Timor, this dish is typically made with goat meat. In other parts of Indonesia, pork is the preferred meat. Soak the bamboo skewers in water for 1 hour before using to prevent them from burning.

PEANUT SAUCE:
4 ounces tamarind paste
1 cup vegetable oil
12 cloves garlic, minced
1 medium onion, grated
2 tablespoons smooth
   peanut butter
¾ cup soy sauce
4 tablespoons sugar
1 tablespoon white vinegar
1 to 2 tablespoons ground
   red pepper

MEAT SKEWERS:
2 pounds lean goat meat,
   cut into 1-inch cubes
24 bamboo skewers
Vegetable oil for the grill

FOR THE PEANUT SAUCE: Soak the tamarind paste in 2 cups of hot water for 10 minutes. Meanwhile, heat the oil in a frying pan with the garlic and onion, and sauté until the onion is golden. Add the peanut butter and let simmer for about 2 minutes. Add the tamarind paste with the water, soy sauce, sugar, vinegar, and red pepper and simmer for 30 to 40 minutes or until the sauce darkens and thickens. Set aside.

FOR THE MEAT SKEWERS: Heat the charcoal in grill, until it turns white hot, or preheat a gas grill to high level. Brush the grate with oil. Place 5 or 6 pieces of meat on each skewer. Brush with the peanut sauce. Grill the skewers 4 to 5 minutes on each side or until tender. Remove and serve with the remaining sauce.

Seafood Soup

Sopa de Mariscos
6 servings

this recipe is very similar to an Angolan soup called Caldeirada de Peixe. Both have Portuguese origins but are typically Timorense.

½ cup olive oil
4 tomatoes, peeled and quartered
1 onion, thinly sliced
6 cloves garlic
2 tablespoons chopped fresh parsley
2 teaspoons minced red chili pepper
Salt to taste
4 cups white wine
1 cup orange juice
2 tablespoons brandy or *aguardente*
1 smoked pork sausage, sliced into 1-inch pieces
2 fish steaks (grouper or other white fish), cut into 1-inch cubes
6 squid sacs, cleaned and cut open into fourths
6 raw prawns, peeled
2 whole blue crabs, cut into fourths
2 pounds cockles
2 tablespoons chopped fresh cilantro
2 tablespoons chopped fresh mint

eat the oil in a large pot and sauté the tomatoes, onion, garlic, parsley, hot pepper, and salt. Before the vegetables become golden, add the wine, orange juice, and brandy. Mix well.

One at a time add, in this order: the smoked sausage, fish, and squid. Cook 5 minutes and then add the remaining seafood. Cook for 20 minutes.

Pour the soup into a terrine and sprinkle it with the cilantro and mint leaves. Serve hot.

Sautéed Cabbage

Modo-Fila
2 servings

tétum is one of the languages spoken in East Timor, and in that language modo-fila means "stewed vegetables." Modo-fila is to the Timorense what bread is to the Portuguese. This dish is part of their daily diet and can be made with a variety of vegetables and even some fruits. Modo-fila is served with many lunches or dinners. The secret for successful modo-fila is to fry the garlic cloves in their skins, then peel and use them to flavor the greens. Add a little meat to this dish and you have a complete meal. Serve it with white rice, piripiri or Tomato Preserve (page 188).

3 tablespoons vegetable oil
4 large cloves garlic,
    smashed in their skins
½ spring cabbage (napa),
    cut into small pieces
1 teaspoon salt

In a large frying pan, heat the oil to 365 degrees F. Add the garlic cloves and sauté until lightly golden. Remove the garlic, peel, and set aside.

Add the cabbage to the oil and sauté for 1 minute, stirring constantly until all the cabbage is coated with oil. Add 2 tablespoons of water, the salt, and garlic; cover and simmer for 2 minutes until the cabbage is soft. Serve with rice and fish or meat.

Mountain Meal

Seduk

4 servings

Seduk *is a very popular dish in the mountain region of East Timor. It is a good main dish and can also be served as an accompaniment to pork or lamb kabobs (page 186) or a pork roast with a rich tomato sauce.*

1 cup dried black-eyed peas, washed and sorted
2 cups dried hominy
1 tablespoon vegetable oil
2 pounds pumpkin leaves, stemmed and chopped (see note)
1 teaspoon salt

refrigerate the peas overnight in water to cover.

The next day, drain the peas. Cook the peas, hominy, and oil in a medium pot with water to cover for 1½ hours. Do not let the peas dry out. When they are tender, add the greens and salt. Continue cooking until the greens are wilted, adding water as necessary. The finished result should be as dry as cooked rice.

NOTE: Since pumpkin leaves are difficult to find, you can substitute kale or collard greens.

Rice Chau Chau

Arroz Chau Chau
4 to 6 servings

*t*here is a similar dish in Macao with the same name. Since the Portuguese traveled the trade route from Goa to Macao to East Timor and beyond, and carried the cuisine from one area to another, this is not surprising. In Macao, arroz chau chau *is served as an accompaniment to different meat dishes. In East Timor, it is usually the main dish and includes dried shrimp, sausage, and chicken.*

1 cup dried shrimp
2½ cups uncooked white rice
¼ cup vegetable oil
4 eggs
1 whole boneless chicken breast
¼ cup soy sauce
2 cloves garlic, minced
2 green onions, cut into small pieces
2 Chinese sausages, cut into small pieces

*S*often the dried shrimp in warm water for 20 minutes. Add the rice to 5 cups of boiling water, cover, and simmer for 20 minutes, or until tender and the grains are separate.

In a medium skillet, heat 1 tablespoon of the vegetable oil. Beat the eggs in a bowl and pour the mixture into the skillet. Cook the eggs, without stirring, over low heat, forming a pancake. Remove and set aside.

Drain the shrimp and cut into small pieces. Cut the chicken into small pieces and season with the soy sauce and garlic. In a large skillet, heat 2 tablespoons of the vegetable oil and sauté the onions until translucent. Remove the onions and set aside. Add the shrimp and sauté until pink. Remove and set aside in a large bowl. Add the chicken and sauté until tender. Remove and add to the shrimp. Add the sausages to the pan and sauté until cooked through. Remove and add to the other meats.

Wash the skillet and return it to the heat with the remaining 1 tablespoon oil. Cut the omelet into 2-inch strips. Add all the ingredients, including the rice, to the skillet. Heat the mixture for about 5 minutes, stirring constantly to heat through. Serve hot.

NOTE: This dish is a good use for leftover rice. Leftover rice dishes are often stir-fried the following morning and served for breakfast.

East Timor Bean Stew

Feijoada à Timorense

10 to 12 servings

*t*his version of feijoada *comes from East Timor. It calls for kidney beans and leaves from the papaya plant. If not available, collard greens are a good substitute.*

4 cups dried kidney beans, washed and sorted

2 pig's ears, fresh or salted (optional)

2 pig's feet, fresh or salted (optional)

3 tablespoons lard or shortening

3 ripe tomatoes, peeled, seeded, and chopped

1 large onion, minced

6 cloves garlic, minced

2 whole bay leaves

1 teaspoon paprika

2 pounds beef roast, cut into cubes

8 ounces salt pork, cut into cubes

1 pound garlicky pork sausage

1 pound *chouriço*

1 pound blood sausage

Salt to taste

3 pounds collard greens, cut into pieces

*r*efrigerate the beans overnight in cold water to cover. If using salted pig's ears and feet, soak them overnight in cold water also.

The next day, drain the beans, cover them with fresh cold water and bring to a boil. Reduce the heat and simmer until the beans are tender, 1 to 2 hours, depending on the quality of the beans used. Add more water as necessary.

Meanwhile cut the pig's feet and ears into pieces. Place in medium pot, cover with cold water and bring to a boil; cook until tender, about 2 hours.

In a large skillet, melt the lard and add the tomatoes, onion, garlic, bay leaves, and paprika. Mix well and cook on medium-low heat until the mixture forms a purée, about 20 minutes, stirring occasionally.

Add the beef, salt pork, pig's ears and feet, and 1 cup of broth from the beans. When the mixture begins to boil, add the sausages and enough broth from the beans to simmer the sausages. When the sausages are cooked through, remove them and cut into 1-inch pieces while still warm.

Taste the mixture for salt and add the collard greens to the skillet. Let simmer for 20 minutes or until tender. Serve the beans with the meats on the side, accompanied by white rice and Tomato Preserve (page 188).

Fish and Vegetable Stew

Caldeirada de Peixe

4 to 6 servings

i *n Portugal* caldeirada de peixe *is made with a variety of fish, but in Timor they use only one type at a time. Oily fish like mackerel, swordfish, or tuna, is preferred, but grouper—which is very popular in East Timor—can also be used.*

3 pounds fish steaks or fillets such as grouper, mackerel, or tuna
4 cloves garlic, minced
1 teaspoon salt
¼ teaspoon black pepper
1 bay leaf, broken into pieces
1 pound white potatoes, peeled and sliced into ½-inch rounds
4 yellow onions, thinly sliced
4 red bell peppers, sliced
¾ cup olive oil
1½ cups white wine
½ cup chopped fresh parsley

r inse the fish, pat dry, and set aside. Place the minced garlic and salt in a mortar and pound to a paste. Add the pepper and broken bay leaf and rub the mixture into the fish pieces. Set aside for 30 minutes.

In a deep skillet, layer the ingredients, beginning with half the fish, then half of the potatoes, onions, and red peppers. Repeat the layering and pour the olive oil over all, followed by the wine. Sprinkle with the parsley. Cook covered, over low heat until the fish is cooked through and the vegetables are tender. Serve with white rice, Preserved Onions (page 189), and hot sauce.

Grilled Fish, Timor-Style

Saboco de Peixe
4 servings

S aboco *is a traditional Timorense dish favored by the fishermen. In Timor, they drop their nets in the waters off the beaches or cast lines from their dug-out canoes. Upon returning to shore at the end of the day with their catch, they prepare this delicious dish on the beach over an open fire. Pots or pans are not used but instead they cook the* saboco *wrapped in banana leaves over the coals while members of their families sit around the fire. Lacking banana leaves, aluminum foil or collard greens can be substituted. Traditionally this dish is served with white rice, but it can also be served with boiled new potatoes. Large shrimp or prawns can be substituted for the fish.*

2 groupers, about 1½
    pounds each
6 cloves garlic
1 teaspoon salt
3 tablespoons lemon juice
½ teaspoon saffron
1-inch piece fresh ginger,
    grated
½ teaspoon Tabasco or
    other hot sauce
2 banana leaves, pieces
    of aluminum foil, or
    collard green leaves

h eat the charcoal in a grill until it turns white, or preheat a gas grill to high.

Clean the fish and open the cavities.

In a mortar, mash the garlic and salt together to a pulp. Add the lemon juice, saffron, ginger, and hot sauce. Mix well.

Rub the fish inside and out with the mixture and wrap them in the leaves or aluminum foil. Place the fish over the coals and cook for 25 minutes. Remove and serve the fish with white rice or boiled potatoes and additional hot sauce (*piripiri*).

Steamed Fish

Peixe Cozido à Vapor
4 servings

there are many dishes in Timor that are of Chinese origin but have been incorporated into the Timorense diet with a few changes. This steamed fish is such a dish and today it is considered local cuisine.

1 grouper (about 2 pounds)
Salt to taste
1-inch piece fresh ginger,
    grated
2 cloves garlic, minced
1 tablespoon vegetable oil
4 green onions
1 cup fresh cilantro
1 tablespoon sesame oil
1 tablespoon soy sauce, or
    to taste

preheat the oven to 425 degrees F.

Season the fish with the salt, ginger, and half of the garlic. Put the fish in a deep casserole and place the casserole in a baking pan with 1 inch of water, forming a bain-marie. Cover the pan with aluminum foil and bake until the fish flakes easily, about 20 minutes.

Meanwhile, heat the vegetable oil in a frying pan and quickly fry half of the onions and the cilantro (about 30 seconds). Add the sesame oil and soy sauce, stir well, and set aside.

When the fish is done, sprinkle it with the rest of the chopped onions and pour the soy mixture over all. Serve hot with white rice.

Crab Curry

Caril de Caranguejo

6 servings

*t*his curry originated with Goan families who lived in Timor, but was modified and today is a dish considered part of the Timorense cuisine. It is best to prepare this dish a day before serving. The seasonings will have a chance to impregnate the crabmeat and the end result is a wonderful taste.

4 pounds large blue crabs
2 tablespoons olive oil
1 tablespoon curry paste
   (see note)
1 onion, minced
6 cloves garlic, minced
3 lemon leaves
1 bay leaf
1 cup coconut milk

*C*ut the crabs into fourths.

In a frying pan, place the olive oil and curry paste and sauté for 2 minutes. Add the onion, garlic, lemon leaves and bay leaf. Sauté for 3 minutes. Add the crabs and enough coconut milk to cover them. Simmer for 20 or 30 minutes, until the crabs are cooked through. Serve with white rice and Preserved Onions (page 189).

NOTE: The curry paste can be found in the Asian section of most grocery stores.

Chicken Curry

Caril de Galinha
4 to 6 servings

*t*he people from India who lived in Timor were, in a large part, of Goan ancestry, some of whom married Timorense. Obviously, this miscegenation influenced, to a certain degree, the culinary habits of the local population. The dishes that they brought with them were tried by the Timorense and slowly incorporated into the local diet. There is not a party or celebration in Timor that does not serve Indian food, such as curry or sarapatel *(a stew of pork innards)*. Chicken curry is one of the dishes that gained national status.

1 large chicken (3 to 4 pounds), cut into 8 pieces
3 tablespoons lemon juice
2 cloves garlic, minced
Salt and black pepper to taste
Vegetable oil for frying
2 tablespoons olive oil
1 onion, minced
1 hot chili pepper, minced
1 tablespoon curry paste
½ cup fennel leaves
6 lemon leaves
4 cups coconut milk

*S*eason the chicken pieces with the lemon juice, half of the garlic, and some salt and pepper. Let the chicken marinate for 2 hours.

Pour the vegetable oil into a deep frying pan or heavy skillet to a depth of two inches. Heat it over medium-high heat to 365 degrees F on a deep-frying thermometer. Remove the chicken from the marinade and fry in the hot oil until lightly golden. Remove to paper towels to drain.

In a large frying pan, heat the olive oil and sauté the onion, the remaining garlic, and the chili pepper. Add the curry paste, and when the mixture becomes lightly golden, add the chicken, fennel leaves, and lemon leaves. Let simmer for 5 minutes, and then add the coconut milk. Cover and simmer for an additional 20 minutes until the sauce thickens. Serve with white rice and Preserved Onions (page 189).

NOTE: When this dish is prepared a day in advance it is tastier and the seasonings have a chance to meld. Reheat in a covered dish in the oven at 350 degrees F for 30 minutes.

Boneless Stuffed Chicken

Frango Recheado sem Osso
4 to 6 servings

C hicken stuffed with rice is an ancient Portuguese recipe. The Portuguese used capons and stuffed them with rice, onions, port wine, and giblets. The Timorense have adapted that recipe to their taste. They bone the chicken, keeping it whole, and stuff it with rice, giblets, bacon, mushrooms, and green onions. After the bird is stuffed it resumes its original shape.

¼ cup (½ stick) butter, melted
3 tablespoons lemon juice
2 cloves garlic, minced
1 teaspoon salt
1 teaspoon paprika
1 roasting chicken (about 5 pounds), boned

STUFFING:

2 tablespoons olive oil
2 green onions, chopped
2 cloves garlic, minced
10 button mushroom caps, sliced
1 slice smoked bacon, chopped
Giblets from the chicken, chopped
1 cup uncooked white rice

m ix the butter with the lemon juice. In a mortar, mash the garlic with the salt to a purée and mix in the paprika. Add the purée to the butter and mix well. Rub the chicken with the mixture and set aside while you prepare the stuffing.

STUFFING: Heat the olive oil in a large skillet. Add the onions, garlic, mushrooms, and bacon. Sauté for about 5 minutes; add the giblets and rice and stir for 2 minutes. Add 1 cup of water and bring to a boil; cover, reduce the heat to a simmer, and cook for 20 minutes, or until the rice is tender. Remove from heat and let cool. The stuffing should be moist.

Preheat the oven to 400 degrees F. Spoon some of the stuffing into the neck cavity and close the opening using toothpicks. Spoon the remaining stuffing into the body cavity and close with toothpicks. The chicken should return to its original shape. Place in a baking pan and roast for 20 minutes. Reduce the heat to 350 degrees F and continue roasting for 2 hours, or until the internal temperature reaches 160 degrees F.

Remove the chicken from the pan and let it cool for 30 minutes. Slice the chicken and serve with Puréed Turnip Greens (page 28).

Fried Chicken

Frango Frito

4 to 6 servings

t his is Timor's answer to fried chicken. This dish is always served with white rice and accompanied by Tomato Preserve (page 188), and Sautéed Cabbage (page 175).

8 cloves garlic, minced
6 tablespoons lemon juice
¼ cup soy sauce
½ teaspoon black pepper
1 chicken (about 3 pounds), cut into 8 pieces
Oil for frying (see note)

i n a mortar and pestle, pound the garlic to a pulp and add the lemon juice, soy sauce, and pepper. Season the chicken with the sauce and marinate for 1 hour.

Pour the oil into a deep frying pan or heavy skillet to a depth of two inches. Heat it over medium-high heat to 365 degrees F on a deep-frying thermometer. Fry the chicken in the hot oil, a few pieces at a time, until the skin is golden. Remove to paper towels to drain.

NOTE: In Timor, coconut oil is often used for the frying.

Lamb Kabobs, Timor-Style

Sassate
4 servings

i n Timor, sassate *is the local term for "shish kabob" or "meat on a skewer." Traditionally goat is the preferred meat, but you can also use other meats. Many Portuguese who lived in Timor during colonial times preferred lamb. This recipe reflects that influence.*

8 bamboo skewers, soaked in water for 30 minutes
2 pounds lamb shoulder, trimmed of fat and cut into 1-inch cubes
⅓ cup raw unsalted peanuts
6 cloves garlic
3 tablespoons vegetable oil
1 medium onion, minced
2 tablespoons tamarind paste
1 tablespoon soy sauce
2 teaspoons red pepper flakes, or more to taste
1 teaspoon sugar

h eat the charcoal in a grill until it turns white, or preheat a gas grill to high. Skewer the lamb cubes and grill them to the desired doneness. Meanwhile prepare the sauce.

Finely grind the peanuts and garlic in a meat grinder or food processor. Heat the oil in a skillet and sauté the peanut mixture for 2 minutes over medium heat. Add the onion and the tamarind paste mixed with ¼ cup of water. Bring the mixture to a boil and add the soy sauce, pepper flakes, and sugar. Simmer for 2 minutes, or until the sauce thickens.

Serve the lamb kabobs with the sauce and white rice.

Goat, Timor-Style

Tukir de Cabrito

8 to 10 servings

t ukir de Cabrito *is one of Timor's most traditional dishes and is always served at family celebrations. It can be made with almost any kind of meat, but the most favored is goat. The traditional way to cook this dish is in a hollowed-out bamboo trunk over coals. Since this trunk is not readily available here, I have used a Chinese bamboo steamer wrapped in aluminum and placed over coals. You can also use a deep casserole and cook the stew over medium heat on top of the stove. Either way, the result is deliciously exotic.*

½ cup tamarind paste

4 pounds goat meat, cubed

1 pound goat innards (such as liver, kidney, and heart), cubed

4 large red onions, chopped

12 cloves garlic, smashed

2-inch piece fresh ginger, grated

1 tablespoon saffron

1 teaspoon salt

¼ teaspoon black pepper

3 tablespoons lemon juice

p lace the tamarind paste in 2 cups of hot water and set aside for 20 minutes.

Mix the meat and innards with the onions, garlic, ginger, saffron, salt, and pepper. Add the tamarind paste with the water and the lemon juice and place all the ingredients in a large pot or bamboo steamer. Cover and cook over medium-low heat until the goat meat is tender, about 1 hour. Serve with white rice.

Tomato Preserve

Budo de Tomate
Makes about 5 cups

budo, *a word meaning "preserve," is from Tetum, the major language of East Timor. There are several kinds of budos and they can either be for long-term or short-term use. A* budo *usually accompanies a meal, but some can be served as the main dish. The accompaniment* budo *typically has more hot sauce (piripiri) than the entrée* budo. *This recipe for Tomato Budo is a wonderful accompaniment to East Timor Bean Stew (page 178).*

4 medium tomatoes
1 large onion, sliced paper thin
2 cloves garlic, minced
3 green onions, minced
¼ cup fresh mint, minced
3 tablespoons lemon juice
1 teaspoon salt
Minced piripiri or chili peppers to taste

mince the tomatoes with the seeds, and combine in a large bowl with the onion slices, garlic, green onions, and mint.

Season the vegetable mixture with the lemon juice, salt, and hot peppers. Mix well and serve.

NOTE: This dish can also be made with cucumbers. In that case, omit the green onions, mint, and hot peppers.

Preserved Onions

Budo de Cebola

Makes 3½ cups

budos *are preserves that are placed on the table in little bowls and guests take a small amount and place it on the edge of their plates. On those same plates will be rice, meat, or fish, and* piripiri *sauce. Each forkful will have a little of each item, which will be topped with the preserves. This is a typical Timorense meal. Budos are made with many different ingredients: papaya, tomato, giblets, cucumber, lemon, and mango.*

3 large onions, thinly
    sliced
6 tablespoons lemon juice
2 red chili peppers, minced,
    or 2 tablespoons red
    pepper flakes
Salt and black pepper to
    taste

in a medium bowl, place the onion slices and season with the lemon juice, red peppers, salt, and pepper. Stir to incorporate the spices and serve.

Coconut Pudding

Pudim de Côco

8 to 10 servings

Coconut desserts are very popular throughout the Portuguese-speaking world. This delicious dessert from Timor is similar to traditional Portuguese flan, but with a coconut flavor. The pudding can also be cooked in individual pastry tins or individual muffin tins.

3 cups sugar

6 eggs

2 tablespoons flour

2 cups unsweetened coconut milk

¼ cup freshly grated coconut (optional)

Preheat the oven to 350 degrees F.

Slowly heat 1 cup of the sugar in a heavy skillet, stirring constantly with a wooden spoon until the sugar melts and is free of lumps. When the sugar turns a caramel color, remove it from the heat and pour it into a 6-cup ovenproof mold. Turn to coat the bottom. Set aside.

Beat the eggs with the remaining 2 cups sugar until fluffy. Place the flour in a small bowl and add 2 tablespoons of the coconut milk, one at a time until the mixture is smooth. Add the flour mixture to the remaining coconut milk, mix well, and then add to the egg mixture. Pour into the mold over the caramelized sugar.

Place the mold in a large baking pan filled with 1 inch of hot water, creating a bain-marie. Bake for 40 minutes, or until a toothpick inserted in the center comes out clean. Remove from the water bath immediately and cool on a rack for 30 minutes. Chill for 6 to 8 hours. Run a knife around the edge and invert onto a serving dish. To serve, sprinkle with freshly grated coconut, if desired.

Banana Cake

Bolo de Banana
10 servings

Portuguese settlers in East Timor brought with them the custom of entertaining at home. They took advantage of local foods, such as bananas, and substituted them in traditional recipes that they brought from Portugal. This cake is a good example.

2 cups sugar
1 cup (2 sticks) butter, softened
5 eggs
2½ cups all-purpose flour
1 teaspoon baking powder
½ cup oats, ground
5 ripe bananas
5 tablespoons heavy cream

In a large bowl, beat 1 cup of the sugar and the butter together until creamy. Add the eggs one at a time, beating after each addition. Mix the baking powder with the flour and add the flour mixture to the batter a little at a time, then add the ground oats and 2 bananas, mashed. In another bowl, beat the cream to firm peaks and fold into the batter.

Preheat the oven to 350 degrees F. In a small pot, slowly heat the remaining 1 cup sugar, stirring constantly, until caramelized. Pour the liquid caramel into a 2-quart mold. Turn the mold until the bottom is completely covered.

Peel and slice the 3 remaining bananas into ½-inch slices. Arrange the banana slices over the caramel and up the sides of the mold.

Pour the batter into the mold and bake for 30 minutes, or until a tester or wooden skewer inserted in the cake comes out clean. Remove the cake from the oven and cool for 15 minutes. Invert onto a serving platter while still warm and serve.

Layered Cake

Bibinca
10 to 12 servings

bibinca *is a dessert of Goan origin that the Portuguese took to Timor. Bibinca tastes like a cross between a cake and a pudding, but looks like a stack of pancakes. Seven layers make up this delicious cake.*

2 cups sugar
1 cup plus 2 tablespoons
    flour
12 egg yolks
1½ cups unsweetened
    coconut milk
1 teaspoon ground nutmeg
1 cup (2 sticks) butter,
    melted

preheat the oven to 350 degrees F.

Put the sugar, flour, and egg yolks into a large bowl and beat with a wooden spoon until well mixed. Slowly add the coconut milk and nutmeg and stir well. Add the melted butter, stirring constantly.

Grease a deep round 8-inch cake pan with butter and pour in ½ cup of the batter for the first layer. Bake the layer for about 5 minutes, or until golden. Remove from the oven, turn out onto a plate. Pour ½ cup into the pan for the second layer. Continue until all 7 layers are cooked, stacking the layers on the plate, one on top of the other. Invert onto a serving dish while still warm.

NOTE: Some cooks make only 5 layers, and once they are stacked cut them into triangles.

CUISINE OF
Goa

early in the sixteenth century, the Portuguese sought to colonize India and gain a foothold in the spice trade. They landed on the west coast of India in 1510 at the port of Goa, which controlled the spice trade. Before the Portuguese arrived, the Muslims were in control. But by the end of the sixteenth century, the Portuguese had created an eastern territory around the port with Goa as its capital. Portugal's rule of Goa lasted for 450 years. Because of this control, Christianity became one of the three religions of Goa—Hinduism and Islam being the other two. The arrival in 1542 of Father Francis Xavier, a Jesuit, was responsible for the degree of tolerance that existed among the three faiths. Before his arrival, early attempts to convert the Goans to Christianity had resulted in temples and mosques being demolished. Today, the people belonging to all three religions respect each others customs and rituals. In fact, Christian and Hindu festivals are celebrated by nearly all Goans.

Goa has the privilege to have assimilated the culinary arts of many cultures, the most important being those of the Indian subcontinent, but also those of Portugal and other parts of the Portuguese-speaking world. Soup is probably the best example of the assimilation of Portuguese cuisine. Soup was never a part of the menu anywhere in India before the Portuguese arrived. The recipe for Fish Head Soup (page 202) came about as a way to utilize the heads of fillets that were used to prepare other dishes. Other soups that have become part of the Goan cuisine are *Caldo Verde* (Collard Green Soup, page 22), and *Canja* (Chicken Soup, page 203).

Vegetables play a quantitatively and qualitatively important role in the diet of the Goans even though they are not vegetarians. Goa boasts a large variety of locally grown vegetables. Among those most consumed are okra, spinach, cabbage, cauliflower, eggplant, and green beans. These vegetables are usually cooked in coconut milk, and some are stuffed with shrimp or ground meat.

The Goan coast is rich in seafood. There are shrimp, prawns, crabs, lobsters, squid, mussels, oysters, and cockles. The most popular of these are shrimp prepared in curries, stuffed, fried, and cooked simply in water. The Portuguese influence in the preparation of seafood is apparent in such dishes as shrimp turnovers, oyster pie, shrimp balls, stuffed squid, sautéed or stuffed prawns, and stuffed crab. The recipes are basically Portuguese, but with Goan seasonings. Even the use of more than one type of fish in a dish is from the Portuguese. The variety of fish in Goa is enormous. Most of the fish that we know are found there along with a number of indigenous varieties. Tilapia and codfish are dried and used in many dishes of Portuguese origin.

Goans eat more pork than beef, mainly because in years past the houses were large as were the backyards and pigs were easy to farm. Roast suckling pig, sausages, and such dishes as *vindaloo*, *balchão*, and *sarapatel* are very popular even today. Beef is usually roasted, cooked in stews, and used as fillings for pastry. Sheep are rarely consumed because they are raised in other parts of India. Goat is eaten, but most often only in stews. In the past, lard or coconut oil was used for frying. Today, peanut oil, sunflower oil, corn oil, and butter are the norm.

In Goa, poultry is more expensive than other meat and therefore is not eaten as much. But a few dishes, such as chicken *cafreal* of Mozambican influence (page 309), are enjoyed by all. Duck and turkey are often served during the Christian holidays.

Desserts are where the greatest Portuguese influence is found. Egg yolk desserts and cakes are evolved from recipes of the Portuguese nuns in the convents. Coconut and bananas are commonly used in cakes and puddings. During the festivals in the churches and the Hindu temples, the nuns set up stalls and sell the desserts and cakes for the holidays, therefore these are rarely prepared in homes.

This chapter gives a sampling of traditional Goan dishes, and shows the influence on the cuisine by Portuguese, Indian, and African culinary cultures. The end result is an aromatic, savory, and exotic cuisine that tantalizes the palate.

Fish Puffs

Sonhos de Peixe
24 croquettes or 12 appetizer servings

this is one of the small savory appetizers so popular in Goa. Any white fish is suitable for these puffs. I often use orange roughy or tilapia because they are mild-tasting fish and the seasonings work well. The filling can be prepared a day in advance and chilled overnight. These puffs, fully cooked, can be kept in the freezer for several months. To eat as an appetizer, form the filling into croquettes and serve with relishes or chutney. To prepare as a side dish, form the filling into patties and serve with garlic rice and spinach.

1 pound boneless white fish
    fillets, such as orange
    roughy or tilapia
12 ounces white potatoes,
    peeled
2 tablespoons vegetable oil
1 medium onion, minced
6 large cloves garlic, minced
1-inch piece fresh ginger,
    peeled and grated
2 red chili peppers, seeded
    and chopped
2 teaspoons ground
    coriander
1 teaspoon ground turmeric
1 teaspoon garam masala
1 teaspoon pure chili
    powder
⅓ cup finely chopped fresh
    cilantro
½ teaspoon salt
¼ cup all-purpose flour
1 egg, beaten
1 cup soft white bread
    crumbs
Vegetable oil for frying

Cut the fish into 1-inch pieces. Grind the fish and the potatoes in a meat grinder on small grind. If a grinder is not available, use a food processor and pulse until the mixture resembles cornmeal.

Heat the 2 tablespoons vegetable oil over medium heat in a small skillet and fry the onion until soft. Add the garlic, ginger, chilies, coriander, turmeric, garam masala, and chili powder. Stir and cook for 3 minutes. Add the cilantro and salt. Mix well and remove from the heat.

Place the potato and fish mixture in a large bowl and fold in the onion mixture until it is well mixed. Cover the mixture and chill overnight.

To make patties, use ⅓ cup of the fish mixture and shape into round cakes. For croquettes, use 2 tablespoons to form the mixture into ovals. Roll the cakes or croquettes in flour, then dip in the beaten egg and roll in bread crumbs. Pour vegetable oil into a deep frying pan or heavy skillet to a depth of two inches. Heat it over medium-high heat to 365 degrees F on a deep-frying thermometer. Fry the cakes until golden on both sides. Drain on paper towels. Serve warm or at room temperature.

Shrimp Balls

Almondegas de Camarão
2 dozen appetizer servings

these tasty little appetizers are very popular in Goa and are found on the menu of many restaurants. They are served with a spicy tomato sauce.

2½ pounds raw shrimp with shells
1 large onion, chopped
1 head garlic, separated and peeled
3-inch piece fresh ginger, peeled and grated
1 tablespoon red pepper flakes
6 whole cloves
¼ cup chopped fresh cilantro
1 tablespoon vinegar
1 teaspoon turmeric
1 teaspoon ground cumin
½ teaspoon black pepper
2 eggs, beaten
1 cup all-purpose flour for dusting
Vegetable oil for frying

SAUCE:
2 tablespoons vegetable oil
1 large onion, minced
2 green bell peppers, minced
5 cloves garlic, minced
½ teaspoon saffron
⅔ cup coconut milk
1 can (16-ounce) crushed tomatoes

reheat the oven to 350 degrees F.

Slit the shrimp down the back, place them in a colander, and rinse well. Arrange the shrimp on baking sheets and bake in the oven for 15 minutes, or until the shrimp turn pink. Allow to cool and then peel the shrimp. In a food processor or meat grinder, combine the shrimp, onion, garlic, ginger, pepper flakes, and cloves. Add the cilantro, vinegar, turmeric, cumin, and pepper. Mix well. Form the mixture into balls the size of walnuts and roll them in the beaten eggs and then in the flour. Place in the refrigerator to chill for 30 minutes.

Meanwhile, prepare the sauce. Heat the oil in a large frying pan. Add the onion and cook until translucent. Add the green peppers, garlic, and saffron. Stir and cook for 3 minutes. Add the coconut milk and the crushed tomatoes; cook uncovered, for about 20 minutes, or until the sauce thickens.

Pour some vegetable oil into a deep frying pan or heavy skillet to a depth of two inches. Heat it over medium-high heat to 365 degrees F on a deep-frying thermometer. Fry the shrimp balls for about 3 minutes, turning constantly, until golden on all sides. Remove and drain on paper towels. Serve warm with the tomato sauce on the side.

| Cuisines of Portuguese Encounters

Broccoli Fritters

Pakode
15 to 20 appetizer servings

Pakode *can be made with any vegetable, but I would suggest using broccoli, cauliflower, eggplant, thickly sliced potatoes, or string beans. You can make a beautiful buffet platter by using some of each of the vegetables. Chickpea flour is the basis of this spicy batter and can be found in health food stores and select supermarkets. These vegetable fritters are related to the tempura of Japan, which originated in Portugal. The word "tempura" comes from the Portuguese* tempero, *which means "seasoning."*

1 small onion, coarsely chopped
2 green chilies, seeded
¼ cup finely chopped fresh cilantro leaves and stems
1-inch piece fresh ginger, peeled and chopped
2 cloves garlic, peeled
2 teaspoons ground coriander
1 teaspoon cumin seeds
½ teaspoon salt
¼ teaspoon chili powder
1 tablespoon uncooked white rice
⅔ cup chickpea flour, sifted
Vegetable oil for frying
1 bunch broccoli, cut into florets (about 30 florets)

Place the onion, fresh chilies, cilantro, ginger, and garlic in a blender or food processor. Add 2 tablespoons water and blend to a smooth paste. Transfer the paste to a mixing bowl and add the coriander, cumin seeds, salt, and chili powder. Mix well.

Place the rice in a blender or coffee grinder and grind for 10 seconds, or until the rice looks like cornmeal. Add the ground rice and chickpea flour to the paste. Gradually add ⅔ cup water and mix until the batter is smooth. Add more water if the batter is too thick.

Pour the oil into a deep frying pan or heavy skillet to a depth of two inches. Heat it over medium-high heat to 365 degrees F on a deep-frying thermometer, or when a drop of the batter floats to the surface immediately without browning. Dip each broccoli floret in the batter, making sure that it is completely coated. Fry the broccoli in the hot oil until golden brown, 4 to 6 minutes. Drain on paper towels. Serve with mango chutney.

NOTE: *Pakode* can also be served as a side dish with chicken, lamb, pork, or fried sardines.

Miniature Pork Pies

Empadinhas de Porco
20 servings

t hese miniature pork pies are seen at buffet parties and picnics in Goa but are also found on party tables from Portugal to Brazil. This recipe can also be made into one large pie and served as a light lunch or supper with a green salad. Don't let the long list of ingredients scare you. This recipe is really easy to prepare and well worth the effort. The pastry, made with butter and eggs, is ideal for pork pies. It can also be used for many other recipes, including empadas and tortes. The uncooked pies can be frozen before baking.

PASTRY:
1¾ cups self-rising flour (or all-purpose flour plus 1 teaspoon baking powder)
1 tablespoon sugar
1 teaspoon salt
1 teaspoon caraway seeds
½ cup (1 stick) butter, melted
3 large eggs, beaten

FILLING:
2 tablespoons red pepper flakes
3-inch piece cinnamon stick, broken up
6 green cardamom seeds
6 whole cloves
2 teaspoons cumin seeds
2 teaspoons coriander seeds
½ teaspoon black peppercorns

FOR THE PASTRY: Place the flour, sugar, salt, and caraway seeds into a large bowl and mix thoroughly. Add the melted butter and eggs and mix until a stiff dough forms. Knead the dough until it is smooth. Cover with a damp cloth or plastic wrap and set aside for 30 minutes.

FOR THE FILLING: Finely grind together in a blender or coffee grinder the red pepper flakes, cinnamon pieces, cardamom seeds, cloves, 2 teaspoons cumin seeds, coriander seeds, and peppercorns. Set aside.

Heat the oil over medium heat in a large skillet and add the 1 tablespoon cumin seeds. When they begin to crackle, add the onion and fry until translucent. Add the ginger, garlic, and green chilies. Stir and fry for 1 minute. Add the ground spices; stir and sauté for 1 more minute.

Add the pork, salt, and sugar and mix well. Sauté over medium heat, for 6 minutes stirring occasionally. Add 6 tablespoons of warm water, the tomatoes and vinegar. Bring to a boil and simmer for 15 minutes, uncovered, to reduce the liquid. The mixture should be moist but not wet. Stir in the cilantro and remove from the heat. Let cool completely.

2 tablespoons sunflower oil
1 tablespoon cumin seeds
1 medium onion, finely
　chopped
1-inch piece fresh ginger,
　peeled and grated
2½ teaspoons minced garlic
1 or 2 fresh chilies, seeded
　and chopped
1 pound lean pork, minced
1 teaspoon salt
1 teaspoon sugar
¾ cup chopped canned
　tomatoes and juice
2 tablespoons cider vinegar
2 tablespoons chopped
　fresh cilantro
1 egg yolk, beaten

ASSEMBLE PIES: Preheat the oven to 400 degrees F. Brush a 12-cup mini-muffin tin with vegetable oil. Divide the dough into 4 portions and roll each portion into a 10-inch circle. Using a 3½-inch cookie cutter, cut circles in the dough and line each muffin tin with 1 circle. Fill each muffin tin with 1 tablespoon of the pork filling and moisten the edges with water. With a 3-inch cookie cutter, cut the same number of dough circles to use as lids. Moisten the undersides with water and place the lids on top of the filled pies. Press the edges of the dough lightly together to seal. Brush each pie with egg yolk and make 2 slits in the top. Bake for about 15 minutes or until golden. Continue making these pies until all the dough and filling is used. Cool on a rack for 15 minutes. Serve warm or at room temperature as part of a buffet.

Apple Salad with Garlic Dressing

Salada de Maçã com Molho de Alho

4 first course servings

g*ranny Smith or any other tart apple are a good choice for this easy and tasty salad from Goa. Serve this salad as a first course or as a side dish with roast pork.*

2 Granny Smith or other
   tart apples
1 teaspoon salt
2 large cloves garlic,
   minced
2 tablespoons olive oil
1 teaspoon sugar
½ teaspoon white pepper
½ teaspoon mustard powder
2 teaspoons cider vinegar
4 large lettuce leaves

p eel and core the apples and slice into eighths. Place the apples in a bowl and set aside.

Pound the salt and garlic into a paste in a mortar. Place the paste in a small bowl and add the olive oil, sugar, pepper, and mustard powder. Blend thoroughly and add the vinegar. Pour the mixture over the apples and toss to mix well.

Arrange the lettuce on four salad plates. Divide the apples evenly among the plates and pour any remaining dressing over the apples.

Cucumber Salad

Salada de Pepino

4 to 6 side-dish servings

This is a traditional Goan salad that normally accompanies fish. It is also served with meatballs and other meats.

3 cucumbers
1 teaspoon salt
2 jalapeño peppers, seeded and thinly sliced
¼ cup white vinegar

Peel the cucumbers and slice very thinly. Place the cucumbers in a colander; sprinkle with the salt and let stand over a bowl or the sink for 1 hour, or until all the water has drained out.

Press the cucumbers lightly and place in a bowl. Add the jalapeño peppers to the vinegar and pour over the cucumbers. Mix well and serve with fried fish.

Fish Head Soup

Sopa de Cabeça de Peixe

2 to 3 servings

this soup is perhaps the best example of Portuguese culinary assimilation by the Goans, because soup was not part of the Goan cuisine before the Portuguese arrived. Today, this dish is one that appears most on lists of Goan specialties. Saffron and ginger are two ingredients that dominate the Goan cuisine and are known to cure certain illnesses. But the Goans also use saffron as a disinfectant and to eliminate the strong odor of fish.

1 large fish head (about 1 pound)
Salt to taste
2 teaspoons saffron
2 tablespoons vegetable oil
1 clove garlic, peeled
1 medium onion, peeled
2 tablespoons uncooked white rice
½ cup fresh cilantro leaves

Sprinkle the fish head with salt and 1 teaspoon of the saffron. Heat the vegetable oil in a large frying pan and fry the head until golden on both sides.

In a large pot, place the fish head, garlic, whole onion, remaining 1 teaspoon saffron, and 6 cups water, and cook over medium heat for 10 minutes, or until fragrant. Strain the broth and save the fish head.

Return the broth to the pot and add the rice. Cover and cook for 20 minutes.

Meanwhile, remove the meat from the head of the fish and set aside.

Remove the soup from the heat and sprinkle with the cilantro leaves and the meat from the fish head. Serve hot with Goan Flat Bread (page 223).

Chicken Soup

Canja de Galinha
4 servings

Chicken broth was, long ago, one of the foods reserved for convalescents. In Goa, according to custom, a woman gives birth to her child in the home of her parents. Before the birth of her first child, her mother-in-law sends a basket to the home which contains a bottle of port wine and six chickens to prepare this famous broth. The broth is prepared with rice and is eaten at eleven o'clock in the morning on the day of the birth. It is accompanied by curry leftovers from the day before, salt fish, and a preserve called manguinha de chetnim. At the same time, young children take the broth in a clay pot to share with their parents and older siblings who are working in the fields.

1 whole chicken or pieces
    to equal 2 pounds
8 ounces smoked pork
    sausage, cut in ½-inch
    slices
2 onions, peeled
5 cloves garlic, unpeeled
3 tablespoons uncooked
    white rice
Salt to taste

Remove the skin from the chicken and cut it into 8 serving pieces.

In a large pot, place the chicken pieces, sausage, onions, garlic cloves, rice, and 6 cups of water. Place over high heat, bring to a boil, reduce heat to a simmer, and cook until the chicken almost falls off the bone, about 1 hour.

Remove the onions and garlic and discard. Remove the chicken from the broth and place on a platter. Pull the chicken off the bones and shred. Return the chicken to the broth, season with salt, and reheat if necessary. Serve hot.

Goan Rice

Arroz Pilau
4 to 6 servings

pilau, *a word of Hindi origin, and the Portuguese word* arroz, *both mean "rice." So the name of this dish is obviously redundant. This method of preparing a pilau comes from the Turks, and this way of preparing rice comes from the Portuguese, which results in this wonderful combination of culinary cultures.*

4 spicy sausages, about 1
  pound (see note)
4 tablespoons (½ stick)
  unsalted butter
1-inch piece fresh ginger,
  peeled
5 cloves garlic, sliced
4 whole cloves
1 cinnamon stick
5 green cardamom pods
10 black peppercorns
2 medium onions, thinly
  sliced
2 green chilies, seeded
2 cups uncooked white rice
½ teaspoon ground turmeric
4 cups beef broth
3 tablespoons chopped
  fresh cilantro
1 teaspoon salt
3 hard-boiled eggs, shelled
1 cup black olives

prick the skin of the sausages; add 2 tablespoons of water to a skillet and cook the sausages until cooked through, turning frequently. The sausages will brown in their own fat. Cool and cut diagonally into 1-inch pieces; set aside.

Melt 3 tablespoons of the butter in a skillet over low heat and add the ginger, garlic, cloves, cinnamon stick, cardamom pods, and peppercorns. Fry for 1 minute, stirring constantly. Increase the heat to medium and add the onions and chilies; mix well with the spices and sauté for 2 minutes. Cover and simmer for 5 minutes. Add the remaining 1 tablespoon butter and mix well.

Add the rice and turmeric to the onion mixture and sauté until the rice turns a golden color, about 3 minutes. Stir in the beef broth, cilantro, and salt. Bring to a boil, cover, reduce the heat to a simmer, and cook for 15 minutes. Fold the sausages into the rice mixture and continue cooking for 5 more minutes, until the rice is tender. Remove the cinnamon stick from the skillet. Turn the rice and sausage mixture onto a serving platter. Decorate the platter with egg wedges and black olives.

NOTE: This dish calls for a Goan sausage not readily available in the United States. You can use, with excellent results, smoked Chinese sausage or Italian sausage with fennel, chili peppers, cumin, peppercorns, and coriander.

Stir-Fried Rice

Arroz Refogado

8 servings

arroz refogado *is a dish of Portuguese origin. In Goa, stir-fried rice is frequently prepared for casual meals.*

3 tablespoons vegetable oil
2 medium onions, minced
2 medium tomatoes, peeled, seeded, and chopped
3 cloves garlic, minced
1 teaspoon salt
2 cups uncooked white rice
4 cups beef broth
8 ounces smoked sausage (*lingüiça*), cut into thin slices
1 teaspoon lemon juice
4 whole cloves
½ cup cooked peas
¼ cup black olives, sliced

preheat the oven to 350 degrees F.

Heat the oil in a large skillet. Add the onions and cook, stirring, for 2 minutes. Add the tomatoes, garlic, and salt. Mix well. Add the rice and stir-fry for 3 minutes, or until lightly golden. Add the beef broth, sausage, lemon juice, and cloves (saving a few slices of sausage for decoration). When the broth begins to boil, lower the heat, cover the skillet, and cook for only 15 minutes.

Remove from the heat and place in a casserole. Cover and bake until the rice is cooked, about 10 minutes. Remove the cover to let the steam escape. Decorate with the reserved sausage slices, cooked peas, and olives. Serve hot.

Okra in Coconut Milk

Quiabos em Leite de Coco

4 servings

t he Goan diet is rich in vegetables, due to the fact that there is a large variety from which to choose. Thanks to the Portuguese, okra is plentiful and savored by a large majority of the population. It is prepared in many ways, but mainly in curries. This recipe combines okra with coconut milk, saffron, onion, shrimp, and malagueta peppers. The result is an exotic flavor that I am sure many will enjoy.

1½ cups coconut milk
3 cloves garlic
1 tablespoon minced fresh cilantro leaves
1 teaspoon ground cumin
1 teaspoon saffron
3 tablespoons peanut oil
3 medium onions, chopped
8 ounces small raw shrimp, peeled
¼ teaspoon sugar
1 pound okra, trimmed and cut into 2-inch pieces
2 tablespoons tamarind juice or white vinegar
2 green malagueta or hot peppers, thinly sliced
1 teaspoon salt

i n a blender combine ½ cup of the coconut milk, the garlic, cilantro, cumin, and saffron, and blend until the mixture becomes creamy. Set aside.

In a large skillet, heat the peanut oil and sauté the onions until they become translucent. Add the shrimp and sauté until light golden. Add the remaining 1 cup coconut milk and the sugar. Bring to a boil and add the okra and tamarind juice. Lower the heat and simmer for 15 minutes.

Add the mixture from the blender, the malagueta peppers, and the salt to the okra. Continue simmering for another 10 minutes, stirring occasionally. Serve as a side dish to grilled meats or fish.

NOTE: Goans like to cook their vegetables in coconut milk. This is a basic recipe for all vegetables. You can substitute cabbage, eggplant, green beans, spinach, or cauliflower for the okra.

Spicy Roasted Vegetables

Legumes Assados
8 side-dish servings

t his is another recipe that takes advantage of the numerous vegetables consumed in Goa.

2 pounds white potatoes
1 medium eggplant (about
    2 pounds)
1 pound Brussels sprouts
2 green bell peppers
2 medium onions
¼ cup clarified butter, melted

SPICE MIXTURE:

2 tablespoons red wine
    vinegar
1 tablespoon grated fresh
    ginger
2 cloves garlic, minced
2 teaspoons ground
    cinnamon
2 teaspoons mustard seeds,
    crushed
2 teaspoons salt
1½ teaspoons cayenne
    pepper
1 teaspoon turmeric
½ teaspoon ground cloves
½ teaspoon black pepper

p reheat the oven to 350 degrees F.

Peel and cut the potatoes and eggplant into 2-inch cubes. Trim the bottoms of the Brussels sprouts and cut them in half lengthwise. Cut the bell peppers and onions into thin wedges. Place the vegetables in a large bowl and toss with the melted butter.

Combine all the ingredients for the spice mixture and sprinkle over the vegetables; toss to coat evenly. Spread the vegetables on a baking sheet and bake for about 35 minutes, or until tender. Serve hot.

Eggs, East Indian-Style

Ovos à Indiana
6 servings

i n Goa, eggs poached, fried, or scrambled, with or without an accompaniment, are enjoyed at breakfast, lunch, and dinner. This dish features poached eggs over rice with a curried tomato sauce. It can stand alone or enhance a Cucumber Salad (page 201) or a meat curry.

1½ cups uncooked white rice
6 eggs
¼ cup (½ stick) butter or margarine
1 medium onion, finely chopped
3 cloves garlic, chopped
5 medium tomatoes, peeled and chopped
1 teaspoon salt
¼ cup all-purpose flour
1 tablespoon curry powder
¾ cup coconut milk

i n a 2-quart pot, bring 3 cups of water to a boil. Add the rice, stir, cover, and simmer for 20 minutes, or until tender. Set aside.

Bring 4 cups of water to a boil in a large fry pan. Break open the eggs and slip them, 1 at a time, into the boiling water. Poach the eggs for 3 to 4 minutes, or until desired doneness. Remove the eggs from the water with a slotted spoon and keep warm.

Melt the butter in a medium frying pan. Add the onion and garlic and sauté until soft. Purée the tomatoes in a food processor or blender and add to the onion mixture. Simmer for about 5 minutes, or until the sauce thickens. Season the sauce with the salt.

Mix the flour and curry powder together in a small bowl. Slowly pour the coconut milk into the mixture, beating continuously with a wire whisk. When the flour mixture is smooth, add it to the tomato mixture and simmer for 3 minutes, stirring constantly. Transfer the rice to a deep serving platter. Arrange the eggs strategically on top of the rice and pour the tomato sauce over the rice. Serve immediately.

Eggs Poached in Red Wine

Ovos Escalfados com Vinho Tinto
4 to 5 servings

*t*he Portuguese occupation of Goa for 450 years has definitely left its mark on their cuisine. This dish is an adaptation of a similar one in Portugal in which poached eggs are the main ingredient. Try this dish with a green salad for breakfast, brunch, or a light supper.

2 cups red wine
1 medium onion, minced
1 teaspoon salt
½ teaspoon ground nutmeg
¼ teaspoon pepper
2 cloves garlic, minced
1 tablespoon butter, melted
1 tablespoon flour
8 to 10 eggs
8 to 10 slices peasant-type
    bread, toasted (see note)

*p*our the red wine into a large skillet and add the onion, salt, nutmeg, pepper, and garlic. Bring to a boil and simmer until the onions are soft. Mix the butter and flour together and add to the skillet.

Carefully break the eggs, 1 at a time, into the wine sauce and poach them to the desired doneness, basting occasionally. Place 2 slices of toast on each plate; top each slice with a poached egg and pour the wine sauce over the eggs. Serve immediately.

NOTE: You can substitute any bread, even an English muffin for the peasant-type.

Fish Curry

Caril de Peixe
Serves 4 to 6

*i*n Goa, this dish is usually prepared with kokums, *a variety of plum that has a bitter taste and is pitted and dried. In Macao, this bitter plum is known as* mangosteen. *Since neither is readily available in the United States, I have substituted tamarind with good results.*

2 pounds white fish steaks, such as halibut or grouper
1 teaspoon salt
1 large coconut, grated, or 2 cups frozen, grated, unsweetened coconut
8 to 12 dried red chilies
1 tablespoon coriander seeds
2-inch piece fresh ginger
4 cloves garlic, minced
1 tablespoon ground turmeric
1 teaspoon ground cumin
1 tablespoon black peppercorns
4 green chilies, seeded
1 large onion, sliced
1 cup tamarind paste

Sprinkle the fish with the salt and set aside.

In a blender or food processor, grind together the coconut, red chilies, coriander seeds, ginger, garlic, turmeric, cumin, and peppercorns, adding a little water if necessary to form a paste. Place the mixture in a medium pot on low heat and cook for 5 minutes, stirring constantly. Add water as necessary to keep the mixture from sticking.

Add the green chilies and onion to the spice mixture and continue to simmer for another 10 minutes. Mix the tamarind paste with 1 cup of warm water and add to the pot. Simmer for 5 minutes.

Add the fish steaks and cook for about 5 minutes or until the fish flakes easily. Taste and adjust the seasonings if necessary. Serve with white rice.

Codfish Chutney

Chutney de Bacalhau

2 to 4 servings

Chutney is an Indian specialty that was adopted by early Portuguese settlers in Goa. The most popular chutneys are made from mango, lemon, and tomato and are served as an accompaniment to curry dishes. Codfish chutney is a Luso-Indian dish that the Goans serve, not as an accompaniment but as a main dish. This is called a Luso-Indian dish because the Portuguese were responsible for introducing the codfish.

1 pound dried salt codfish fillets
2 tablespoons lard or shortening
1 white onion, minced
2 green onions, thinly sliced
1 teaspoon saffron
2 malagueta or jalapeño peppers, seeded and thinly sliced
1 cup coconut milk

Soak the dried salt cod in cold water to cover for 24 hours in the refrigerator, changing the water frequently.

Preheat the oven to 350 degrees F. Cook the codfish in boiling water to cover for 5 minutes. Remove the fish from the water and let cool. Remove any skin and bones and flake. Spread the codfish on a baking sheet and place in the oven for 10 minutes to dry out.

Heat the lard in a skillet and sauté the white and green onions until lightly golden. Add the saffron and stir to incorporate well. Stir in the cod and half of the malagueta peppers. Add the coconut milk. Reduce the heat and simmer until the mixture dries out, about 10 minutes. Be careful to not let the mixture stick to the pan or burn. Add the rest of the malagueta peppers and serve hot with white rice.

Oyster Pie

Empada de Ostras
6 servings

this recipe is yet another example of east meeting west and yielding delicious results. Although the dish is basically of Portuguese origin, it was enhanced in Goa by the addition of local spices.

FILLING:

2 tablespoons olive oil, plus extra for dish
4 medium onions, chopped
30 cloves garlic, minced
2 malagueta or jalapeño peppers
2-inch piece fresh ginger, peeled and thinly sliced
1 ounce (about 1½ teaspoons) saffron threads
1 teaspoon salt
½ teaspoon sugar
2 medium white potatoes, peeled and cubed
4 pounds shucked oysters with liquid
1 teaspoon white vinegar
3 hard-boiled eggs, chopped
½ cup chopped black olives

TOPPING:

1 cup semolina flour
1 tablespoon sugar
2 to 3 egg yolks

FOR THE FILLING: Heat the oil in a large skillet and sauté the onions, garlic, peppers, ginger, and saffron, stirring constantly. When the onions become translucent, add the salt and sugar; mix well. Add the potatoes and 1 cup of water; cover, and cook for 15 minutes, or until the potatoes are tender. Check occasionally to make sure that there is enough liquid to cook the potatoes; if not, add a little more water. When the potatoes are tender add the oysters and vinegar. Stir and cook until the oysters are opaque. Preheat the oven to 350 degrees F.

FOR THE TOPPING: Heat a large skillet and toast the flour until lightly brown, shaking the skillet occasionally. Remove from the heat and let cool. Place the flour in a bowl, add the sugar, and mix with your hands just to blend. Add the egg yolks, 1 at a time, folding them into the flour. This will give a crumbly mixture.

Rub a 3-quart baking dish with olive oil. Spoon the oyster mixture into the dish and top with the hard-boiled eggs and olives. Sprinkle the topping over the oyster filling and bake for 20 minutes, or until the topping is golden. Be careful not to let it burn. Remove from the oven and let cool for 20 minutes before serving. A green salad is a nice accompaniment.

Goan Shrimp Curry

Caril de Camarão
4 to 6 servings

g oa is known for its fish and seafood recipes. This dish, made with shrimp, is a mild curry that is consumed almost on a daily basis. You can substitute any firm fish for the shrimp, such as monkfish or halibut.

2 pounds medium raw
  shrimp, peeled
2 tablespoons cider vinegar
Salt to taste
½ teaspoon chili powder
1 teaspoon ground turmeric
1 teaspoon ground cumin
2 teaspoons ground
  coriander
½ teaspoon black pepper
3 tablespoons sunflower or
  vegetable oil
1 onion, finely chopped
1-inch piece fresh ginger,
  peeled and grated
6 cloves garlic, peeled and
  crushed
1½ cups coconut milk
4 jalapeño peppers, seeded
  and sliced lengthwise
¼ cup chopped fresh
  cilantro leaves

p lace the shrimp in a large bowl with the vinegar and ½ teaspoon salt. Mix well and set aside for 10 minutes.

In a small bowl, mix together the chili powder, turmeric, cumin, coriander, and black pepper and set aside.

Heat the oil over medium heat in a large skillet, and sauté the onion until pale gold, about 6 minutes, stirring constantly. Add the grated ginger and garlic and sauté for 1 minute. Add the reserved ground spices and sauté for another 2 minutes. Add the coconut milk, jalapeño peppers, and salt to taste. Simmer for 5 minutes, or until the liquid thickens a little.

Add the shrimp, stir, and simmer until the shrimp are just cooked, about 5 minutes. Pour the curry into a serving dish and sprinkle with the cilantro leaves. Serve with white rice.

Squid in Cream

Lulas com Natas
6 to 8 servings

*t*his recipe for squid is very similar to a Portuguese dish for salt cod *with cream*, bacalahau com natas. *The Goans have substituted squid for the codfish and added tomatoes and hot green peppers.*

4 pounds squid, or 3½
    pounds cleaned frozen
    calamari sacs
2 teaspoons salt
1 teaspoon white vinegar
¼ cup plus 3 tablespoons
    olive oil
3 large onions, minced
3 medium tomatoes, peeled
    and chopped
4 large cloves garlic,
    minced
2 jalapeño peppers, sliced
    in half lengthwise and
    seeded
2 large white potatoes,
    peeled and thinly sliced
2 tablespoons white wine
¼ cup olive oil
1 cup heavy cream,
    whipped into firm
    peaks

*t*o clean the squid, pull the head off the body of the squid. Cut off the tentacles just below the eyes. Discard the transparent quill from inside the body sac, rinse the body sac well, and peel off the purple membrane covering it. Pull off the flaps gently from the body sac to avoid tearing it and reserve them.

Cut the sacs into ½-inch rings. Place the rings and flaps in a deep clay or ceramic dish and sprinkle with 1 teaspoon of the salt and the vinegar. Mix well and set aside.

In a large skillet heat 3 tablespoons of the olive oil and sauté the onions until translucent. Add the tomatoes, garlic, peppers, and remaining 1 teaspoon salt. When the tomatoes cook to a purée, add the squid, potatoes, and ¼ cup water. Cover and cook over low heat until the squid is tender, about 10 minutes. Add the wine and mix well.

Preheat the oven to 350 degrees F. Oil a 3-quart baking dish and fill it with the squid mixture. Pour the remaining ¼ cup olive oil over the mixture and top with the whipped cream. Bake the squid for 30 minutes, or until the cream is lightly golden. Serve hot.

Prawns in Tomato Sauce

Lagostins com Molho de Tomate

4 servings

*t*his is but another example of the Goans' wonderful use of prawns. This recipe calls for the prawns to be simmered in a rich tomato broth.

1½ pounds raw prawns, shelled
1 tablespoon cider vinegar
Salt to taste
¼ cup vegetable oil
2 large onions, finely sliced
8 cloves garlic, minced
1-inch piece fresh ginger, peeled and grated
1 tablespoon ground coriander
1 teaspoon ground turmeric
1 teaspoon ground cumin
½ teaspoon chili powder
½ teaspoon ground cinnamon
¼ teaspoon ground cloves
1 can (14-ounce) diced tomatoes, pureed in the blender
1¼ cups coconut milk
6 fresh red chili peppers
¼ cup chopped fresh cilantro

*p*lace the prawns in a large bowl and add the vinegar and ¼ teaspoon salt. Mix well and set aside.

Heat the vegetable oil in a large skillet over medium heat. Sauté the onions until translucent, stirring frequently. Lower the heat, add the garlic and ginger and fry for 1 minute.

Add the coriander, turmeric, cumin, chili powder, cinnamon, and cloves and sauté for 1 minute to release the flavors.

Add the prawns, tomato purée, and coconut milk. Cover and simmer for 6 minutes, or until the prawns turn pink. Add the whole chilies and salt to taste. Simmer for 2 more minutes. Pour into a serving dish and sprinkle with the cilantro leaves. Serve with white rice.

Chicken with Coconut

Chacuti de Galinha
4 to 6 servings

this recipe originated in Goa and traveled to Mozambique with the Portuguese. It has since become a part of Mozambique's national cuisine. This recipe was given to me by Maria José Knopfli, wife of Rui Knopfli, a Luso-Mozambican writer of considerable talent. Prepared by her Goan cook, this chicken dish was a favorite in the Knopfli household. The original recipe calls for a whole coconut. After grating the coconut meat, half is used to make the milk and the other half for toasting. I have used both fresh and frozen grated coconut and canned coconut milk, and both work fine for this recipe.

1 cup frozen, grated, unsweetened coconut (see note)
2 tablespoons red pepper flakes
1 tablespoon ground coriander
1 tablespoon ground cumin
1 tablespoon saffron
1 tablespoon ground cinnamon
10 green cardamom pods
1 tablespoon ground nutmeg
½ teaspoon ground cloves
3 tablespoons lard or shortening
3 large onions, chopped
1 whole chicken (3 to 4 pounds), cut into parts
1 tablespoon tamarind paste
1 cup coconut milk
2 tablespoons curry powder
1 tablespoon kosher salt

preheat the oven to 350 degrees F. Thaw the grated coconut and place it in a bowl along with the pepper flakes, coriander, cumin, saffron, cinnamon, cardamom, nutmeg, and cloves. Mix well and place on a baking sheet; toast in the oven until the coconut is a light golden brown. Cool and place in a food processor or blender and grind to a powder.

Heat the lard in a large skillet; add the chopped onions and sauté until transparent, stirring occasionally. Add the pieces of chicken and cook until they are golden on both sides. Mix the tamarind paste with 1 tablespoon of warm water and add to the pan along with the coconut milk, curry powder, ground seasonings, and salt. Cover and simmer for 30 minutes, or until the sauce thickens. There should be plenty of sauce. Serve with white rice.

NOTE: Grated unsweetened coconut can be purchased in the freezer section of your local Asian supermarket.

Ceremonial Chicken

Galinha de Cerimônia
4 to 6 servings

Chicken and duck are the most popular types of poultry in Goa. This recipe, like most Goan chicken recipes, is of Portuguese origin or from the Portuguese-speaking world. This dish is usually served at weddings, anniversaries and special dinner—as the name suggests.

1 whole chicken (about 3 pounds), or parts
Salt to taste
2 pounds white potatoes, cut into julienne strips
1 pound onions, thinly sliced
8 ounces fresh button mushrooms, thinly sliced
3 tablespoons vegetable oil
1 tablespoon butter
1 teaspoon cornstarch
1 cup milk
2 tablespoons grated parmesan cheese

Place the chicken in a large pot with water to cover and bring to a boil. Add the salt and cook over medium heat until the chicken is cooked through, about 30 minutes. Remove the chicken from the pot and save the stock. Let the chicken cool and remove all the meat from the bones; discard the skin and the bones.

Meanwhile sauté the potatoes, onions, and mushrooms separately in the vegetable oil until they are each golden. Set aside.

To make the sauce, melt the butter in a frying pan and add the cornstarch, stirring until it thickens. Add the cup of milk and mix well. Add some of the reserved chicken stock a little at a time until the sauce thickens. The sauce should not be too thin or too thick.

Preheat the oven to 350 degrees F. Cover the bottom of a large 3-quart casserole with a layer of the fried potatoes. On top, place a layer of the onions, then some chicken, and some mushrooms. Continue with layers of potatoes, onions, chicken, and mushrooms, ending with a layer of potatoes. Add the grated cheese to the sauce and pour the sauce over the potatoes and bake for about 30 minutes. When the top is golden but not dry, the dish is ready. Serve with a green salad.

Pork Vindaloo

Vindaloo de Porco

4 to 6 servings

Vindaloo *is one of the most popular curries in Goa and its fame has traveled around the Portuguese-speaking world and beyond. I first tasted this dish in 1971 in a little Goan restaurant in Lorenço Marques, formerly the name of Mozambique's capital city, now called Maputo. Since then, I have made it both in Mozambique and in the United States. This recipe is an adaptation of four different recipes that I have tasted in Mozambique and comes closest to the one I remember from 1971.*

2 pounds lean pork, cubed

MARINADE:
1 cup cider vinegar
10 cloves garlic, crushed
2 tablespoons red pepper flakes
1-inch piece fresh ginger, peeled and grated
1 teaspoon salt
1 teaspoon ground turmeric

Place pork cubes in a non-reactive bowl.

FOR THE MARINADE: Mix together all the ingredients and pour over the pork cubes. Mix well and refrigerate overnight or for at least 4 hours.

FOR THE PORK SAUCE: Heat the oil in a large skillet over medium heat and sauté the onions with the cinnamon until the onions are soft. Finely grind together the cloves, cardamom pods, nutmeg, cumin seeds, coriander seeds, fenugreek seeds, and bay leaves. Add the ground spices to the onions and fry for 1 minute. Add 2 tablespoons of water; mix well and fry for 2 minutes.

Remove the pork from the marinade with a slotted spoon, reserving the marinade. Add the pork to the onions. Raise the heat and fry the pork for 5 minutes, stirring occasionally. Stir in the tomato paste, paprika, chili powder, and reserved marinade. Stir in 2 cups of warm water; bring to a boil, reduce the heat, and simmer, uncovered, for 30 minutes.

PORK SAUCE:

2 tablespoons vegetable oil
2 large onions, chopped
2-inch piece cinnamon
8 whole cloves
8 green cardamom pods
2 teaspoons ground nutmeg
2 teaspoons cumin seeds
2 teaspoons coriander seeds
2 teaspoons fenugreek
    seeds
2 bay leaves
1 tablespoon tomato paste
1 teaspoon paprika
½ teaspoon chili powder

2 large baking potatoes,
    peeled and cubed
2 teaspoons brown sugar
1 teaspoon salt
3 green chilies, seeded and
    minced
2 tablespoons chopped
    fresh cilantro

Add the potatoes, sugar, and salt to the pork. Bring to a boil, cover, and simmer for 20 minutes more, or until the potatoes are tender. Add the chilies and cilantro and simmer, uncovered, for 5 minutes. Serve with white rice.

NOTE: This dish can be prepared ahead of time and frozen for up to 4 weeks. Prepare the recipe up to the point before the potatoes are added. When ready to serve, reheat the vindaloo and add the potatoes, chilies and cilantro according to the directions.

Beef and Pork Stew

Cozido Goesa

4 to 6 servings

*g*oan Christians eat both beef and pork; Muslims are forbidden to eat pork; Hindus will not eat beef. This recipe calls for beef, pork, and chicken and is served in many restaurants throughout the country, so it is mainly for the Christian population.

8 ounces Goan or other spicy sausages
8 ounces stew beef, cut into 1-inch cubes
¼ cup sunflower oil
1 large onion, thinly sliced
8 ounces lean pork, cut into 1-inch cubes
5 cloves garlic, minced
1-inch piece fresh ginger, peeled and grated
1 teaspoon ground turmeric
6 cups beef broth or water
4 whole cloves
4-inch piece cinnamon stick, broken
8 ounces boneless, skinless chicken thighs
8 ounces white potatoes, peeled and cubed
1 teaspoon ground cumin
½ cup heavy cream
Salt and black pepper to taste

*g*rill or fry the sausages until well browned. Cool and cut into 1-inch slices.

Place the beef cubes in a saucepan with water to cover. Bring to a boil, cover, reduce the heat, and cook until beef is tender and water has evaporated.

In a large skillet, heat the oil over medium heat and sauté the onions until limp. Add the boiled beef, pork, garlic, ginger, and turmeric. Stir and cook for 5 minutes. Add the broth, cloves, and cinnamon. Cover and simmer for 20 minutes.

Add the chicken, mix well, and bring to a boil. Reduce the heat, cover, and simmer for 10 minutes. Add the potatoes, sausages, and cumin. Stir, cover, and cook for 20 minutes, or until the potatoes are tender.

Add the cream, salt, and pepper, and mix well. Simmer uncovered for 5 minutes, to heat through. Remove from the heat and serve with white rice, *Apas* (page 223), or *Chapatti* (page 222).

Prawn Preserve

Balchão de Camarão
Makes 2 cups

this sauce is common in both Goa and Macao. Though there may be a slight variation of the recipe in the two colonies, the balchão is used to season meat, poultry, and fish dishes. The preserve will keep for up to four months in tightly sealed jars kept in a cool place. You can substitute clams or mussels for the shrimp.

12 ounces small raw shrimp
2 teaspoons salt
1 tablespoon olive oil
1 small onion, chopped
½ cup cider vinegar
1 head garlic, peeled
2-inch piece fresh ginger, peeled and chopped
2 tablespoons red pepper flakes
2-inch piece cinnamon stick, broken into pieces
10 whole cloves
2 teaspoons ground turmeric
1½ teaspoons cumin seed
1 teaspoon peppercorns
1 tablespoon saffron
½ teaspoon black or yellow mustard seeds
1 tablespoon tomato paste

preheat the oven to 200 degrees F. Peel and clean the shrimp. Rinse, squeeze out all the water, and arrange them on a rack on a baking sheet. Sprinkle with 1 teaspoon of the salt. Place the shrimp in the oven to dry out. The process takes about 2 hours.

Heat the olive oil in a skillet and sauté the dried shrimp for 5 minutes. Place the shrimp in a food processor or meat grinder along with the onion, vinegar, garlic, ginger, red pepper flakes, cinnamon, cloves, turmeric, cumin, peppercorns, remaining 1 teaspoon salt, saffron, and mustard seeds, and pulse to a purée.

Pour the mixture into a small skillet, add the tomato paste, and cook over low heat, stirring constantly with a wooden spoon, until the mixture is well heated, about 3 minutes. Let the mixture cool. Spoon the mixture into a clean bottle or jar and cap tightly. Store the preserve in a cool place.

Unleavened Bread

Chapatti
8 pieces

C hapatti, *Indian whole-wheat flour, lends its name to this bread. It is a wholesome bread that is a staple of northern India. The bread is similar to flour tortillas except that it is always made with whole-grain flour with the germ and bran intact. But I have used regular whole-wheat and white flour as a substitute and it works fine. The* chapatti *is made by rolling out the dough into a thin circle and baking it on a hot griddle. Because significant numbers of Goans have settled in Mozambique, the bread is very popular there and is also served in many restaurants and homes of that east African country. Chapattis are traditionally served at breakfast but can be eaten at any meal.*

1½ cups chapatti flour, or
　　¾ cup whole-wheat and
　　¾ cup all-purpose flour
　　(see note)
½ teaspoon sugar
½ teaspoon salt
5 tablespoons vegetable oil
3 tablespoons clarified
　　butter for brushing

m easure the flour into a bowl and mix in the sugar and salt. Add 2 tablespoons of the vegetable oil and mix into the flour until the mixture resembles cornmeal. Slowly add ¾ cup warm water and knead until the dough is soft. Add the remaining 3 tablespoons oil and knead the dough for about 5 minutes, or until smooth. Place the dough in an oiled bowl; cover with a damp cloth and let rest for 30 minutes.

Divide the dough into 8 portions. Roll each between your palms into a ball. Heat a griddle over medium-high heat. Roll out each ball into a flat 6-inch disk. Place one on the griddle and cook for 10 seconds. Turn with a spatula and cook on the other side for about 2 minutes, or until brown spots appear. Place the cooked chapatti on a plate and brush with butter. Keep warm while cooking the rest of the dough. Serve immediately with curries, or keep warm in a low oven.

NOTE: Chapatti flour, also called *atta*, can be found in Indian grocery stores.

Goan Flat Bread

Apas
10 pieces

apas, *like rice and* chapattis, *accompany many Goan dishes and are a favorite at afternoon teas. This Goan bread is also enjoyed in Mozambique, where it is usually served with any main dish cooked or accompanied by a sauce. Goan flat bread is but another of several examples of the Indo-Portuguese culinary influence in Africa.*

2 cups all-purpose flour
¼ cup vegetable oil
1 teaspoon salt
¾ cup hot water
½ cup (1 stick) butter, melted

measure the flour into a large bowl; add the oil and salt. Mix the flour with a fork until it looks like coarse meal. Add the hot water a little at a time, stirring until the mixture forms a ball of dough. Knead for 3 minutes, or until the dough is smooth and elastic.

Separate the dough into 10 small balls. Roll out each ball on a floured surface to about ½ inch thick. Shake off any excess flour and cover the apas with a damp cloth to prevent them from drying out.

Heat a nonstick skillet over high heat. When the pan is smoking, add the apas one at a time to the pan and cook for 10 to 15 seconds. They will puff up and should be turned 2 or 3 times as they brown. Place the apas on a warm plate, brush each one with melted butter, and cover to prevent them from drying out. Serve hot.

NOTE: *Apas* can also be served as a snack. Sprinkle each one with a little sugar or jam and roll up like a cigar. Serve at room temperature.

Banana Fritters

Filhós
Makes about 30

f*ilhós are a light, fluffy confection of Spanish origin. The Portuguese adopted this fritter dough and eventually exported it to Goa, where it became a tropical dessert.*

⅔ cup all-purpose flour
2 tablespoons sugar
1 teaspoon ground
    cinnamon
½ teaspoon ground nutmeg
½ teaspoon salt
2 large eggs
1 teaspoon vanilla extract
⅔ cup milk
6 large, ripe bananas,
    mashed
Vegetable oil for frying
Confectioners' sugar for
    dusting (optional)
1 tablespoon brandy
    (optional)
1 tablespoon apricot jam
    (optional)
1½ tablespoons toasted
    sliced almonds
    (optional)

Combine the flour, sugar, cinnamon, nutmeg, and salt in a large bowl. Beat the eggs in a medium bowl with the vanilla and gradually add the milk. Add the egg mixture to the flour mixture. Stir until well mixed. Fold in the mashed bananas.

Pour some vegetable oil into a deep frying pan or heavy skillet to a depth of two inches. Heat it over medium-high heat to 365 degrees F. Fry the dough by spoonfuls in the oil until golden all over. Drain on paper towels.

Arrange the fritters on a serving dish. Dust with confectioners' sugar or brush with brandy. If using apricot jam, heat the jam until warm and drizzle it over the fritters. Sprinkle with the toasted almonds, if desired. Serve warm or at room temperature.

CUISINE OF
Guinea-Bissau

t iny Guinea-Bissau is located on the west coast of Africa. Most of the country is located on the mainland, between Senegal and the Republic of Guinea, and the rest is a string of islands called the Bijagó Archipelago. In 1446, a Portuguese adventurer named Nuno Tristão, was the first European to disembark in this future colony, to be known as Portuguese Guinea. Down through the centuries, the Portuguese established trading stations in the towns of Bolama, Cacheu, and Bissau, which later became the capital of the colony.

In colonial times, the people living in the coastal region existed essentially on the cultivation of rice, fishing, and commerce. Besides rice, vegetables such as corn, okra, manioc, and beans became part of Guinean agriculture. Sugarcane also became a major crop. In the rural interior, many of the residents raised cattle for food and dairy products.

Today, the salient food ingredients are rice, peanuts, okra, spinach, palm oil, and manioc. Rice is usually just boiled in water or broth. Peanuts (*mancarra*), introduced by the Portuguese, serve as the basis of various preparations, both for main dishes and desserts. They are usually roasted, ground, and used in sauces for meats, fish, and poultry. A traditional preparation is *kru-kru*—ground fish with spices made into meatballs and cooked in a peanut sauce. Peanut oil is also used to sauté meats and vegetables. The red fruit from the African palm, *chabéu* is crushed and the oil called *citi* is extracted and used for most traditional local dishes. Among the most popular sweets are peanut balls, peanut brittle, and peanut cake.

Black corn, known as *futo*, also serves as a basic ingredient for many dishes. A traditional dish served at most festivals in the northern part of the country is *bringe*—especially popular among the *Cacheu* peoples (Creoles), who seek to maintain their former pre-colonial image as high Guinean society. *Bringe* can be prepared a number of ways, including with cockles, duck, fish, or chicken sautéed with garlic, onions, piripiri peppers, tomatoes, and rice in peanut or vegetable oil.

Fish and seafood are plentiful and are part of many Guineans' daily diet including tuna, *bicuda* (a long-beaked fish), grey mullet, shrimp, oysters, and crab, among others. The most popular way to prepare fish and seafood is grilled over coals or roasted in a clay oven. Even oysters in the half shell are grilled over coals and served with a hot sauce. Chicken, duck, and pork are part of the Guinean diet, but very little beef is consumed.

Fish and Peanut Balls

Bolinhos de Mancarra com Peixe
Makes about 30 pieces

i t seems that mancarra *(peanuts) are found in at least one dish at every meal in Guinea-Bissau. They are usually toasted and ground into a powder and then added to a broth to make a sauce. In this recipe, fish and the ever-present peanuts are mixed to form a delicious appetizer.*

1 cup raw unsalted peanuts
2 pounds tilapia or other
   white fish
6 thin slices onion
3 tablespoons lemon juice
2 teaspoons salt
¼ teaspoon black pepper
1 tablespoon vegetable oil
2 medium onions, grated
½ cup parsley, chopped
About ¼ cup chicken broth
Vegetable oil for frying

p reheat the oven to 350 degrees F. Spread the peanuts on a baking sheet and bake until lightly golden, about 10 minutes, shaking occasionally. Remove the peanuts from the oven, cool and finely grind in a food processor. Set aside.

Season the fish with the onion slices, lemon juice, 1 teaspoon of the salt, and pepper. Set aside for 30 minutes. Heat the oil in a medium skillet and sauté the fish until golden on both sides. Remove and cool.

Flake the fish and place it in a large bowl. Add the grated onions, parsley, remaining 1 teaspoon salt, and ground peanuts. Mix well. Add enough broth to hold the ingredients together. Shape the mixture into balls the size of golfballs.

Pour some vegetable oil into a deep frying pan or heavy skillet to a depth of two inches. Heat it over medium-high heat to 365 degrees F on a deep-frying thermometer. Fry the balls in the hot oil until golden on all sides. Drain on paper towels. Serve the balls warm or at room temperature with drinks.

Avocado and Tuna Salad

Salada de Abacate com Atum
4 servings

a *vocados are as abundant in Guinea-Bissau as they are in Cape Verde, and there are many wonderful recipes for salads that are enjoyed in both countries. In Cape Verde they stuff the avocados with dates (page 146) or with lobster. And in Guinea-Bissau they like them stuffed with tuna with a sauce made from coconut, condensed milk, and tomato sauce. It is an interesting and tasty combination.*

2 large ripe avocados
1 can (6-ounce)
    water-packed tuna,
    drained
¾ cup unsweetened
    condensed milk
½ cup freshly grated
    coconut or fresh frozen
3 tablespoons tomato
    sauce
½ teaspoon salt
¼ teaspoon black pepper
2 lemons, quartered

C ut the avocados in half lengthwise; remove the seeds and pulp, being careful not to tear the shells. Reserve shells. Cut the pulp into small cubes and place it in a bowl.

Add the tuna, condensed milk, coconut (except for 1 tablespoon), and tomato sauce. Season with the salt and pepper and mix well.

Stuff the avocado shells with the tuna filling and sprinkle with the remaining grated coconut. Serve with lemon quarters on the side.

Guinean Fish Stew

Caldo de Peixe
4 to 6 servings

*i*n Guinea-Bissau, this soup is normally eaten after a cocktail party. It is said to help one sleep well and stave off a hangover.

Boiling water
3 pounds green bananas
3 medium onions, sliced
3 green bell peppers,
    sliced
2 pounds white potatoes,
    peeled and sliced
6 medium tomatoes, peeled
    and sliced
3 pounds white fish fillets,
    such as tilapia, cod, or
    grouper
Salt to taste
Piripiri or hot sauce to
    taste
1¼ cups olive oil

drop the unpeeled bananas into boiling water to scald them. This will make it easier to remove the skins. Peel and slice the bananas lengthwise and then across in quarters.

In a large pot with a cover, layer one-third each of the onions, green peppers, potatoes, tomatoes, fish fillets, and bananas. Season each fish layer with salt and piripiri. Continue layering until all the ingredients are used. Pour the olive oil over the ingredients and add 8 cups of water. Place the pot over low heat, cover, and simmer for 35 minutes or until sauce thickens and vegetables are tender, shaking the pot occasionally to prevent the vegetables from sticking. Do not uncover during cooking.

Serve the stew in the same pot in which it was cooked, accompanied by white rice and Puréed Turnip Greens (page 28).

Oyster Stew

Pitche-Patche de Ostras
4 servings

t his is a unique and delicious version of the traditional Portuguese oyster stew. My good friend Deolinda Mendes, wife of the former Guinean ambassador to the United States, prepared this dish for me at her home in Bissau. This is her recipe and it is quick and easy to make. Shrimp or fish can be substituted for the oysters, in which case, use fish stock instead of water.

⅔ cup uncooked white rice
½ cup peanut oil
2 large tomatoes, peeled, seeded, and chopped
1 large onion, minced
2 pounds shucked oysters, or 3 containers (10-ounce) oyster meat with juice
6 tablespoons lemon juice
1 teaspoon salt
½ teaspoon cayenne pepper
¼ teaspoon black pepper

Soak the rice in 1 cup of warm water for 20 minutes. Drain the rice and dry in a cloth. Place the rice in a food processor and pulse for 10 seconds to make a coarse meal.

Heat the peanut oil in a large pot and add the tomatoes, onions, and ground rice. Mix well and sauté for about 3 minutes.

Strain the liquid from the oysters and add enough water to the juice to make 2 quarts. Add this liquid to the onion mixture and simmer for 2 minutes. Add the oysters and simmer until the oysters are opaque, about 8 minutes. Sprinkle with the lemon juice, salt, cayenne pepper, and black pepper; stir and serve hot with crusty peasant bread.

Okra and Spinach Sauté

Bagique
2 side-dish servings

This typical dish of Creole origin is served as a side dish with chicken, pork, or beef.

8 ounces okra, trimmed and sliced into ½-inch pieces
8 ounces fresh spinach leaves
1 cup beef stock
1 teaspoon salt
½ teaspoon black pepper

Cook the okra in water to cover for 10 minutes. In another pot, cook the spinach in ¼ cup of water until it is just wilted. Drain the okra and spinach and purée in a food processor for 30 seconds.

Place the spinach mixture in a pot with the beef stock, salt, and pepper. Bring to a boil, reduce the heat to a simmer, and cook for 2 minutes. Mix well.

Manioc Fries

Mandioca Frita
4 servings

manioc fries are Guinea-Bissau's answer to French fries. They are also popular in Brazil, Cape Verde, and Angola. What makes these fries unusual is that they are fried in palm oil, which gives the manioc a reddish tint and a very distinctive flavor. They are delicious served as a side dish with grilled meats and a salad, or with drinks as an appetizer.

2 pounds manioc root
1 teaspoon salt
Palm oil for frying, or
    half palm oil and half
    vegetable oil

Peel the manioc root and cut the tuber into 3-inch pieces. Place the pieces in a pot and cover with water. Bring to a boil, add the salt, reduce the heat and simmer for 15 minutes. Remove the manioc pieces from the water and set aside to cool.

Pour the palm oil into a deep frying pan or heavy skillet to a depth of two inches. Heat it over medium-high heat to 365 degrees F on a deep-frying thermometer. Cut the manioc pieces lengthwise in half and then into wedges or julienne strips, removing the center core. Fry the slices in the hot palm oil until crisp. Drain on paper towels. Serve hot.

Rice with Tomatoes

Arroz de Tomate

4 side-dish servings

this is a very popular way to prepare rice in Guinea-Bissau and in Portugal. It is usually served with poultry, meat, and seafood.

1 medium onion, chopped
2 cloves garlic, minced
½ cup peanut oil
4 plum tomatoes, peeled and seeded
1 teaspoon salt
1 teaspoon ground red pepper
1 bay leaf
1 cup uncooked white rice

place the onion and garlic in a skillet with the peanut oil over medium heat. Cook, stirring occasionally, until the onion is translucent.

Add the tomatoes, salt, red pepper, and whole bay leaf. Simmer for 5 minutes, or until the tomatoes are almost puréed.

Stir in 2 cups of water and bring to a boil. Stir in the rice, cover, and cook for 20 minutes, or until the rice is tender.

Fried Fish in Spicy Sauce

Peixe Escabeche
4 servings

e scabeche *is the term usually applied to a method of conserving fried fish. It can be kept for up to two weeks in a tightly covered container.* Escabeche *is also used as a sauce for cooked meats.* Manioc Fries (page 232) *are the preferred accompaniment.*

FISH:
4 (6-ounce) white fish
   fillets, such as tilapia,
   grouper, or snapper
3 tablespoons lemon juice
1 teaspoon salt
2 tablespoons butter

SAUCE:
2 tablespoons butter
2 large onions, thinly
   sliced
3 tablespoons lemon juice

FOR THE FISH: Season the fish with the lemon juice and salt on both sides. Let the fish stand for 20 minutes. Melt the butter in a large skillet and fry the fish until golden on both sides. Remove the fish from the pan and keep warm.

FOR THE SAUCE: Melt the butter in the same skillet and add the onions. Sauté the onions until lightly golden, stirring occasionally. Add the lemon juice, heat and pour over the fish.

Smoked Fish with Vegetables

Maafe
4 servings

S moked fish is enjoyed throughout Guinea-Bissau. When prepared with spinach, onions, and tomatoes in a spicy palm oil sauce, it is a great one-dish meal.

1 pound fresh spinach
2 teaspoons salt
¾ cup palm oil, or half
    palm oil and half
    vegetable oil
4 medium tomatoes, peeled
    and seeded (see note)
2 onions, minced
2 cloves garlic, minced
1 pound smoked white fish
    (such as mackerel),
    skinned and boned
1 teaspoon Tabasco or
    other hot sauce
¼ teaspoon black pepper

b ring a pot of water to a boil. Wash the spinach well and remove the stems. Place the spinach in the boiling water with 1 teaspoon of the salt and cook for 5 minutes. Drain and set aside.

In a large skillet, heat the palm oil and add the tomatoes, onions, and garlic. Mix well and cook for 5 minutes. Add the spinach, smoked fish, remaining 1 teaspoon salt, Tabasco sauce, and pepper. Add 1 cup of water; lower the heat to a simmer, and cook until the sauce is reduced and thickened, about 15 minutes. Serve with white rice cooked with 1 tablespoon of lemon juice and 1 teaspoon salt.

NOTE: Instead of the 4 fresh tomatoes, you can substitute 1 can (14-ounce) chopped tomatoes with or without diced jalapeño peppers.

Shrimp with Okra

Sigá de Candja com Camarão
4 servings

Sigá *is a Creole term which means "stew." There are many ways to prepare* Sigá. *It can be made with beef, chicken, shrimp, or oysters. No matter which* Sigá *you choose, the preparation is quick and easy and the end result is always delicious. If you substitute chicken, marinate the pieces in three tablespoons of lemon juice for one hour before adding to the boiling water.*

2 pounds medium raw
  shrimp, peeled and
  cleaned
1 large onion, minced
1 tablespoon red pepper
  flakes
1 teaspoon salt
1 pound okra, trimmed and
  sliced into ½-inch
  pieces
8 ounces fresh tomatillos,
  peeled, seeded, and
  sliced
½ cup palm oil

bring 4 cups of water to boil in a large pot. Place the shrimp, onion, red pepper flakes, and salt in the boiling water. When the water returns to a boil, reduce the heat, and simmer until the shrimp are just pink, about 3 minutes.

Add the okra, tomatillos, and palm oil. Cover and simmer for 15 minutes, or until the vegetables are cooked and the sauce thickens. Serve with white rice.

Shrimp, Bissau-Style

Camarões à Guineense
4 servings

this is a very common way to prepare shrimp in Bissau, the country's capital city. Use large or jumbo shrimp for this dish and serve over a bed of rice.

½ cup peanut oil
1 large onion, finely chopped
2 pounds large or jumbo raw shrimp, peeled and cleaned
1 large cucumber, peeled, seeded, and cut into thin slices
3 tablespoons lemon juice
1 teaspoon salt
¼ teaspoon black pepper
½ cup chicken broth

heat the oil in a large frying pan and sauté the onion until it is lightly golden.

Add the shrimp and cucumber, stir, and simmer for 2 minutes.

Add the lemon juice, salt, and pepper and stir.

Add the broth, and cook until the shrimp just turns pink and the sauce thickens a little.

Chicken in Palm Oil

Chabéu de Galinha
4 to 6 servings

Chabéu *is the tiny red fruit from which palm oil is extracted. It is found in clusters at the top of a certain species of palm tree. This recipe calls for the berries to be boiled to extract the juice for the sauce. Since these berries are not available in the United States, I have substituted the imported oil that is made from the berries and can be found in many international and specialty markets.*

1 chicken (3 to 4 pounds), or 4 pounds bone-in chicken thighs
1 large onion, thinly sliced
1 teaspoon salt
1 to 2 teaspoons ground red pepper
8 ounces okra, trimmed and halved crosswise
¼ cup palm oil
4 ounces tomatillos, husked and thinly sliced
3 tablespoons lemon juice

Wash the chicken and cut it into 8 serving pieces. Place in a glass dish or bowl and season with the onion slices, salt, and red pepper. Marinate for 30 minutes.

Place the chicken and onions in a large skillet; add water to barely cover and simmer over medium heat until the chicken is cooked through, about 20 minutes.

Add the okra, palm oil, and tomatillos. Simmer for 10 minutes, or until the vegetables are tender. Remove from the heat, and sprinkle with the lemon juice. Serve with cooked white rice.

Chicken in Ground Peanut Sauce

Caldo de Mancarra

4 to 6 servings

C aldo de Mancarra *is a favorite dish of my good friend Deolinda Mendes. I first sampled it in 1995 at her home in the city of Bissau, and she finally gave me her recipe in 1998 while living in Washington, D.C., with her ambassador husband. She occasionally adds ½ pound of flaked dried white fish to the pot during the last 10 minutes of cooking.*

1 chicken (3 to 4 pounds), or 4 pounds bone-in chicken parts (see note)
1 large onion, thinly sliced
2 red chili peppers, minced, or 1 teaspoon red pepper flakes
3 tablespoons lemon juice
1 teaspoon salt
1 cup raw unsalted peanuts
3 large tomatoes, peeled, seeded, and puréed
8 ounces dried white fish, skinned and flaked (optional)

W ash the chicken and cut it into 8 pieces. Put it in a glass bowl or dish and season with the sliced onions, chili peppers, lemon juice, and salt; marinate for 1 hour.

Place the chicken in a large pot with 2 cups of water and cook over medium heat for 20 minutes, or until cooked through. Remove the chicken and set aside. Reserve the broth.

Finely grind the peanuts in a blender. Add the tomatoes to the peanuts and blend until the mixture forms a paste. In a medium saucepan, heat 2 cups of water to boiling and add the tomato mixture; blend well. Add the broth from the chicken pot to the tomato mixture and incorporate well.

Return the mixture to the chicken pot, along with the reserved chicken, and simmer for 10 minutes to blend well. If using dried fish, add it to the pot now. Mix well. Remove the pot from the heat, pour into a warm deep serving dish and serve.

NOTE: This *caldo* (sauce) can also be made with beef instead of chicken. Use 2 pounds of roast beef cut into cubes and omit the dried fish.

Chicken with Spinach

Frango com Bagique
4 servings

C hickens in Guinea-Bissau tend to be a little on the scrawny side and not as tender as the ones we get in the States. So proper seasoning is crucial, as is the length of cooking time. Otherwise, this recipe is easy to prepare and very tasty.

1 chicken (3 to 4 pounds),
   or 4 pounds bone-in
   chicken parts (see note)
1 medium onion, chopped
½ cup palm oil
Juice of 1 lemon
   (3 tablespoons)
2 cloves garlic, chopped
1 bay leaf
1 teaspoon red pepper
   flakes
1 pound spinach leaves

Wash the chicken; cut it into 8 serving pieces and remove the skin. Place the chicken pieces in a large bowl and set aside.

In a blender or food processor, purée the onion, palm oil, lemon juice, garlic, bay leaf, and red pepper flakes. Pour the mixture over the chicken, coating well. Let marinate for 30 minutes.

Place the chicken and the seasonings in a pot with 1 cup of water. Simmer, covered, until the chicken is tender, about 20 minutes. Add the spinach leaves and continue simmering for 10 minutes. Serve over white rice.

NOTE: If you use chicken breasts, simmer for only 15 minutes before adding the spinach.

Duck, Bissau-Style

Bringe de Pato
4 servings

bringe *should be prepared a day in advance so that the duck can marinate overnight. The broth from cooking the duck is used to cook the rice, giving it a wonderful flavor. This dish is usually served at weddings, anniversaries, and special occasions.*

1 duck (4 to 5 pounds)
6 large cloves garlic
1 teaspoon salt
1 red chili pepper, chopped
1 teaspoon paprika
½ teaspoon black pepper
1½ cups white wine
¼ cup white vinegar
½ cup vegetable oil
2 large onions, thinly
    sliced
3 tomatoes, peeled, seeded,
    and chopped

SAUCE:

½ cup peanut oil
2 medium onions, chopped
4 medium tomatoes,
    peeled, seeded, and
    chopped

1½ cups uncooked white
    rice
3 cups duck broth (from
    cooking the duck)

rinse the duck inside and out; dry well. In a mortar, pound the garlic and salt to a paste. Add the chili pepper and continue pounding to incorporate the pepper into the paste. Add the paprika and black pepper; stir and mix in the wine and vinegar. Rub this mixture over both the inside and outside of the duck; cover and refrigerate overnight.

The following day, heat the oil in a large pot and sauté the onions and tomatoes. When the onions become limp, add the duck and sear on all sides. Add enough water to cover the duck; cover the pot and simmer until the duck is cooked through, about 35 minutes. Remove the duck from the broth and cut it into serving pieces. Keep warm. Strain the broth in which the duck was cooked and reserve the broth and onions.

FOR THE SAUCE: Heat the oil in a large skillet and sauté the chopped onions and tomatoes. When the onions turn golden, remove half of the mixture and pour it over the duck.

To the remaining onion mixture, add the rice and sauté until the rice is golden, stirring constantly. Add 3 cups of the reserved duck broth and bring it to a boil; cover and simmer until the rice is tender, about 20 minutes.

To serve, arrange the sliced onions in the center of a platter and surround them with the rice mixture. Place the duck on top of the onions.

Pork Cubes with Okra

Sigá de Carne
4 servings

i n Guinea-Bissau, this dish is usually served for lunch on Saturdays and Sundays, and for special festivals.

1 cup palm oil
1 medium onion, minced
3 cloves garlic, minced
3 or 4 malagueta or chili peppers
1 teaspoon salt
1 pound pork loin, cut into 1-inch cubes (see note)
12 ounces okra, trimmed and cut into 1-inch slices
8 ounces green tomatoes, chopped
3 tablespoons lemon juice

i n a large skillet, heat the palm oil over medium heat. Add the onion, garlic, hot peppers, and salt. Mix well and sauté for 5 minutes or until the onions are translucent.

Add the pork cubes, okra, tomatoes, lemon juice, and 2 cups of water. Cover and simmer until the pork is tender, about 30 minutes.

NOTE: This dish can also be prepared with oysters instead of pork. See Oyster Stew (page 230) for preparation of oysters.

Green Onion Sauce

A Palha de Cebola
2 servings

t he palha, *which literally means "straw," is the long green part of the green onion. This sauce made with the green onions is used as a side-dish with smoked fish, grilled chicken, or roast meat, or served with rice.*

10 green onions
2 red chili peppers, seeded
   and minced
3 tablespoons lemon juice
½ teaspoon salt
¼ cube chicken bouillon

C ut the green stems from the onions and place them in a food processor. Reserve the white bulbs for another use.

Add the peppers, lemon juice, salt, and bouillon, and blend until the mixture forms a purée.

Manioc Cake

Bolo de Mandioca
10 to 12 servings

this tasty cake originated in Brazil and has traveled to Guinea-Bissau as well as other African countries. It is made with grated manioc root and coconut milk and is a favorite at parties and festivals.

1¼ pounds manioc root
1 cup coconut milk
3 eggs
2 cups sugar
½ cup (1 stick) butter, melted
¼ cup manioc flour

preheat the oven to 350 degree F. Peel the manioc root, slice in half lengthwise, and remove the center core. Grate the pieces on the medium holes of a grater. You should have 2 cups. Place the grated manioc in a large bowl and add the coconut milk, beating with a whisk. Add the eggs, 1 at a time, then the sugar, butter, and manioc flour, mixing well.

Butter and flour a 2-quart baking dish. Pour the batter into the dish and bake for 40 to 45 minutes, or until a wooden skewer inserted in the center comes out clean. Cool on a wire rack for 10 minutes before unmolding onto a plate.

NOTE: For a beautiful presentation, drizzle the cake with warm apricot preserves and top with sliced almonds.

CUISINE OF
Macao

the cuisine of Macao derives from various cultural influences through the centuries from the geographic areas that the Portuguese claimed. The Portuguese had the greatest impact, second were the Chinese, and then the Goans, Japanese, English, Africans, and finally South Americans—especially Brazilians.

Beguiled in 1499 by the profits and dietary benefits of the spice trade initiated in India as a result of the voyages of Vasco da Gama, the Portuguese were inspired to sail further east searching for new lands. By 1513 they had made trading and land contracts with China, and by 1542 with Japan. But they were still seeking a permanent base in East Asia to facilitate their international trade. In 1557 they signed an agreement with China for a peninsula at the entrance of the Pearl River Delta. Two adjacent islands would be added in the nineteenth century. This contract gave Portugal the only permanent western port in China's empire. From 1560 to 1640, the Portuguese trading route included Canton, Macao, Nagasaki, Malacca, Goa, Lisbon, Manila, and Mexico. This was not only a lucrative silk, spice, and silver trade route, but also the carrier of foods and cultures from one area to another.

The early Portuguese settlers in Macao were principally sea-fearing traders and priests. They were supplied fish and seafood by their neighbors the Fukienese because they were not adept at farming or fishing due to the challenges of the heat, humidity, or periods of drought and the summer months of typhoons and heavy rains.

This dependency on the Fukienese and other native peoples led to cross-cultural dietary customs that contributed to the current cuisine. The Portuguese introduced the Chinese to a fish sauce known as *balichão*, which became a staple in the Macanese kitchen. Vegetables were imported from European countries and some of their colonies. From South America came sweet potatoes, peanuts, and corn (maize). From Portugal's African colonies and from Brazil came pineapples, papayas, custard apples, guava, lettuce, green beans, sprouts, and watercress. To these ingredients the Macanese added herbs and spices also brought by the Portuguese from a number of far-away sites, including Brazil, Timor, Angola, Mozambique, Goa, and Malaysia.

The Chinese, in turn, introduced the Portuguese to rhubarb, celery, ginger, soy sauce, lychee nuts, and petite oranges, which later became known as tangerines. In the early 1600s, Chinese boars were cross-bred with Europe's indigenous pigs, and became an export that raised Western pork standards.

In turn, the Portuguese were also responsible for introducing tea to Europe. To the Chinese it was known as *"tcha"* and to the Portuguese as *"chá."*

During the first thirty years of the Portuguese presence in Macao, they cultivated farm products. The Portuguese contracted Chinese laborers who gradually took over and turned some of the fields into rice paddies, while others were used to raise cabbages, potatoes, pumpkins, peas, and beans.

The traditional food of Macao basically differs from typical Chinese cuisine in that it is largely comprised of traditional Portuguese dishes, although enhanced by local ingredients. This is also true of the cuisines of Goa and Malaysia, where dishes like *Vindaloo* (page 218), spicy sausages, and sweet rice with coconut milk were introduced by the Portuguese. These dishes, whose base was Portuguese, gradually influenced the cuisine of Macao. One of the best-known dishes in Macao is *Cozido*, also called *Tacho*, which is an adaptation of the traditional *Cozido à Portuguesa* (page 42).

This chapter invites you to discover the wonderful food of Macao that is a mélange of cultures, traditions, and eating customs brought by the Portuguese. Down through the ages the cuisine was not only enriched and seasoned due to the influence of various regions where the Portuguese sailed but also by the Amerindian, African, and Goan women who accompanied them to Macao.

Pork Balls

Boullettes
12 servings

i n 1989 I sampled this tasty appetizer at the Hilton Hotel in Macao at what is known as chá gordo, which translates literally as "fat tea." At 4 p.m. in the afternoon a beautiful table is spread with appetizers and sweets, and, of course, tea. These little pork balls are a favorite item on the menu for those occasions.

8 ounces lean pork, cut into cubes
1 medium onion
¾ cup fresh bread crumbs
3 tablespoons grated Parmesan cheese
1 teaspoon chopped fresh parsley
1 teaspoon salt
½ teaspoon black pepper
2 eggs, or ½ cup egg substitute
2 cups dry bread crumbs
Vegetable oil for frying

g rind the pork and onion together in a meat grinder or food processor. Wet the fresh bread crumbs with 1 tablespoon of water and stir in the cheese and parsley. Mix well and add to the pork. Season the mixture with the salt and pepper.

Shape the pork mixture into 1-inch meatballs. Beat the eggs. Roll the meatballs in the eggs and then in the dry bread crumbs. Place the balls on waxed paper.

Pour some vegetable oil into a deep frying pan to a depth of two inches. Heat it over medium-high heat to 365 degrees F on a deep-frying thermometer. Fry the balls in the hot oil until golden on all sides. Drain on paper towels. Serve with toothpicks.

Half Moon Pastries

Chilicote

Makes 2 dozen

i n many cultures we find appetizers in the shape of a half moon. Chilicotes *are very similar to the Mozambican chamuças (page 290) except that they don't call for hot peppers. The filling can be beef, curried chicken, or pork.*

FILLING:
1 onion, minced
2 tablespoons vegetable oil
½ pound ground pork
1 teaspoon saffron
1 teaspoon salt
½ teaspoon black pepper
1 teaspoon cornstarch
½ cup cooked minced
    potato or turnip
    (optional)

DOUGH:
6½ cups self-rising flour
1 teaspoon salt
8 egg yolks
½ cup lard, softened

2 egg whites, lightly beaten
Shortening or oil for frying

FOR THE FILLING: Sauté the onion in the vegetable oil for 2 minutes over medium heat until translucent. Add the ground pork, saffron, salt, and pepper. Sprinkle the mixture with the cornstarch and mix well. Sauté until the mixture is dry and the pork is broken into small pieces. Add the minced potato or turnip here, if desired. Set aside.

FOR THE DOUGH: Sift the flour with the salt into a large bowl. Add the egg yolks, one at a time, kneading after each addition. Add the lard a little at a time, kneading after each addition. Continue kneading until the dough no longer sticks to your hands. Let rest for 30 minutes.

Roll out the dough on a lightly floured surface to ⅛-inch thick, and cut circles with a 3-inch cutter. Place 1 teaspoon of filling in the center of each circle and moisten the edges with a little of the egg whites. Fold over to form a half moon and press the edges to seal. Continue making the half moons until all the dough and filling are used.

Pour some oil into a deep frying pan to a depth of two inches. Heat it over medium-high heat to 365 degrees F on a deep-frying thermometer, or until a piece of dough rises to the surface. Fry the pastries in hot oil until golden. Drain on paper towels. Serve hot or at room temperature.

Eggs Stuffed with Ground Meat

Ovos Recheados com Minche
6 servings

i n Macao this dish is often served at a "cha gordo" translated as "fat tea," as part of an elaborate buffet that might also include Boullettes (Pork Balls, page 247). The Portuguese word minche comes from the English "to mince." In Macao, minche is very common and has many uses. It is used to stuff rolls, omelets, and potato balls; or served over white rice or fried with vegetables. This recipe for stuffed eggs is similar to the Portuguese dish called Ovos Verdes (Green Eggs, page 17), but with the addition of minced meat.

7 eggs, at room temperature
1 cup Minced Meat,
    Macao-Style (page 262)
Vegetable oil for frying
Flour for dusting
Lettuce leaves for serving

p lace 6 of the eggs in cold water; bring to a boil, cover, reduce the heat, and simmer for 10 minutes. Drain the eggs and place them under cold running water. Peel the eggs as soon as they are cool enough to handle. Slice the eggs lengthwise and remove the yolks, being careful not to tear the whites.

Mash the yolks and mix them with the minced meat. Use a tablespoon to stuff the white halves with the mixture, forming a mound to make each half look like a whole egg.

Pour some vegetable oil into a deep frying pan to a depth of two inches. Heat it over medium-heat to 365 degrees F on a deep-frying thermometer. Beat the remaining egg with 1 tablespoon water. Dip the stuffed eggs in the beaten egg to cover. Roll the eggs in flour and deep-fry until golden. Drain on paper towels. Serve on a platter lined with lettuce leaves.

Shrimp Salad

Salad de Camarões
4 servings

the Portuguese-influenced cuisine of Macao is rich, delicious, and usually quite easy to prepare, as is the case of this shrimp salad. It is often served with hot Portuguese rolls and a good Dão wine.

DRESSING:

1 cup small curd cottage cheese
1 hard-boiled egg, halved
¼ cup tomato juice
1 teaspoon prepared mustard
1 teaspoon hot pepper sauce

SALAD:

1 pound medium cooked shrimp, peeled
1 avocado, peeled and cut into 1-inch strips
1 cucumber, cut into 1-inch strips
1 can (8 ounces) black olives, halved
1 head Romaine lettuce

FOR THE DRESSING: Combine all ingredients in a food processor or blender and blend for 10 seconds until smooth. Chill.

FOR THE SALAD: Combine the shrimp, avocado, cucumber, and olives in a large bowl. Arrange the lettuce leaves on a platter in a decorative manner. Fold the dressing into the shrimp mixture carefully and spoon on the lettuce leaves. Serve.

Cuisines of Portuguese Encounters

Shrimp and Rice Noodle Soup

Sopa de Lacassa
4 to 6 servings

his soup originated in Malacca, where it was known as laksá and was traditionally served on Christmas Eve. It is basically rice noodles cooked in a shrimp broth. There are many thoughts on the original use of the soup in Macao. Some say that this soup was eaten by the Catholic Macanese on Christmas Eve, which was a day of abstinence without meat. Others say that it replaced the Bacalhau on Christmas Eve for the Consoada, and still others say that it was only served during Carnival. One thing that they all agree on is that this soup calls for Prawn Preserve. Despite this confusion, Lacassa is on the menu of many restaurants in Macao.

12 ounces small raw shrimp with shells
1-inch piece fresh ginger, peeled
6 ounces thin, dried rice noodles
2 tablespoons olive oil
2 tablespoons Prawn Preserve (page 221)
8 ounces crabmeat (optional)
1 teaspoon sea or coarse salt
¼ teaspoon black pepper
½ cup chopped green onions

eel and clean the shrimp, saving the shells. Slice the shrimp in half lengthwise and set aside. Place the shrimp shells in a pot with 8 cups of water and the ginger. Bring to a boil, reduce the heat, and simmer for 5 minutes. Strain the broth and save.

Soften the noodles in hot water for 10 minutes. Rinse in cold water and drain.

Heat the olive oil in a large pot and sauté the prawn preserves for 2 minutes. Add the reserved broth and bring to a boil. Reduce the heat; add the shrimp and crabmeat (if using) and simmer for 5 minutes, just until the shrimp are pink. Just before serving, add the noodles, salt, and pepper. Mix well. Serve hot, topped with the chopped green onions.

Meat and Bread Soup, Macao-Style

Açorda à Moda de Macau
4 to 6 servings

açorda, *a dry soup, was created in Portugal in the mid-1500s. It then traveled to Macao with the Portuguese. Seafood was plentiful on Macao but provisions like olive oil, smoked sausages, olives, vegetables, and fruits were scarce. They did occasionally arrive by ship and were stored for future use, enabling the Portuguese to enjoy their favorite dishes. This recipe varies from the Portuguese version in that it calls for prawn purée, beef, ham, and olives.*

1 pound piece roast beef
8 ounce piece ham or lean bacon
1 loaf (1 pound) white bread
2 cups boiling water
½ cup lard or shortening
2 medium onions, thinly sliced
1 green onion, chopped
2 cloves garlic, minced
1 tablespoon Prawn Preserve (page 221)
½ teaspoon black pepper
½ cup black olives
4 to 6 hard-boiled eggs, sliced

Cut the beef and ham into 1-inch cubes. Set aside.

Break the bread into large pieces; place in a bowl and add the boiling water. Squeeze the water from the bread and set aside.

Heat the lard in a large skillet and add the onions, green onion, and garlic and sauté until golden. Remove the onions and garlic and set aside.

Add the preserve to the skillet and cook over low heat for 5 minutes, stirring occasionally. Return the onion mixture to the skillet along with the meats. Sauté the mixture for 5 minutes or until the meats are heated through.

Add the bread in small batches, stirring constantly, until the mixture is dry. Sprinkle the top of the mixture with the pepper and serve hot, decorated with black olives and sliced hard-boiled eggs.

Watercress Soup

Caldo de Agrião
2 servings

i t was the Portuguese who took watercress on its journey to China, and it was they who popularized its use in the region which is now Macao. The watercress that is found in Macao is smaller than what is sold in Portugal. It is this smaller variety that is sought after for home remedies.

4 ounces pork roast or loin, cut into 1-inch cubes (see note)
1 tablespoon peanut oil
2 cloves garlic, minced
1 pound watercress leaves, washed
1 teaspoon salt

b lanch the cubes of pork in boiling water for 3 minutes. Drain.

In a medium pot, heat the oil with the garlic for 1 minute. Add the pork cubes and sauté until the cubes are lightly golden.

Add 6 cups of water and bring to a boil. Add the watercress and salt, lower the heat, and simmer covered for 2 hours, or until the pork is tender. Serve hot.

NOTE: You can substitute 4 duck gizzards for the pork. In that case, blanch the gizzards in boiling water and place them in the pot at the same time you add the watercress.

Fat Rice

Arroz Gordo
8 to 10 servings

*t*he name of this dish derives from the fact that it is traditionally made with several different kinds of meats (literally, "fat with ingredients"). In the Portuguese city of Porto, there is a similar dish, called arroz de sustância, literally "rice of substance."

1 chicken (about 3 pounds), cut into serving pieces
1 pound pork roast
8 ounce veal roast
Salt and black pepper to taste
1 bay leaf
2 tablespoons olive oil
2 large onions, chopped
1 pound (about 4) medium tomatoes
1 pound *chouriço* (Portuguese) sausage
4 cups uncooked white rice

GARNISH:
1 cup fresh bread cubes
2 tablespoons olive oil
3 or 4 hard-boiled eggs, sliced
¼ cup raisins
¼ cup currants
¼ cup black olives

place the chicken pieces in a large bowl. Cut the pork and veal roasts into 1-inch cubes and place in the bowl with the chicken. Season with salt, pepper, and whole bay leaf. Mix well and set aside.

Heat 1 tablespoon of the olive oil in a large skillet; add the onions and tomatoes and sauté until the onions are translucent. Set aside.

In a large pot, heat the remaining 1 tablespoon olive oil and sauté the pork, veal, and chicken pieces for 5 minutes, turning to brown on all sides. Add the sausage and enough hot water to cover the meats. Reduce the heat and simmer until the meats are cooked through, about 30 minutes.

Pour the meats and water from the pot into a strainer over a large bowl, leaving a little oil in the pot. Add the rice to the pot and sauté until golden. Add a pinch of salt and the liquid from the meats plus enough water to equal 8 cups. Bring to a boil, reduce the heat, cover the pot, and cook until the rice is dry, 20 to 25 minutes. Add the onion and tomato mixture and the meats to the rice. Mix well and simmer for 10 minutes.

Fry the bread cubes in the olive oil and set aside. Pour the rice mixture onto a large deep platter. Arrange the meats around the edge and garnish with the fried bread cubes, slices of egg, raisins, currants, and olives.

Moorish Rice

Arroz Mouro

6 servings

*t*his dish, introduced by the Moors during their occupation of Portugal, was later taken to Macao where it was modified to fit within that area's food culture.

2 cups uncooked white rice
4 slices white, day-old
    bread
3 tablespoons lard
1 tablespoon butter
1 medium onion, chopped
3 green onions, chopped
½ cup raisins
1 whole roasted chicken
    with juice
1 teaspoon salt
½ teaspoon black pepper
½ cup unsalted peanuts,
    roasted
4 hard-boiled eggs

*t*hree hours before preparing this dish, cook the rice in 4 cups of water for 20 minutes, until tender. Refrigerate until ready to use.

Cut the bread into 1-inch cubes and sauté in 2 tablespoons of the lard until golden. Set aside.

In a large skillet, heat the butter and remaining 1 tablespoon lard. Sauté the onion for 2 minutes and add the green onions and raisins. Cook for 5 minutes, or until they are tender. Add the cold rice and stir with a fork. Drizzle half of the juice from the chicken over the rice, and sprinkle with the salt and pepper. Remove the pan from the heat and add ½ of the toasted bread cubes.

Arrange the rice on a large platter. Sprinkle the rice with the roasted peanuts and the remaining toasted bread cubes. Cut the chicken into serving pieces and place on the rice. Slice the hard-boiled eggs and place around the platter decoratively. Serve hot.

Fish Torte, Macao-Style

Empada de Peixe
8 servings

by adding port wine to the dough you get a subtle, delicate flavor in this elegant dish. This torte, or pie, is often served for lunch on Christmas Eve day when, traditionally, the devout abstain from eating red meat and poultry.

PASTRY:

4½ cups all-purpose flour
1 teaspoon baking powder
¼ cup shortening, melted, hot
5 egg yolks, plus 1 egg
⅔ cup sugar
⅔ cup port wine
1¼ cups ground pine nuts
½ teaspoon salt

FILLING:

2 tablespoons olive oil
2 tablespoons shortening
2 pounds white fish fillets
2 medium onions, coarsely
    chopped
2 tablespoons white vinegar
1½ teaspoons ground ginger
1½ teaspoons ground cumin
1½ teaspoons ground
    coriander
1¼ cups blanched whole
    almonds
1 cup pitted black olives,
    sliced
2 hard-boiled eggs, chopped

FOR THE PASTRY: Combine the flour and baking powder in a large bowl. Make a well in the center and pour in the hot shortening. Mix well, and while the dough is still warm add the egg yolks and egg, one at a time, beating well after each addition. Add the sugar, port wine, pine nuts, and salt. Knead well and set aside, covered.

FOR THE FILLING: Heat the oil and shortening in a large skillet and fry the fish until slightly golden on both sides. Remove the fish from the pan and drain on paper towels; cool slightly and flake. Sauté the onions in the same skillet until translucent; then add the vinegar, ginger, cumin, and coriander. Return the flaked fish to the skillet and add ½ cup of water. Mix well and bring to a boil; reduce the heat and cook for 5 minutes. Fold in the almonds, black olives, and eggs.

Preheat the oven to 350 degrees F. Divide the pastry in half and roll out one half at a time on a lightly floured pastry cloth or board to ⅛-inch thick. Line the bottom of a 9-inch pie plate or a round Pyrex dish with half of the dough. Add the filling and cover with the remaining dough. Wet your fingers and pinch closed the edges of the torte. Make 3 slits in the top crust. Bake for 35 minutes, or until a golden brown. Serve hot or at room temperature with a green salad.

Stuffed Crab

Caranguejo em Casquinha
6 to 8 servings

t*his dish has traveled from Macao to Goa and as far as Brazil. In Brazil it is called* Caranguejos Recheados.

12 large blue crabs,
    or 3 cups crabmeat
2 tablespoons lard
1 white onion, chopped
2 green onions, chopped
1 teaspoon saffron
1½ slices white bread
12 large pitted black olives,
    coarsely chopped
2 teaspoons curry powder
½ teaspoon black pepper
12 puff pastry shells, if
    needed (see note)
2 eggs
¼ cup dry bread crumbs
Lard for frying
Shredded lettuce for serving

IF USING FRESH CRABS: Wash the crabs well and drop them into enough boiling water to cover. Return the water to a boil and cook for 8 minutes per pound. Remove the crabs from the water and cool completely. Pull off the legs and claws and extract the meat. Clean out the body and remove all the meat, being careful not to break the shells. Shred the meat and set aside. Wash and save the shells for stuffing.

PREPARE STUFFING: Heat 2 tablespoons lard in a skillet and sauté the white and green onions until golden. Sprinkle in the saffron and mix well. Add the crabmeat to the pan. Moisten the bread slices with 2 tablespoons of water, squeeze out the water, and shred the bread. Add the bread to the mixture and stir, making sure it doesn't stick or burn. Add the olives, curry powder, and pepper and mix well.

Stuff the crab shells (or pastry shells) with the crab mixture and smooth the mixture with the back of a spoon. Beat the eggs and brush only the filling with the beaten eggs. Sprinkle with the bread crumbs.

If using crab shells, heat 1 cup of lard in a large skillet and fry the stuffed crab shells, shell side down until golden. (If using store-bought pastry shells, place them on a baking sheet and bake in a 350 degree F oven for 20 minutes, or until the pastry is golden.) Arrange the shells on a bed of shredded lettuce and serve.

NOTE: If you cannot find fresh crabs, use fresh or frozen crabmeat and store-bought puff pastry shells.

Chicken for the Mother of a Newborn

Galinha Chau-Chau Parida
4 to 6 servings

traditionally this is a dish for women who have just given birth. Legend has it that ginger and wine have powers that enable the new mother to regain her strength quickly. Today the dish is still popular, although served at get-togethers for men as well as women. Chau-Chau *is a term of Mandarin Chinese origin that translates literally as "to confuse," which in a culinary context means the mixing of several ingredients. In current Macao culinary usage,* chau-chau *refers to a kind of fried sauce, usually made from a mixture of meat and vegetables. There are many variations of this dish, some using chicken gizzards or pork ears instead of chicken. The most commonly used meat however is pig's kidneys. I believe that the version that calls for chicken is the most delectable. To make a complete meal, serve with white rice and sautéed Chinese cabbage.*

1 tablespoon vegetable oil
4 cloves garlic, minced
1 large onion, chopped
1-inch piece fresh ginger, peeled and thinly sliced (julienned)
1 chicken (3 to 4 pounds), cut into 8 serving pieces
1 tablespoon ground ginger
½ cup white wine vinegar
1 teaspoon salt
¼ teaspoon black pepper
½ cup dry white wine

heat the oil in a large skillet. Sauté the garlic, onion, and sliced ginger until the onion is translucent. Remove the onion mixture from pan and set aside.

Add the chicken to the skillet and brown lightly (about 2 minutes on each side). Mix the ground ginger with the vinegar and add to the chicken. Return the onion mixture to the pan and add 1 cup of water. Season the mixture with the salt and pepper. Cover and simmer until the chicken is cooked through, about 20 minutes (see note). Add the wine and mix well. Serve immediately.

NOTE: If you use bone-in chicken breasts, be sure to reduce the cooking time to 15 minutes. This will keep the chicken from becoming too tough.

Curry, Macao-Style

Caril à Moda de Macau

4 servings

this is a basic recipe for curry that is popular throughout Macao, and has traveled to Mozambique and Portugal. You can add chicken, shrimp, or any meat of your choosing.

1 large onion, chopped
3 or 4 malagueta peppers, seeded
1 large clove garlic
¼ cup lard or shortening
1 tablespoon curry powder
1 tablespoon tamarind paste
¼ cup warm water or vinegar
1½ teaspoons salt
2 cups coconut milk
½ teaspoon black pepper

MEAT:

For chicken curry use one whole chicken cut into eight serving pieces.
For shrimp curry, use two pounds medium shrimp, peeled and deveined (see note).
For meat curry, use two pounds of beef or lamb, cut into 1-inch cubes.

purée the onion, peppers, and garlic in a food processor.

Heat the lard in a large skillet and add the mixture from the processor. Stir the mixture until it becomes lightly golden, then add the curry powder and mix well. If using chicken or meat add it to the skillet here.

Combine the tamarind with the water or vinegar and ½ teaspoon of the salt and blend it into the mixture. Pour in the coconut milk and season with the remaining 1 teaspoon salt and the pepper. Simmer until the meat is tender.

NOTE: For shrimp curry, boil the shrimp shells (and heads if using whole shrimp) with 2 cups of water until the liquid is reduced to 1 cup. Strain the mixture. Reduce the coconut milk to 1 cup and use the one cup of shrimp broth. Add the shrimp when you add the broth and coconut milk to the curry and simmer until the shrimp are cooked.

Duck with Pineapple

Pato com Ananás

4 servings

*f*or the best results always use fresh pineapple for this recipe, never canned.

1 duck (about 3 pounds)
1 teaspoon salt
¼ teaspoon black pepper
1 teaspoon soy sauce
1 pound piece smoked
  bacon
2 tablespoons lard or
  shortening
1 white onion, minced
1 green onion, minced
1 whole pineapple, peeled,
  cored, and cubed
1 teaspoon grated lemon
  peel

Wash the duck, remove the skin (see note) and cut it into 8 serving pieces. Season the duck with the salt, pepper, and ½ teaspoon of the soy sauce. Cut the bacon into 1-inch cubes and season with the remaining ½ teaspoon soy sauce. Set aside the duck and bacon for 30 minutes.

Meanwhile, heat the lard in a large skillet and sauté the white and green onions. When the onions are golden, add the bacon and cook for 5 minutes, stirring occasionally. Add the pieces of duck and the pineapple; stir and let cook for 5 minutes. Add 1½ cups of water and bring to a boil. Cook for 20 minutes. Reduce the heat to medium and simmer for another 20 minutes, or until the liquid is reduced to 2 tablespoons and the duck is cooked through. Add the lemon peel, stir, and cook another 3 minutes.

NOTE: Removing the skin gives the seasonings a chance to penetrate the meat and also means less fat in the broth.

Meat and Vegetable Stew, Macao-Style

Cozido Macanese
8 to 10 servings

i n Macao, the greens used for this dish are similar to the couve galego *greens used in the Portuguese* cozido. *The major difference between the two dishes is that the* cozido *from Macao calls for sweet potatoes and different meats.*

1 whole chicken (3 to 4 pounds)
1 pound veal roast
1 pound pork roast
2 teaspoons salt
½ teaspoon black pepper
3 tablespoons lard or shortening
1 large onion, chopped
3 green onions, chopped
2 large sweet potatoes
1 large yam
1 pound Chinese (napa) cabbage
2 pounds mustard greens
1 pig's foot (optional)
8-ounce piece of ham
3 cups white rice

S eason the whole chicken, veal roast, and pork roast with the salt and pepper and let macerate for 2 hours.

Heat the lard in a large pot and sauté the onion and green onions until golden. Add the chicken and veal and pork roasts. Add enough water to cover the meats and simmer over medium heat until the chicken is cooked through, about 1 hour and 25 minutes. Remove the chicken from the pot and set aside. Cook the pork and veal for another 15 minutes, then remove from the broth.

Add the sweet potatoes, yam, Chinese cabbage, and mustard greens to the broth; cook about 30 minutes until tender. Remove the vegetables and keep warm. Return the chicken, pork, and veal to the pot. Add the pig's foot (if using) and the ham and cook for another 45 minutes until the meats are tender. Remove the meats and skim off all the fat from the broth.

Meanwhile bring 6 cups of water to a boil in another large pot. Add the rice and cook for 25 minutes, or until the water has been absorbed.

Cut the chicken into 8 serving pieces, the roasts into thin slices, the pig's foot into slices, and then place the meats on a large platter. Slice the sweet potatoes and yam. On another platter, place the sliced potatoes and the greens, uncut. Serve the broth first as a soup. Then serve the meats and vegetables accompanied by the white rice.

Minced Meat, Macao-Style

Minche
4 to 6 servings

minche *is the national dish of Macao. The word comes from the English "mince," and rice with minche is for the Macanese what salted fish with rice is for the Chinese, or beans with rice is for the Brazilians. Minche is easy to prepare, delicious, and rather exotic. A combination of East and West, it can be served alone or to enhance other dishes, used to fill omelets or stuff eggs (see page 249), be fried with vegetables, or eaten with bread or white rice. The choices for* minche *are virtually limitless.*

MINCHE:
- 2 tablespoons vegetable oil
- 1 medium onion, thinly sliced (see note)
- 2 cloves garlic, mashed
- 1 pound ground beef or turkey
- 1 tablespoon soy sauce (see note)
- 1 tablespoon dark soy sauce (see note)
- 1 teaspoon sugar
- ½ teaspoon black pepper

FOR THE MINCHE: Heat 1 tablespoon of the oil in a medium skillet and sauté the onion slices until golden. Remove the onion from the skillet and set aside.

Add the remaining 1 tablespoon oil to the skillet and sauté the garlic until slightly golden. Add the meat and crumble with a fork or chopsticks. Sauté the meat until all the liquid is absorbed.

Add the sautéed onions, soy sauces, sugar, and pepper. Mix well, reduce the heat, and simmer until all the liquid has evaporated, stirring occasionally with a fork. Set aside.

FRIED RICE:

1 tablespoon plus
   1 teaspoon vegetable oil
4 beaten eggs, or
   1 teaspoon egg
   substitute
6 cups cooked and chilled
   basmati rice
3 green onions, chopped
4 ounces ham or Canadian
   bacon, chopped

FOR THE FRIED RICE: Heat 1 teaspoon of the oil in a small frying pan. Pour the beaten eggs into the pan and let them cook until set. Cut into thin strips and set aside. Heat the remaining 1 tablespoon oil in a large skillet. Add the cold rice and green onions and stir-fry until the rice is well heated, about 5 minutes. Add half of the *minche*, half of the egg pieces, and half of the chopped ham. Mix well, heat thoroughly, and place on a serving dish. Top the rice with the remaining minche, egg, and chopped ham, all arranged in a decorative manner.

NOTES:

SOY SAUCES: In Macao there are two kinds of soy sauce—white and black. The black soy sauce is sweeter and when used, less sugar is required in the recipe.

ONIONS: Macao cooks use an onion that is dryer than those available in the United States. However, our yellow or white onion does not alter the taste of the dish.

VARIATIONS: (1) Prepare the recipe with 8 ounces beef and 8 ounces pork; (2) use ground turkey instead of the beef; (3) mix cubed fried potatoes with the meat just before serving; (4) serve green peas in a ring around the meat.

The Devil's Pot

O Diabo
10 to 12 servings

the Devil's Pot is almost always made with the leftovers from a large party or banquet. How rich and varied the pot is depends on the quantity and quality of the leftovers. The ideal pot includes left-over roast turkey, roast pheasant, capons, roast beef, roast leg of lamb, pork or veal chops, roast pork, and perhaps some stewed meats. The juices from all the different meats are also used. If you are not fortu-nate enough to have seven or eight leftover meats, you can make do with some turkey meat, a couple of chicken legs, and some leftover sausages. Prepare this dish in the morning so that the flavors will have melded by dinnertime.

6 to 7 pounds cooked mixed meats (see above)
3 tablespoons olive oil or vegetable oil
2 large onions, chopped
8 medium tomatoes, chopped
1 (32-ounce) jar mixed sweet pickles, drained and chopped, reserving juices
Reserved juice from the meats (see above)
3 pounds white potatoes, peeled and quartered
18 hard-boiled eggs
6 tablespoons sugar
6 tablespoons mustard powder
1 cup white wine

remove any bones from the meats and cut the meat into 1-inch square pieces. Set aside.

Heat the oil in a large pot over medium heat and sauté the onions until lightly golden. Add the toma-toes and cook until the liquid has evaporated. Add the pickles and chopped meats. Mix well, cover, and cook over low heat for 10 minutes to blend the fla-vors. Add the reserved meat juices and enough water to barely cover the meats. Place the potatoes over the meats, cover, and cook until the potatoes are ten-der, about 20 minutes.

Meanwhile, peel the eggs and separate the yolks from the whites. Mash the whites with a fork and add to the pot. Mash the yolks and mix them with the sugar and the mustard. Add enough of the juices from the pickle jar to form a paste (about ½ cup).

When the potatoes are tender, stir in the egg yolk mixture. Cook 5 minutes more. Add the white wine, increase the heat, and bring to a boil. Cook another 3 minutes. Remove from the heat and let it set, cov-ered, until dinner is served. Serve hot with rice.

Golden Crown

Capela
6 to 8 servings

t he Portuguese word capela *means "chapel." This dish is so named because it is said to resemble a circular golden chapel. To me it looks like a small golden crown because of the crust of cheese covering the top.* Capela *is an aromatic, spicy, and easy-to-prepare dish. The secret to a successful outcome is to use pork that has very little fat. Fatty pork tends to crumble. Parmesan cheese is used in Macao, but in Portugal they prefer the cheese from the island of São Jorge in the Azores. As with many dishes from Macao, each cook has his or her own way of preparing* capela. *Depending on the ingredients, it can be elaborate or relatively simple. This version is fit for a king.*

2 pounds lean ground pork
   (see note)
3 tablespoons lemon juice
1 teaspoon salt
¼ teaspoon black pepper
1 medium onion, grated
1 cup shredded Parmesan
   or Swiss cheese
¼ cup chopped black olives
2 tablespoons ground
   almonds
2 tablespoons ground pine
   nuts
1 egg, or ¼ cup egg
   substitute
1 slice white bread, soaked in
   water and squeezed dry
6 slices lean bacon, cut in
   half crosswise
2 egg yolks, beaten
⅓ cup dry bread crumbs

p reheat the oven to 350 degrees F. Place the ground pork in a large bowl. Season the pork with the lemon juice, salt, and pepper. Add the onion, ¾ cup of the cheese, black olives, nuts, egg, and bread. Mix well. Roll the meat mixture into a 4-inch-wide sausage shape and connect the ends to form a ring. Place the ring on a lightly greased baking pan or in a Bundt pan. Decorate the top of the ring with the bacon half slices, placing them a few inches apart around the ring. Brush the top with the yolks and sprinkle with the bread crumbs and 2 tablespoons of the cheese. Bake for 45 minutes until the ring is dry with a golden crust.

Remove from the oven; drain and place on a platter. Sprinkle with the remaining 2 tablespoons cheese. This dish is traditionally served with white rice cooked with 1 teaspoon salt.

NOTE: If you use pork that has a little fat, place a rack in the baking pan and layer a piece of aluminum foil over the rack. Punch a few holes in the aluminum foil and place the ring of pork on top. This way any fat will drain away from the meat.

Pickled Cucumber

Sun-Kua

2 to 4 side-dish servings

*t*his traditional recipe, which originated in China, is an example of the ease with which the Macanese have adapted to the cuisines of foreign cultures and appreciated the cuisines that have influenced their own. The pickled cucumber will keep for a couple of weeks if covered and kept in a cool place.

2 cucumbers, long and narrow
1 teaspoon salt
4 ounces minced pork
1 tablespoon soy sauce
1 tablespoon corn flour (see note)
¼ teaspoon black pepper
2 tablespoons vegetable oil
1 medium onion, minced
3 cloves garlic, minced
1 teaspoon saffron
1-inch piece fresh ginger, peeled and thinly sliced
1 tablespoon vinegar
2 red chili peppers, cut into thin strips

Wash the cucumbers and cut them into ½-inch slices, leaving the skin on. Sprinkle with the salt and leave in a sieve to release the juices, about 30 minutes.

Place the pork in a bowl and season it with the soy sauce, corn flour, and pepper. Set aside.

Heat 1 tablespoon of the oil in a skillet and sauté the onion, garlic, and saffron until the onion is golden. Add the pork and cook until the mixture is dry.

In another skillet, heat the remaining 1 tablespoon oil and when the oil is hot, toss in the cucumbers and ginger, stirring well for about 1 minute. Add the vinegar, chilies, and pork mixture. Cook for only 1 minute, just to heat through, so that the cucumber remains crisp. Serve as a side dish with rice and shrimp.

NOTE: Corn flour can be found in Latin American or Asian markets and even some supermarkets. If not available, use a finely ground cornmeal.

Sweet Potato Pudding

Batatada
8 to 10 servings

his dessert is a good example of how the Portuguese carried food crops, like the sweet potato, from South America to other parts of the world where they were incorporated into the local cuisine.

3 pounds sweet potatoes, peeled and cubed
2 cups sugar
1½ cups all-purpose flour
12 egg yolks
1 cup (2 sticks) butter, melted
1 cup coconut milk
¾ cup sweetened condensed milk
½ cup ground almonds
4 egg whites
½ cup sliced toasted almonds for decoration

preheat the oven to 350 degrees F.

Boil the potatoes with barely enough water to cover. When the potatoes are tender, drain and put them through a ricer or food mill until puréed. Add the remaining ingredients (except the toasted almonds), one at a time, mixing well after each addition. Butter a 2-quart tube mold and pour the batter into the mold. Bake for 1 hour and 15 minutes, or until a toothpick inserted in the center comes out clean.

Remove the *batatada* from the oven and cool in the pan on a rack for 10 minutes. Invert the pudding onto a serving platter and sprinkle with the toasted almonds. Refrigerate until ready to serve. Slice and serve cold.

NOTE: Some cooks add ½ cup freshly grated coconut to the batter before cooking. I like to drizzle 2 tablespoons of honey over the top of the pudding before sprinkling on the toasted almonds.

Bean Balls Rolled in Sesame Seeds

Fritos de Sésame e Feijão
24 pieces

during the Chinese Lunar New Year, this is one of the desserts the Macanese most enjoy. In Chinese, the bean balls are called tchin-tôi.

8 ounces sweet potatoes, peeled and cubed
4 cups rice flour
1½ cups all-purpose flour
3 tablespoons sugar
2 cups canned red beans, mashed
1 cup sesame seeds, soaked in 1 cup water and drained
Oil for frying

Cook the sweet potatoes in a pot with water to barely cover until tender. Place in a bowl and mash with a fork. Add both flours and the sugar. Add ¾ cup of water, mixing well to form a dough.

Take 1 tablespoon of the dough and make a ball about 1 inch in diameter. With your finger, make a hole in the ball and fill it with a teaspoon of mashed beans. Close the hole and roll the ball in the sesame seeds. Continue making the balls until all the dough is used.

Heat the oil in a deep pot to a depth of two inches. Fry the balls until they are golden. Remove and drain on paper towels. Cool and serve.

CUISINE OF
Malacca

the Portuguese first landed in Malacca on a trip from Goa in 1509. They were looking to establish a trading post, but they were attacked by local traders who were defending their own commercial interests. It wasn't until 1511 that the Portuguese finally were able to capture the city and build a fort over the Strait of Malacca to protect their new possession. The fort was called *A Famosa* (The Famous). This rule lasted for about 130 years. Throughout that period the Portuguese established a policy of interracial and cultural relationships with local females and the relatively few women who came from Portugal often married indigenous men. From these interethnic relationships emerged a people possessing an exotic blend of Latin and Asian characteristics. Many of these Creoles identified themselves as Portuguese and occupied a favorable position in the social hierarchy. Outside of the fort they formed an enclave in a prestigious district called Upeh.

By 1639 the Dutch had taken over Malacca, and they ruled until 1795, when the British gained control. During this time the *Cristangs* (i.e., the Portuguese Creoles) lost nearly all they had possessed, but because of their European heritage many were able to secure positions both in the Dutch and British administrations. They were given other land and encouraged to build a new community. Slowly the primitive settlement in the swamp evolved and schools, churches, etc. were established. The area became known as the "Portuguese Settlement."

Cristang culture in large part was based on religious practices, including cuisine. The Catholic holidays were celebrated with food and drink. Given their origins and association with the Malays, Chinese, and Indians of Malaysia, it is understandable that the Cristangs were recognized as an indigenous people. To be a Cristang one had to be a Christian and have a European name. Moreover, Cristangs needed to have at least one blood ancestor who was a Malaccan-Portuguese. And a Cristang had to know the Creolized language of their Creole ancestors.

When the Portuguese arrived, Malaccan cuisine already was a hybrid of several cultures, among them Malay, Chinese, Indian, and Arab. Combining these influences with the Portuguese cooking methods the Cristangs created their own unique cuisine. The end result was a combination of East and West.

The Portuguese introduced onions, garlic, chilies, and the marinating of foods in lemon, vinegar, and lime. They also brought lemon grass, lime, and tamarind from other colonies to use in their curries, soups, and vegetable dishes. Meat was usually marinated, then sautéed to seal in the juices. Even today, pork, the preferred meat, is usually cut into bite-size pieces and fried with vegetables or added to curries.

The Cristangs use large chunks of beef for their curries, but it is then shredded and stir-fried. The vegetables most often consumed are broccoli, cauliflower, celery, leeks, spinach, green beans, eggplant, carrots, bamboo shoots, radishes, cucumbers, and cabbages. The preferred methods for cooking meats and vegetables include frying, stir-frying, braising, stewing, and broiling. The use of butter, margarine, and vegetable oil is preferred for cooking. Coconut milk is added to vegetables, curries, and cakes. Rice is prepared white and fluffy.

The recipes in this chapter give you just a sampling of the exotic cuisine of this former Portuguese territory in Asia.

Vegetable Turnovers

Empadas de Verduras
About 20 pieces

these vegetable fritters are as popular in Malacca as similar ones are in Goa and Portugal.

PASTRY:
2½ tablespoons butter
1 teaspoon salt
2 cups all-purpose flour

FILLING:
3 tablespoons vegetable oil
2 ounces firm tofu, diced
5 dried black mushrooms, soaked in water
2 medium onions, finely chopped
6 cloves garlic, minced
1 cup shredded jicama
½ cup shredded carrot
1 teaspoon black pepper
⅛ teaspoon ground nutmeg
⅛ teaspoon ground cinnamon
⅛ teaspoon ground cloves
3 tablespoons beef stock
2 teaspoons sugar
1 teaspoon salt

CHILI-VINEGAR SAUCE:
¼ cup chili pepper flakes
¼ cup lime juice
¼ cup white wine vinegar
10 cloves garlic, minced
1 teaspoon sugar
½ teaspoon salt

Oil for frying

FOR THE PASTRY: Melt the butter in 3 cups of hot water with the salt. Slowly pour the flour into the water mixture. Stir well. Fold out onto a lightly floured surface and knead until the mixture forms a soft dough. Divide the dough into 20 balls about 1 inch in diameter and set aside, covered.

FOR THE FILLING: Heat the vegetable oil in a large wok or pan. Fry the tofu until golden; drain on paper towels. Drain the mushrooms, dry, and dice into ½-inch cubes. Place the mushrooms in the wok and sauté for 1 minute. Add the onions and garlic and stir-fry until the onions are translucent. Add the jicama, carrot, pepper, nutmeg, cinnamon, and cloves. Stir-fry for 2 minutes over medium heat. Add the beef stock, cover, reduce the heat and cook for 5 minutes. Add the sugar and salt, cover, and cook for about 3 minutes, or until all the liquid is absorbed. Fold in the tofu, remove from the heat, and set aside to cool.

FOR THE CHILI-VINEGAR SAUCE: Combine all the ingredients in a bowl. Mix well.

TO ASSEMBLE: Flatten each pastry ball until it measures 4 inches in diameter. Place 1 tablespoon of filling in the center of each pastry circle. Fold the pastry over the filling and seal the edges by pinching the dough together. Place the turnovers on a baking sheet. Heat some oil in a deep pot or wok until almost smoking. Fry the turnovers, 3 at a time, until golden. Drain on paper towels. Serve with the Chili-Vinegar Sauce.

Shrimp Fritters

Pastéis de Camarão
8 to 10 servings

t hese fritters are similar to Portuguese Codfish Croquettes (page 9).
The Cristangs (Malaccans of Portuguese descent) use flour instead
of potatoes, and chili spice to give it a tang. The Portuguese were
responsible for bringing this type of cooking to Goa, Macao, East Timor
and Malacca. The Cristangs also use a small shrimp called "krill" to
make these fritters. They are usually served with Belachan, which is
similar to the Goan Prawn Preserve (page 221).

1 pound baby raw shrimp,
   peeled
3 tablespoons all-purpose
   flour
2 teaspoons salt
1 teaspoon black pepper
3 eggs, lightly beaten
1 large onion, minced or
   coarsely grated
1 tablespoon red pepper
   flakes
1 teaspoon sugar
Vegetable oil for frying

m ince the shrimp or put them through the
coarse grind of a meat grinder. Set aside. In a
large bowl, mix the flour, salt, and pepper. Add the
beaten eggs and 2 tablespoons of water slowly to
form a batter. Fold in the shrimp, onion, pepper
flakes, and sugar; mix well.

Heat some oil in a wok or deep pot. Drop heaping
tablespoons of batter into the hot oil and fry until
golden brown. Drain on paper towels. Serve on a bed
of lettuce with chili sauce on the side.

NOTE: The Cristangs also ladle the dough into the
hot oil to form a small flat pancake. It is then cut into
fourths and served over shredded lettuce and sliced
cucumbers.

Minced Meat Croquettes

Empadas de Carne
About 20 croquettes

*t*hese appetizers, popular in Malacca, are similar to the codfish and meat croquettes so popular in Portugal. The Indian spices and the addition of Parmesan cheese give these croquettes an exotic twist.

2 baking potatoes
1 teaspoon salt
¼ teaspoon black pepper
2 tablespoons vegetable oil
8 ounces minced beef
1 medium onion, minced
3 cloves garlic, minced
⅛ teaspoon ground
  cinnamon
⅛ teaspoon ground nutmeg
⅛ teaspoon ground cloves
1 teaspoon sugar
1 egg, separated
3 tablespoons dry bread
  crumbs
3 tablespoons grated
  Parmesan cheese
1¼ cups vegetable oil for
  frying

*p*rick the potatoes, wrap them in paper towels, and microwave for 7 minutes; or bake in the oven for 20 minutes; or boil for 20 minutes, until tender. Cool for 10 minutes; peel and mash while still warm. Season with ½ teaspoon of the salt and the pepper and set aside.

Heat the 2 tablespoons vegetable oil in a medium skillet and sauté the beef for 2 minutes; add the onion, garlic, cinnamon, nutmeg, and cloves and mix well. Add the sugar and remaining ½ teaspoon of salt and continue cooking until the beef is cooked through and the mixture is dry. Remove the skillet from the heat and set aside to cool.

Mix the egg yolk with the mashed potatoes. Add the minced beef and 1 tablespoon bread crumbs. Mix well. Form 1 tablespoon of the potato mixture into an egg shape. Repeat with the remaining mixture. Slightly beat the egg white and place in a shallow bowl. Combine the remaining 2 tablespoons bread crumbs and the cheese and place in another dish. Dip the croquettes first in egg white and then in the breadcrumb mixture to cover completely. Place the croquettes on a baking sheet.

Pour the vegetable oil into a deep skillet to a depth of two inches. Heat it over medium-high heat to 365 degrees F on a deep-frying thermometer. Fry the croquettes, a few at a time, until golden brown. Remove the croquettes with a slotted spoon to paper towels to drain. Serve the croquettes on a bed of shredded lettuce with a side dish of chili sauce.

Old-Fashioned Chicken Broth

Caldu Galinha
4 servings

this soup is traditionally recommended to mothers after childbirth and to invalids, as it is thought to help restore one's strength. The meat from the chicken can be shredded and added to the soup; mixed with salt, pepper, and mayonnaise and used as a filling for sandwiches; or mixed with curry and used as a filling for empanadas.

1 chicken (about 3 pounds)
6 cloves garlic, finely
   chopped
2 tablespoons brandy
1 teaspoon sugar
½ teaspoon Dry Spice Curry
   Powder (page 284)
½ teaspoon black pepper
¼ cup vegetable oil
1 teaspoon salt
1 egg white, lightly beaten
4 cups croutons

Cut the chicken into 8 serving pieces. Combine the garlic, 1 tablespoon of the brandy, the sugar, dry spice, and pepper, mixing well. Coat the chicken pieces with the mixture and set aside for 5 minutes.

Heat the oil in a large skillet or wok. Stir-fry the chicken pieces for 1 minute. Add 6 cups of water and bring to a boil. Cook for 20 minutes. Remove the chicken pieces from the broth and set aside. Lower the heat and add the salt. Stir well. If a scum rises to the surface, add the egg white, stir, and skim off the scum. The broth should be clear.

Just before serving, strain the soup into a tureen. Add the remaining 1 tablespoon brandy, stir well, and sprinkle with the croutons. If desired, shred the chicken breasts and add to the broth.

Okra with Dried Shrimp Sauce

Quiabo com Camarão Seco
4 side-dish servings

Okra, originally from Africa, has traveled to Europe, Asia, and the Americas in the holds of sailing ships. This dish bears something of a resemblance to the Chicken Stew with Okra (page 336) of São Tomé, and Bahian-Style Shrimp and Okra (page 113) of Brazil. Serve as a side dish to fish curry with white rice.

1 cup dried shrimp, soaked
in hot water
1 medium onion, chopped
6 cloves garlic, chopped
1 to 2 tablespoons red
pepper flakes
1 tablespoon shrimp paste
or Prawn Preserve
(page 221)
2 teaspoons white vinegar
½ teaspoon baking powder
8 ounces whole okra,
trimmed
2 tablespoons lime juice
1 teaspoon salt
½ teaspoon sugar
6 shallots, thinly sliced

drain the dried shrimp and place them in a food processor or blender along with the onion, garlic, pepper flakes, and shrimp paste. Blend to a course paste (about 30 seconds) and set aside.

Bring 6 cups of water to a boil in a stainless steel or glass pot with the vinegar and baking powder. Add the okra pods and cook for 8 minutes; remove from the water and immerse them in ice water to stop cooking. Drain and set aside.

Add 1 tablespoon of the lime juice, the salt, and sugar to the shrimp paste mixture. Mix well. Place the okra pods on 4 plates, spread the shrimp paste on top of the okra, and sprinkle the tops with the remaining 1 tablespoon lime juice and the sliced shallots.

Macao Rice

Arroz Macau
6 to 8 side-dish servings

a s the name suggests, this dish was originally from Macao and was brought by the Portuguese to Malacca. The dish is actually a variation of a combination of Macao's Fat Rice (page 254) and Moorish Rice (page 255). The main difference is in the spices. In Malacca the original Macanese dish was further enhanced by the addition of ginger, cinnamon, nutmeg, and cloves. This recipe is a true Portuguese, Goan, and Macanese mixture.

4 bone-in chicken thighs
¼ cup vegetable oil
1 medium onion, minced
6 cloves garlic, chopped
1-inch piece fresh ginger, peeled and grated
5 dried black mushrooms, soaked in warm water, drained, and thinly sliced
½ teaspoon coarse ground black pepper
⅛ teaspoon ground cinnamon
⅛ teaspoon ground nutmeg
⅛ teaspoon ground cloves
1½ cups uncooked white rice
3 eggs, lightly beaten
1 green onion, chopped

p lace the chicken thighs in a medium pot and add 5 cups of water. Bring to a boil and simmer until the chicken is cooked through, about 20 minutes. Remove the chicken and save for another dish (see note). Set the broth aside to cool.

Heat the oil in a deep skillet or wok over medium-high heat. Add the onion, garlic, and ginger and stir-fry for 30 seconds. Add the mushrooms, pepper, cinnamon, nutmeg, and cloves. Stir-fry for 30 seconds. Add the rice and stir to mix well.

Pour 3½ cups of the cooled chicken broth into a medium pot. Add the rice mixture, bring to a boil, cover, and reduce the heat. Cook until all the liquid has been absorbed, about 20 minutes. Set aside to cool.

Preheat the oven to 325 degrees F. Fold the beaten eggs into the cooled rice and mix well. Spoon the rice into a 2-quart ring mold and press gently to pack. Smooth the top with the back of a spoon. Bake for 8 minutes to cook the eggs. Invert the rice onto a serving dish and sprinkle with the chopped green onion. Serve with roast chicken or chicken curry.

NOTE: Shred the cooked chicken and use with vegetables for a stir-fry.

Fisherman's Stew

Caldu Pescador
6 to 8 servings

*t*he fishermen of Malacca, like their counterparts in East Timor, often cook their catch on the beach at the end of the day. Timorenses grill their catch wrapped in banana leaves (see Grilled Fish, page 180) and the Malaccans cook theirs in large pots over coals. This recipe calls for a variety of fish and shellfish. The Malaccan fishermen are known to add a bit of brandy to the stew as a kind of toast to a successful day's catch.

1 pound medium raw shrimp
1 teaspoon sea or other coarse salt
1 pound squid sacs, cleaned
8 ounces white fish fillets
3 tablespoons lemon juice
1 tablespoon tamarind pulp
6 shallots, chopped
3 stalks lemon grass, chopped
3 cloves garlic, minced
1 tablespoon red pepper flakes
½ cup chopped fresh cilantro leaves

*p*eel the shrimp, clean, rinse, and sprinkle with ½ teaspoon of the salt. Set aside for 10 minutes. Rinse the shrimp and blot dry.

Cut the squid sacs into 1-inch pieces. Cut the fish fillets into 1-inch cubes. Sprinkle the squid and fish with the remaining ½ teaspoon of salt and 1 tablespoon of the lemon juice and set aside.

Add ½ cup of water to the tamarind pulp. Mix well and set aside.

Bring 8 cups of water to boil in a large pot. Add the shallots, lemon grass, and garlic. Boil for 4 minutes. Add the tamarind water and red pepper flakes; lower the heat and simmer for about 10 minutes. Add the shrimp, squid, and fish to the pot. Cook for 3 minutes. Add the remaining 2 tablespoons lemon juice and the cilantro leaves. Stir and serve immediately.

Fried Crabs with Chilies and Soybeans

Caranguejos Fritos
6 servings

t his fried crab recipe is one of the many ways the Malaccans pre-pare crabs. It is customary to eat these crabs with your fingers, even in the best of restaurants. Finger bowls are usually kept handy, containing Chinese tea with lemon slices to clean the fingers during the meal.

3 large fresh blue crabs
1 cup vegetable oil
2 onions, chopped
5 fresh red chili peppers, seeded and finely chopped
2 cloves garlic, peeled and chopped
1-inch piece fresh ginger, peeled and chopped
1 teaspoon black pepper
1 tablespoon salted soy-beans, mashed
½ teaspoon sugar

d rop the crabs into a large pot of boiling salted water for about 15 minutes, or until cooked. Remove from the water and cool. When the crabs are cool, remove the backs and the spongy parts (gills) under the shell. Chop each crab into quarters and remove the claws.

Heat the oil in a wok or deep frying pan to a depth of two inches. Fry the crab pieces for about 4 minutes, or until golden. Remove and drain on paper towels. Pour off all but 2 tablespoons of the oil. Add the onions, chili peppers, garlic, ginger, and black pep-per. Stir and add the soybeans. Stir-fry for another 3 minutes. Add the crab pieces, mix well, add 1 cup of water, cover, and cook for 5 minutes to heat through. Add the sugar, stir, and remove from the heat. Serve warm.

Fried Fish

Peixe Frito
4 to 6 servings

in Malacca, the two most popular ways to prepare fish are grilling and frying. This recipe calls for fish steaks and is prepared with a sauce made from tamarind juice and brown sugar.

2 pounds fish steaks, such as halibut, mackerel, or grouper
1 tablespoon salt
1 medium onion
¼ cup blanched almonds
4 red chili peppers
3 cloves garlic
2½ tablespoons tamarind pulp
1 cup vegetable oil
1 teaspoon brown sugar

Sprinkle the fish steaks with the salt. In a blender or food processor, grind together the onion, almonds, chili peppers, and garlic to a purée. Rub the mixture into the fish steaks on both sides.

Place 2 tablespoons of the tamarind pulp in 1 cup of water. Set aside.

Heat the oil in a large frying pan. Add the remaining ½ tablespoon tamarind pulp to the pan and then add the fish steaks. Fry the fish on one side until golden brown. Turn and brown on the other side. Remove the fish from the pan and drain on paper towels.

Empty the oil from the pan and wipe clean. Return the pan to the heat and add the tamarind water; simmer for 2 minutes and add the brown sugar. Stir and remove from the heat. Arrange the fish steaks on a serving platter and pour the tamarind sauce on top. Serve with white rice.

Fried Chicken

Galinha Frita
4 to 6 servings

fried chicken was usually served on Sundays in Malaccan households. It was a day for family gatherings, good times, and good food. Today it is still served for festive occasions.

2 tablespoons soy sauce
1 tablespoon
   Worcestershire sauce
2 cloves garlic, peeled and
   chopped
1 teaspoon salt
1 teaspoon prepared
   English mustard
1 teaspoon Dry Spice Curry
   Powder (page 284)
1 teaspoon sugar
½ teaspoon black pepper
1½ tablespoons butter,
   softened
1 chicken (3 pounds) cut
   into 8 pieces
1 cup vegetable oil
2 onions, peeled and sliced
2 teaspoons corn flour
2 tablespoons white wine
Salt and pepper to taste

GARNISH:
4 large potatoes, boiled
   and quartered
2 tablespoons canned
   green peas, drained
Lime juice

in a large bowl combine 1 tablespoon of the soy sauce, the Worcestershire, garlic, 1 teaspoon salt, mustard, dry spice powder, sugar, and pepper. Add 1 tablespoon of the butter, mix well. Coat the chicken pieces thoroughly with the marinade. Set the chicken aside to marinate for 15 minutes.

Heat the vegetable oil in a large frying pan. Add the chicken pieces and fry for 5 minutes. Add any remaining marinade to the pan. Pour in a ½ cup water and cook until the liquid evaporates. Stir-fry the chicken pieces for another 2 minutes. When cooked through remove from the heat and arrange on a platter.

In another pan heat the remaining ½ tablespoon butter and fry the onions until golden. Add the remaining 1 tablespoon soy sauce and the corn flour and cook until the sauce thickens. Add the wine and salt and pepper to taste. Stir and remove from the heat.

Pour the sauce over the chicken pieces. Garnish with the boiled potatoes and peas. Before serving, sprinkle the chicken with lime juice. Serve with white rice.

Chicken Stew

Ensopada de Galinha

6 servings

t his stew is generally used for the filling for Chicken Pie (page 282). It can also be served with rice. Any other meat may be substituted for the chicken. Brandy can be substituted for the milk for those who may be lactose intolerant or want an interesting taste. Serve with white rice or peasant bread.

2 pounds boneless chicken thighs and/or breasts
1 teaspoon salt
1½ teaspoons black pepper
¼ cup vegetable oil
2 medium onions, quartered
½ star anise
6 whole cloves
1-inch cinnamon stick
1 teaspoon Dry Spice Curry Powder (page 284)
1 carrot, thinly sliced diagonally
3 medium white potatoes, peeled and quartered
1 cup chicken stock
6 large cabbage leaves, stemmed and halved lengthwise
2 tablespoons milk or brandy (optional)

C ut the chicken into bite-size pieces. Season the chicken pieces with the salt and ½ teaspoon of the pepper, and set aside for 5 minutes.

Heat the oil in a large pan or wok and sauté the onions until soft. Add the star anise, cloves, and cinnamon stick. Sauté for 2 minutes and then add the dry spice powder and remaining 1 teaspoon black pepper; mix well.

Add the chicken pieces and stir-fry over high heat until golden on all sides, turning frequently. Add 1 cup of water, cover, and cook for 5 minutes.

Add the carrots, potatoes, and 2 cups of water. Bring to a boil, add the chicken stock, reduce heat, and simmer for 5 minutes. Add the cabbage, salt and pepper to taste, and cook for another 3 minutes. Before serving, mix in the milk or brandy, if desired.

Chicken Pie

Torta de Galinha
4 to 6 servings

C hicken pie has always been served on Christmas Eve as part of the midnight supper meal (consoada in Portugal). Also savored is a sherry-and-anise flavored soup and a ham that is boiled in beer. This dish can be accompanied by a green salad, rustic bread, and a glass of red wine.

DOUGH:
3 cups all-purpose flour
½ teaspoon salt
1 cup butter (2 sticks)
1 egg yolk

FILLING:
1 recipe Chicken Stew
   (page 281)
1 tablespoon brandy
2 hard-boiled eggs, cut
   lengthwise into halves
8 ounces lean bacon, fried
   crisp
4 ounces smoked sausages,
   cooked and thinly
   sliced

¼ cup evaporated milk for
   brushing the crust

FOR THE DOUGH: In a large bowl, sift together the flour and salt. Add the butter and cut into the flour until it resembles cornmeal. Add the egg yolk and ½ cup cold water. Mix into a dough. Knead until just combined. Chill while preparing the filling.

Prepare the chicken stew and cool. Heat the oven to 350 degrees F.

FOR THE FILLING: Stir the brandy into the chicken stew. Fill a deep 10-inch pie pan with the stew. Arrange the slices of hard-boiled egg on top, followed by the bacon pieces. Place the sausage slices around the edge of the pie dish.

Dust a pastry board lightly with flour and roll out the dough large enough to cover the pie. Cover the pie with the dough, trim the edges, and use a fork to flute the edges. Prick the dough with a fork to let the steam escape. Brush the dough lightly with the milk and bake for about 20 minutes, or until the pastry is golden. Remove the pie from the oven and brush again with the milk. Serve hot.

Beef in Wine Sauce

Bife com Vinho d'Alhos
6 servings

this traditional Portuguese dish is also popular in Macao, where a leg of pork is used instead of beef. Today this dish has all but been forgotten by many of the Cristangs; only a small percentage of them remember the recipe and even fewer continue to prepare the dish. But because it is a part of the legacy the Portuguese left, I have included it.

2 pounds beef shoulder or
   leg cuts
3 teaspoons pepper
4 tablespoons ground
   coriander
2 tablespoons ground cumin
1 tablespoon ground fennel
2 tablespoons ground
   turmeric powder
2 tablespoons white vinegar
1 teaspoon salt
1 head garlic (10 cloves),
   peeled and chopped
¼ cup grated fresh ginger
1 star anise
1 cup white wine
½ cup vegetable oil

Cut the beef into thin slices 3 inches long and ½-inch thick.

Place the pepper, coriander, cumin, fennel, turmeric, vinegar, salt, garlic, and grated ginger in a blender, food processor, or mortar and pestle and grind to a paste. Coat each piece of meat with the marinade.

Arrange the beef slices in a glass or ceramic dish. Break off pieces of the star anise and sprinkle over the meat. Pour the wine over the meat and prick the meat with a fork. Cover and marinate overnight in the refrigerator turning once.

The following day, heat the oil in a deep pan. Fry 2 to 3 slices of meat at a time until slightly crispy on the edges. Serve with white rice and any leftover marinade that has been brought to a boil.

NOTE: Two cups of beef broth can be added to the pan after the beef is fried. Cook for 5 minutes. Taste and add salt and pepper if necessary. Pour the sauce over the beef strips and serve.

Dry Spice Curry Powder

Tempero de Caril
Makes 1 cup

U*se this spice with Chicken Stew (page 281), and Fried Chicken (page 280).*

3 tablespoons coriander seeds
2 tablespoons cumin seeds
1 tablespoon fennel seeds
2 teaspoons black peppercorns
Two 2-inch cinnamon sticks
3 green cardamom pods
¼ teaspoon grated fresh nutmeg
5 cloves
1 teaspoon ground turmeric

P lace all the spices, except for the turmeric, in a nonstick frying pan and dry roast for a few minutes over medium heat. Shake the pan occasionally, and don't let the spices burn. Transfer the spices to a plate to cool.

Place cooled spices in a spice mill or blender and grind to a fine powder. Combine the ground spices and the turmeric and mix well. Place in an air-tight jar and keep in a cool place.

Pineapple Tarts

Pastéis de Ananas

About 25 tarts

*a*ll of Malacca's ethnic groups enjoy these delicious pineapple tarts during their respective festivals. Each group will make them in a different shape. The Cristangs top theirs with a three-bladed leaf to symbolize the Holy Trinity; the Peranakan group (the progeny of the Chinese princess' entourage and Malaccan natives) tops theirs with a lattice pattern; and the Chittys (the progeny of unions between Malaccan natives and Indian traders) top theirs with a cut-out piece of dough in the center. No matter which shape or topping is used, they are delicious. The pineapple filling should be prepared the day before serving, as it should cool overnight.

PINEAPPLE FILLING:

2 medium pineapples
   (about 2 pounds each)
1-inch piece cinnamon stick
1 cup rock sugar
5 whole cloves

PASTRY:

3½ cups all-purpose flour
¼ teaspoon salt
1 cup (2 sticks) butter or
   lard, chilled
1 tablespoon corn oil
1 egg yolk
1 teaspoon vanilla extract
2 tablespoons cold water

GLAZE:

1 egg yolk

FOR THE FILLING: Peel the pineapples, remove the eyes, and mince the fruit. Place the fruit in a colander to strain the juice and save. Place the pineapple, cinnamon, sugar, and cloves in a medium non-stick pan and cook over very low heat for 30 minutes, stirring occasionally. Be careful not to let the mixture burn. If the jam becomes too dry and begins to stick to the pan, add ¼ cup of the strained pineapple juice. Simmer until the jam is sticky and light golden. Let the jam cool completely before using.

FOR THE PASTRY: In a large bowl, sift together the flour with the salt. Cut the butter into pieces and add to the flour. Cut the butter into the flour until the mixture is crumbly (you can also use your hands to rub the butter into the flour). Add the corn oil and knead lightly. Add the egg yolk and vanilla extract. Sprinkle the mixture with 2 tablespoons cold water and knead until the dough is soft and pliable. Cover and chill for 2 hours.

(CONTINUED)

ASSEMBLY: Preheat the oven to 350 degrees F. Divide the pastry into four pieces. On a floured surface, roll out each piece of pastry to ¼ inch thick. Cut out circles about 3 inches in diameter with a biscuit cutter. There should be about 25 circles. Place a tablespoon of pineapple jam in the center of each circle. Roll out the remaining pastry to ⅛ inch thick. Cut thin strips, ½ inch wide, and place them around the edge of each tart. Press to seal and flute with your fingers. If there is pastry left over, cut small designs and place them on top of the jam. Brush the tops with the beaten egg yolk.

Bake the tarts on greased cookie sheets for 20 minutes or until the pastries are golden. Cool before storing or serve immediately.

CUISINE OF
Mozambique

t he The Portuguese first arrived in Mozambique in 1498 when Vasco da Gama, en route to India, disembarked on the northern coast and gave it the name of Ilha de Moçambique (Mozambique Island). Within a decade the Portuguese had established a permanent settlement on the island and had gained control of many trading posts formerly occupied by Arab migrants. During the next 200 years, the Portuguese established other trading posts and forts along the coast to secure their position in the gold, ivory, and slave trade.

In a recent survey conducted in Maputo (the capital city) among citizens and tourists, one of the questions asked was, "What is the best thing the country has to offer?" One of the most frequent answers was, "The Afro-Luso-Asiatic food." Mozambican cuisine is a delicious medley of native, Goan, and Portuguese flavors.

Traditional fruit drinks are plentiful in the country and each region has its favorite. The most common are made with cashew, manioc, papaya, coconut, or sugarcane juice. Normally, the fruits are washed and left to ripen completely. They are then cut open, the seeds are removed, and the rind and fruit are cut into pieces and placed in a large receptacle for two days. The mixture is then strained, bottled, and ready for drinking.

Fish and seafood are some of the delicacies that Mozambique has to offer. Maputo is known for its excellent prawns, lobsters, and crayfish. Calamari (*lulas*) is also very popular and usually served grilled or fried. Crabs, cockles, clams, and various fish such as tuna, red snapper, rock fish, and *serra* from the coastal waters are savored and prepared in a variety of ways, but the most common is grilled over coals. They are often just served with a simple sauce made by combining lemon juice, chili peppers, and salt that has been heated for a few minutes. The oils used to cook these delicacies are peanut, olive, and sunflower.

Beans are a staple in Mozambique and are used in many traditional dishes. The most common are *nhemba* (a type of black-eyed bean), the *feijão-manteiga* (butter bean), and *feijão soroco* (a green split pea). The Mozambican secret to cooking beans is not to stir them with a spoon until they finish cooking. The belief is that if you put a spoon or any other object into the pot of beans, they will stop cooking at that point. *Maguinha* and *upswa* are dishes made with dried cassava and cornmeal, respectively. Both are served with a sauce of beans, vegetables, or fish.

The utensils that are essential in a Mozambican kitchen are a *pilão* (mortar and pestle) to pound peanuts and corn, a straw strainer to sift out the small stones and husks from flour, a small mortar to crush garlic and chili peppers, an *mbenga* (clay pot) used to soak corn, and a good wooden spoon. In the countryside, clay pots are the norm.

Some of the local specialties are *Matapa*, manioc or cabbage leaves cooked in a peanut sauce with dried shrimp; *Chamuças* or *Samosas*, curried chicken turnovers served with a mango chutney; *Caril de Galinha*, chicken curry; and *Galinha à Cafreal*, grilled chicken with piripiri sauce. *Matapa* and *Galinha à Cafreal* are dishes native to Mozambique. *Chamuças* and *Caril de Galinha* are of Goan influence. Many of these wonderful dishes are in this chapter. *Bom apetite!*

Peanut Balls

Almondegas de Amendoim
About 20 pieces

*t*hese peanut balls can be served in a chafing dish with toothpicks or as a light lunch with a green salad. The piripiri sauce adds a delightful tang.

2 cups raw unsalted
    peanuts
1 cup finely grated carrots
½ cup grated onion
2 eggs, beaten
2 cups dry bread crumbs
2 teaspoons Tabasco or
    other hot sauce
1 tablespoon chopped
    fresh parsley

SAUCE:
2 cups tomato sauce
2 tablespoons chopped
    fresh parsley
2 tablespoons corn flour or
    finely ground cornmeal
1 tablespoon piripiri sauce
    (page 141), or 2
    teaspoons Tabasco
    sauce

*p*reheat the oven to 350 degrees F. Place the peanuts in a food processor and grind them to a powder. In a bowl mix the peanut powder, carrots, onion, eggs, bread crumbs, Tabasco, and parsley. Form into 1-inch balls.

Mix all the ingredients for the sauce together.

Place the peanut balls in a shallow baking pan. Pour the sauce over them and bake for about 30 minutes, or until the balls are cooked. Serve with toothpicks.

Chicken Turnovers

Chamuças
About 60 pieces

i first tasted these turnovers in 1971 on my first trip to Mozambique, when I was invited to the home of our friends Rui Knopfli, an accomplished poet, and his wife Maria José. Maria's mother had passed this recipe down to her and I understand the recipe originally came from a Goan cook who taught it to Maria's mother. Chamuças are of Indian origin, but are common in much of southeastern Africa. This recipe calls for a chicken filling, but in both Mozambique and Goa, another popular filling is shrimp.

FILLING:
2 pounds bone-in chicken thighs
2 tablespoons vegetable oil
2 large onions, minced
1 large tomato, chopped
1 tablespoon curry powder
1 tablespoon grated fresh ginger
1 tablespoon red pepper flakes
1 tablespoon garam masala
1 teaspoon salt

PASTRY DOUGH:
(see variation)
2 cups all-purpose flour
¾ teaspoon salt
1½ tablespoons oil or clarified butter

Vegetable oil for frying

FOR THE FILLING: Place the chicken thighs in a large pot, cover with water, and bring to a boil. Reduce the heat and simmer until the thighs are cooked through, about 30 minutes. Remove the thighs from the heat and cool in the broth. When the chicken is cool, remove the skin and bones and shred the meat. Heat the oil in a large skillet. Add the shredded chicken and all the other filling ingredients to the skillet and simmer for 30 minutes, stirring frequently. Add a little of the broth if the mixture becomes too dry. Set aside.

FOR THE DOUGH: Sift the flour and salt together. Make a well in the center of the mixture and pour in the oil and ½ to ¾ cup water. Stir briskly until combined, gradually adding more water if necessary. The dough should be slightly moist and stick together. On a lightly floured surface, knead the dough for about 10 minutes until smooth and elastic. Cover with a damp cloth.

PREPARATION: Break off pieces of dough and shape them into balls the size of walnuts. Roll each ball into a circle about ⅟₁₆ of an inch thick and 4 inches across. Cut the circle in half and place a heaping tablespoon of filling on one side of the half circle. Fold over the half circle to form a triangle. Brush a bit of water along the edges and pinch to seal. Continue in the same manner until all the dough and filling is used.

Heat the oil in a large skillet to a 2-inch depth. The oil is ready when a piece of dough sizzles when dropped in. Fry 3 or 4 *chamuças* at a time until golden and crisp on each side. Drain them on paper towels. Serve at room temperature with mango chutney.

VARIATION: You can also use wonton wrappers in place of the pastry dough. In this case, place a tablespoon of the filling in the center of each wonton, brush the edges with egg wash, fold in half diagonally and press the edges together to form a triangle. Fry in hot oil until golden on all sides.

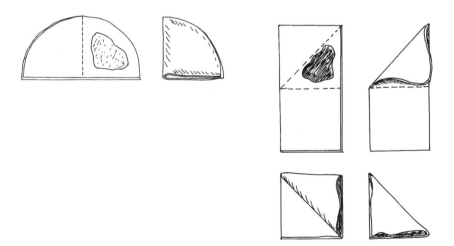

Beet Salad

Salada de Beterraba
4 side-dish servings

t he most common salads in Mozambique are made with cooked vegetables and olive oil. Also popular are salads made with lettuce,
tomato, and cucumber with a vinaigrette sauce. This beet salad
has recently gained popularity and is served in some of the best restaurants. I first tasted it in 1971 at the home of Nelly Honwana, the mother
of Luis Bernado Honwana, a well-known writer. It is easy to prepare
and very tasty. Select medium beets that are smooth and firm. The beets
should be cooked in their skins, as they will lose their bright color if
peeled before cooking, and leave an inch or two of the stem on the beets
when cooking.

1 pound beets
¼ cup olive oil
¼ cup minced parsley
1 large onion, minced
¼ cup lemon juice
1 tablespoon sugar
Salt to taste

W ash the beets and simmer in water to cover for
30 minutes, or until tender. Drain. Place them
in cold water; when cool, trim the tops and peel off
the skins. Dice the beets and place them in a bowl.

Heat the olive oil in a large skillet and sauté the parsley on low heat for 2 minutes. Add the onion, lemon
juice, sugar, and salt. Mix well and pour over the
beets. Serve this salad with poultry or grilled meats.

Seafood Salad

Salada de Mariscos
4 servings

fish and other seafood are some of the culinary delights that Mozambique has to offer. Most Mozambicans enjoy them grilled over charcoal and served with a simple sauce made with lemon juice, chili peppers, and salt. This salad combines local seafood with vegetables for a delicious treat.

1 pound large raw shrimp, peeled
1 tablespoon lemon juice
8 ounces squid sacs, cleaned
8 ounces white fish fillets
½ small cabbage
8 ounces string beans, trimmed
1 medium onion, thinly sliced
1 tablespoon olive oil

DRESSING:
6 tablespoons olive oil
5 tablespoons white vinegar
2 cloves garlic, minced
1 teaspoon salt
¼ teaspoon black pepper

heat the charcoal in a grill until it turns white, or preheat a gas grill to high.

Cook all but 4 of the shrimp in boiling water with the lemon juice until just pink. Grill the squid sacs until golden on both sides. Remove the sacs and slice them into rings. Grill the fish fillets, about 2 minutes each side, and flake them into bite-size pieces. Blanch the cabbage in boiling water for 3 minutes; drain, and slice as for coleslaw. Cook the green beans in boiling salted water for 8 to 10 minutes, depending on their size, just to crisp tender.

In a large salad bowl, mix together the cooked shrimp, squid, fish, cabbage, green beans, and onions. In a small bowl, mix together the dressing ingredients. Pour the dressing over the salad and refrigerate.

Stir-fry the remaining 4 shrimp, still in their shells, in 1 tablespoon of olive oil until pink and set side. When ready to serve, place the fried shrimp pinwheel fashion on top of the salad.

Scrambled Eggs with Fried Eggplant

Beringelas Fritas com Ovos
2 servings

these scrambled eggs are delicious served for breakfast or for a light lunch.

1 medium eggplant (about
    1 pound)
2 tablespoons butter
4 eggs
½ cup dry bread crumbs
1 teaspoon salt
1 tablespoon olive oil

Peel the eggplant and cut into 1-inch cubes. Cook the eggplant in boiling salted water for 3 minutes; drain in a colander.

Heat the butter in a skillet and sauté the eggplant cubes until golden on all sides.

Beat the eggs in a medium bowl; add the bread crumbs, salt, and eggplant. Heat the olive oil in the skillet and pour in the egg mixture. Stir occasionally until the eggs are set. Serve immediately.

Shrimp Omelet

Omeleta de Camarão
2 servings

because shrimp are plentiful in Mozambique, it's no wonder that they appear in many dishes. This omelet, with spicy fries and a green salad, is great for a Sunday brunch.

6 eggs, separated
2 tablespoons butter
1 pound small raw shrimp,
    peeled and cleaned
1 teaspoon Tabasco sauce,
    or ground red pepper
2 tablespoons sunflower oil
¼ cup chopped fresh parsley

place the egg whites in a deep bowl and beat until stiff. In another bowl, beat the yolks.

Heat 1 tablespoon of the butter in a skillet and sauté the shrimp until pink. Sprinkle the shrimp with the Tabasco sauce or ground red pepper.

Heat the oil in a 10-inch omelet pan. Fold the yolks into the beaten whites. When the oil is hot, pour the eggs into the pan. Add the shrimp, lower the heat, and cook, covered, until the omelet begins to set. Fold the omelet in half and let it cook until the eggs are set. Melt the remaining 1 tablespoon butter over the omelet and sprinkle with parsley.

Fried Fish and Manioc Stew

Lumino
4 to 6 servings

i *first tasted this dish at the home of José Craverinha, Mozambique's poet laureate. His daughter-in-law prepared it for our lunch and it has been a favorite of mine ever since. A dish similar to this is found in Brazil. Since manioc originated in the New World, it is very possible that the Portuguese brought it to Africa along with the idea for this stew. It later became a mainstay of the Mozambican diet.*

2 pounds fish steaks such as halibut, grouper, red snapper, or cod
4 cloves garlic, minced
1 teaspoon salt
1 teaspoon ground red pepper
2 pounds manioc root, peeled and sliced ½ inch thick
3 tablespoons vegetable oil
2 large onions, thinly sliced
2 large tomatoes, thinly sliced
2 green bell peppers, thinly sliced
1 bay leaf
1 can (14-ounce) coconut milk

Wipe the fish steaks and season them with the garlic, salt, and ground red pepper. Let them stand for 30 minutes.

Meanwhile, place the manioc in a pot and cover with cold water. Bring to a boil and simmer for 15 minutes, until tender. Drain and set aside.

Heat 1 tablespoon of the oil in a large skillet and fry the fish steaks quickly until golden on each side. Remove the fish from the pan and set aside.

In the same skillet, heat the remaining 2 tablespoons oil and sauté the onions, tomatoes, green peppers, and bay leaf for about 5 minutes. Place the pieces of manioc around the edge of the pan and place the fish on top of the sautéed vegetables. Pour the coconut milk over all, cover, and simmer for 10 minutes, until the fish is cooked through. Serve with white rice.

Mozambican Bean Stew

Feijoada Moçambicana
4 side-dish servings

this is one of several African variations of feijoada—commonly called Brazil's national dish. In Mozambique the recipe calls for dried lima or butter beans, and turnip greens in place of collards. Carrots are also added to the dish. The vegetables are combined with the beans and meats and served in one large dish.

2 cups (1 pound) dried
    lima or butter beans,
    washed and sorted
8 ounces tripe (optional)
1 medium onion, chopped
5 cloves garlic, minced
2 tablespoons vegetable oil
1 pound *chouriço* or other
    spicy sausage, cut into
    ½-inch slices
1 pound pork roast, cut
    into 1-inch cubes
4 ounces salt pork, cubed
3 medium ripe tomatoes,
    seeded and chopped
2 medium carrots, peeled
    and chopped
1 pound turnip greens,
    chopped
2 teaspoons piripiri or
    other hot sauce
2 bay leaves
Salt and pepper to taste

refrigerate the beans overnight in cold water to cover.

Soak the tripe for 1½ hours in salted water; wash well. Chop the tripe into 1-inch pieces and place in boiling water. Reduce the heat and simmer for 2 hours until soft and tender.

Rinse the beans and place them in a large pot with water to cover plus 2 inches. Bring the water to a boil, reduce the heat, and simmer for 2 hours, until tender.

Meanwhile, place the onion and garlic in a large skillet with the oil. Cook over medium heat until the onion is translucent, stirring occasionally. Add the sausage, pork, and salt pork. Continue cooking until the meats brown, adding a little water now and then so that the meat will cook. When the beans are tender, add the meats to the bean pot.

Remove two cups of broth from the beans and place in another pot. Add the tomatoes, carrots, turnip greens, piripiri, bay leaves, and salt and pepper to taste. Cook the vegetables over low heat until tender, stirring occasionally. Add the vegetables to the bean pot, mix well and let simmer for another 30 minutes. Serve with white rice.

Collard Greens with Peanut Sauce

Matapa Saborosa
4 side-dish servings

t his is a very popular Mozambican dish. It was prepared for me by Mrs. Nally Honwana on my first trip to Mozambique in 1971. This is her recipe. This dish goes well with a pork loin and white rice.

1 pound small raw shrimp, shelled and deveined (reserve shells)
2 pounds collard greens
6 cloves garlic
2 cans (14-ounces each) unsweetened coconut milk
1 pound raw unsalted peanuts
1 teaspoon salt
4 large red chili peppers, seeded and minced

p lace the shrimp shells in a pot of cold water and bring to a boil. Boil for 5 minutes; strain the liquid and save.

Wash the collard greens; remove the tough stems and cut the leaves into small pieces. Process the greens and garlic cloves in a food processor or grind in a meat grinder until puréed. In a saucepan, mix the collards, 2 cups of the shrimp water, and 1 can of the coconut milk and cook over medium heat for 30 minutes.

Grind the peanuts in a meat grinder or food processor until they resemble powder. Place the peanut powder in a saucepan with 2 cups of water and the remaining 1 can of coconut milk over medium heat. When it begins to boil, pour the mixture over the greens. Add the salt, red chili peppers, and shrimp; stir, reduce the heat, and simmer for 1 hour. Serve over rice.

Rice with Split Peas

Mucapata
4 to 6 side-dish servings

his dish is an enticing combination of rice, green split peas, and coconut milk from the Zambesia region in central Mozambique, and is prepared there in a clay pot. It is usually served with Grilled Chicken, African-Style (page 309), or Baked Fish with Dried Mango Slices (page 304).

1 cup dried split peas,
    washed and sorted
2 cups uncooked white rice
1 teaspoon salt
3 cups unsweetened
    coconut milk

Refrigerate the peas overnight in cold water to cover.

The following day, rinse the peas and place them in a pot with 3 cups of cold water. Bring to a boil, reduce the heat to simmer, and cook for 20 minutes.

Add the rice, salt, and coconut milk to the peas. Bring to a boil, cover, and simmer for 25 minutes more or until the peas are tender and the sauce is thickened. Serve warm.

Rice with Papaya

Arroz de Papaia

2 to 3 side-dish servings

rice, papaya, and coconut milk might seem like an odd combination but this mixture is a delicious one.

2 cups unsweetened
  coconut milk
1 cup uncooked white rice
½ teaspoon salt
½ teaspoon ground
  cinnamon
1 ripe papaya peeled,
  seeded, and diced
  (about 1 cup)

place the coconut milk, rice, ¼ cup of water, salt, and cinnamon in a medium pot and bring to a boil. Cover, reduce the heat, and cook for 20 minutes. Fluff the rice with a fork and let stand for 10 minutes to absorb the remaining liquid.

Mash half the papaya and mix it and the remaining papaya cubes with the rice. Serve hot with roast pork or grilled chicken.

Brown Rice with Peanut Butter and Bananas

Arroz Integral com Manteiga de Amendoim e Bananas
6 to 8 side-dish servings

t his dish goes well with grilled chicken, pork, or beef.

2 cups uncooked brown rice
2 cups tomato juice
2 medium onions, sliced
2 medium green bell
   peppers, seeded and
   sliced
½ cup peanut oil
1 tablespoon curry powder
1 teaspoon salt
¼ teaspoon black pepper
3 medium tomatoes,
   chopped
½ cup smooth peanut butter
2 medium ripe bananas

pour the brown rice, tomato juice, and 2 cups of water into a 2-quart pot over high heat. When the mixture comes to a boil, cover, reduce the heat and simmer until the rice is tender, 45 to 50 minutes.

Meanwhile, sauté the onions and bell peppers in ¼ cup of the peanut oil until the onions are soft. Add the curry powder, salt, and pepper; mix well and heat for 1 minute. Add ¼ cup of water, the tomatoes, and peanut butter. Simmer for 5 minutes, until the sauce thickens.

In a large skillet, heat the remaining ¼ cup peanut oil. Peel the bananas and cut them into ½-inch slices. Place the bananas in the peanut oil and sauté until lightly golden on both sides.

To serve, place the rice on a serving platter, pour the peanut sauce over the rice and top with the fried bananas.

Green Rice

Arroz Verde
4 to 6 side-dish servings

this is a common way to prepare rice in Mozambique. Cilantro and green bell peppers give the rice its beautiful green color. Serve this dish with grilled chicken or pork.

2 tablespoons olive oil
2 cups uncooked white rice
1 large onion, minced
1 medium green bell
   pepper, finely chopped
½ cup chopped fresh
   cilantro
3 cloves garlic, minced
1 teaspoon salt
¼ teaspoon black pepper
4 cups chicken broth

heat the olive oil in a deep skillet and sauté the rice for 5 minutes stirring continuously.

Add the onion, bell pepper, cilantro, garlic, salt, and pepper. Mix well and continue stirring until the onions are translucent.

Add the chicken broth, stir, bring to a boil, cover, and simmer for 25 minutes, until the rice is tender.

Fried Okra with Shrimp

Quiabos Fritos com Camarão
4 to 6 side-dish servings

O kra is a common ingredient in many dishes in Mozambique. This one, because of the addition of shrimp, can be a complete meal.

2 pounds okra, trimmed
1 teaspoon salt
3 tablespoons vegetable oil
4 medium tomatoes, peeled,
    seeded, and minced
1 large onion, minced
Piripiri to taste (page 141)
2 pounds small cooked
    shrimp, peeled

C ut the okra in half, and season with the salt. Heat 1 tablespoon of the oil in a deep skillet and fry the okra until golden.

In another skillet heat the remaining 2 tablespoons oil and sauté the tomatoes and onions. When the vegetables are tender, add the okra and piripiri. Add ¾ cup of water, bring to a boil, and let simmer for 5 minutes.

Add the cooked shrimp and continue to simmer until the mixture thickens. Serve over white rice.

Baked Fish with Dried Mango Slices

Peixe Assado com Manga Seca
4 servings

his recipe can be prepared with either fresh or dried fish. Although the dish has long been a part of traditional Mozambican cuisine, the mango was introduced to Africa from India by the Portuguese. Dried mango slices can be found in many health food stores and some supermarkets. Serve with white rice, black beans, collard greens, or Rice with Split Peas (page 299).

2 pounds fresh or dried
  fish fillets
3 large tomatoes, peeled
  and chopped
2 large onions, chopped
6 ounces dried mango
  slices
2 teaspoons red pepper
  flakes
1 teaspoon salt

reheat the oven to 350 degrees F.

Butter a 2-quart casserole and layer the fish fillets on the bottom. Top with the chopped tomatoes, onions, mango, red peppers flakes, and salt. Add ½ cup water, cover, and bake for 30 minutes, or until the fish flakes.

Shrimp and Eggplant Bake

Beringela com Camarão

8 to 10 servings

blandina Barbosa, a dear friend from Maputo, prepared this dish for my husband and me at a party in our honor. Her mother used to make it for her when she was a little girl and now she prepares it for her friends. The shrimp and eggplant are a nice combination that is enhanced by the coconut milk. There is a similar dish in Brazil, but it calls for croutons, grated cheese, and broth instead of coconut milk.

2 medium eggplants (about 2 pounds)
2 teaspoons salt
2 tablespoons all-purpose flour, plus additional for dusting
Vegetable oil for frying
1 tablespoon olive oil
8 medium tomatoes, peeled and chopped
1 large onion, minced
8 cloves garlic, chopped
1 tablespoon red pepper flakes
2 cups unsweetened coconut milk
3 pounds medium raw shrimp, peeled and deveined

peel and slice the eggplant into ½-inch slices. Soak them in water to cover with 1 teaspoon of the salt for 20 minutes. Remove the eggplant and wipe dry. Dust the eggplant with flour and fry in hot vegetable oil until golden. Drain on paper towels.

Heat the olive oil in a large skillet. Add the tomatoes, onion, garlic, 1 remaining teaspoon salt, and pepper flakes. Simmer until the vegetables are soft. Add the coconut milk, reserving 2 tablespoons, and simmer another 2 minutes. Mix 2 tablespoons of flour with the reserved 2 tablespoons coconut milk and add to the skillet. Add the shrimp and simmer an additional 15 minutes, until thickened.

Preheat the oven to 350 degrees F. In a 2-quart buttered baking dish, place a thin layer of the sauce without the shrimp, then a layer of eggplant. Top this with a thin layer of shrimp with sauce and then a layer of eggplant. Continue layering the shrimp with the sauce and the eggplant, ending with the eggplant and some sauce without shrimp. Bake for 30 minutes. Serve hot.

Shrimp Laurentina

Camarão à Laurentina

8 to 10 servings

i tasted this dish in 1971 on my first trip to Mozambique. In Lorenço Marques, the capital of colonial Mozambique, we had dinner in the Tropical Hotel and were served this wonderful dish. In 1978, in Maputo—the newly named capital of independent Mozambique—my close friend Suzette Honwana prepared this for me and it was as good, if not better, than the dish I tasted on my visit to Lorenço Marques. This is Suzette's recipe. I have substituted canned coconut milk for the milk made from fresh coconuts. It saves a lot of time and work and tastes just as good.

3 tablespoons olive or vegetable oil

4 pounds medium raw shrimp, peeled and deveined

4 large tomatoes, peeled, seeded, and chopped

2 large onions, chopped

4 cloves garlic, minced

1 tablespoon ground coriander

1 teaspoon paprika

1 teaspoon saffron

1 teaspoon ground cumin

1 teaspoon salt

4 cups unsweetened coconut milk

1 tablespoon fine cornmeal (if needed)

½ cup chopped fresh cilantro leaves

h eat the olive oil in a large skillet and sauté the shrimp until just pink. Remove the shrimp and set aside.

Add the tomatoes and onions to the skillet and sauté for 1 minute. Add the garlic, coriander, paprika, saffron, cumin, and salt. Stir to mix in the spices. Pour the coconut milk over all, stir, reduce the heat, and simmer for 1 hour. If the sauce is too thin at the end of the cooking time, stir in the fine cornmeal and mix well.

Add the shrimp, mix well and heat through. Sprinkle with cilantro. Serve with white rice.

Shrimp and Carrot Pudding

Pudim de Camarão com Cenouras

4 servings

*t*his shrimp pudding with carrots, topped with a curry sauce, makes a delicious light lunch or supper.

1½ pounds carrots, peeled and cut into 1-inch pieces
1 pound medium raw shrimp, peeled and deveined
4 eggs, separated
¾ cup milk
1 tablespoon flour
1 tablespoon butter, melted
Salt and pepper to taste
Shrimp Curry Sauce (page 314)

Preheat the oven to 350 degrees F. Cook the carrots in water to cover until tender. Drain and set aside.

Place the shrimp in boiling water. When the water returns to a boil, remove from the heat, drain the shrimp, save four for decoration, and add the rest to the carrots. Finely grind the carrots and shrimp in a meat grinder or food processor.

Add the egg yolks, one at a time, to the carrot mixture along with the milk, flour, butter, salt, and pepper. Beat the egg whites into stiff peaks and fold into the mixture. Pour into a buttered 2-quart mold.

Place the mold in a larger pan filled with 1 inch of hot water and bake for 30 minutes. Remove the mold from the hot water, place on a rack in the oven, and continue cooking for 20 minutes, or until a toothpick inserted in the center comes out clean. Cool for 15 minutes. Turn the pudding out onto a serving platter. Cover with the curry sauce and decorate with the reserved shrimp.

Seafood Stew

Feijoada de Mariscos
8 servings

*t*oday *this typically Mozambican stew is featured on the menu at various restaurants throughout Portugal. In Lisbon, for example, at the Restaurant Berlenga, this* feijoada de mariscos *is one of the most popular dishes on the menu.*

8 ounces dried Great Northern or cannellini beans, washed and sorted
3 slices bacon, diced
8 ounces smoked pork sausage (*lingüiça*), sliced into 1-inch pieces
1 pound small raw shrimp
2 pounds crab legs
1 pound cockles
3 tablespoons olive oil
1 tablespoon butter
1 onion, chopped
2 cloves garlic, minced
2 teaspoons red pepper flakes
2 tablespoons tomato sauce
1 cup chopped fresh parsley
3 bay leaves
1 cup chopped fresh cilantro leaves
Salt to taste

*r*efrigerate beans overnight in cold water to cover. Drain the beans, put in a pot, cover with fresh cold water, and add the bacon and smoked sausage. Cook until almost tender, about 1 hour. Drain.

Heat 6 cups of water to boiling in a large pot. Add the shrimp and cook until just pink. Remove the shrimp from the water, cool, and remove the shells and the veins. Set 2 of the shrimp aside. Cook the crab legs in the same water until pink. When done, drain, and remove the meat, reserving 2 whole claws. Cook the cockles in the same water until they open. When done, shell and set aside the meat, reserving 4 whole. Save the water in which all the seafood has been cooked.

In a large pan, heat 1 tablespoon of the olive oil, the butter, onion, garlic, and peppers flakes, stirring constantly until it begins to turn golden. Add the tomato sauce, parsley, bay leaves, and 1 cup reserved water from the seafood. Let cook for 3 minutes, add the beans, and continue cooking for 5 more minutes.

Add the shrimp, crab, and cockles and more water if needed. Simmer until heated through. Taste for salt and pepper flakes and add more if necessary. Mix the cilantro with the remaining 2 tablespoons olive oil and add to the stew. Serve with white rice.

Grilled Chicken, African-Style

Frango à Cafreal
2 to 4 servings

there are several versions of this dish in Mozambique, as well as in other parts of the Portuguese-speaking world, including Macao, to which it has been exported. In August 1971, João Honwana took my husband and me to a small restaurant in a suburb of Lorenço Marques (today Maputo), where we savored Frango à Cafreal *for the first time.*

1 chicken (3 to 4 pounds)
4 cloves garlic, minced
1 teaspoon salt
1 teaspoon red pepper
    flakes, African cayenne,
    or ground red pepper
3 tablespoons lemon juice
2 tablespoons olive oil

Wash the chicken well and pat dry. Place the chicken on its back and slit it lengthwise down the breast bone so that it lies flat.

Mash the garlic, salt, and pepper flakes with a mortar and a pestle or in a food processor until it forms a paste. Add the lemon juice and mix well. Rub the chicken on both sides with the mixture and refrigerate for 3 hours.

Heat the charcoal in a grill until it turns white, or preheat a gas grill to high. Arrange the chicken over the coals on a lightly oiled grill. Grill the chicken 10 to 12 minutes on each side, turning as necessary, until nicely browned and cooked through. Brush the remaining seasoning mixture over the chicken several times while grilling. Serve with rice cooked in coconut milk, French fries, and piripiri sauce (page 141).

NOTE: In Maputo, the capital of Mozambique, they use a basting sauce made with ½ cup (1 stick) butter, 2 tablespoons lemon juice, and 3 red peppers crushed in a mortar with 1 teaspoon salt. Baste the chicken with this mixture until it is done. Serve with piripiri sauce on the side.

Chicken Curry, Mozambican-Style

Caril de Galinha à Moçambicana

4 servings

*t*his dish is one of a number of examples of the influence Indian food has had on Mozambican cuisine. The spices used in curries were brought to Mozambique from Asia in the sixteenth century by the Portuguese and have been a part of their cuisine ever since. Maria Craverinha, wife of Mozambique's poet laureate, shared this recipe with me in 1978 after I had enjoyed the dish at her home. Although this recipe can be made with fish, seafood, and all types of meat, chicken curry is the most popular kind.

CHICKEN:

½ cup olive oil
1 large onion, chopped
2 cloves garlic, chopped
½ cup chopped fresh parsley
1 whole chicken (3 to 4 pounds), cut into 8 serving pieces, or 8 bone-in thighs

CURRY SAUCE:

½ cup olive oil
2 cloves garlic, minced
1 large onion, minced
2 medium tomatoes, peeled, seeded, and chopped
1 tablespoon curry powder
1 teaspoon salt
1 tablespoon flour
1 teaspoon red pepper flakes
2 cups unsweetened coconut milk

FOR THE CHICKEN: Heat the oil in a large skillet and sauté the onion, garlic, and parsley, stirring until the onion becomes transparent. Add the chicken pieces; cover with water and cook over medium heat until the chicken is cooked through. Set aside. (See note.)

FOR THE SAUCE: In another large skillet, heat the olive oil over medium heat; add the garlic and onion. When the onion becomes lightly golden, remove it from the skillet and purée in a food processor. Return the purée to the skillet and add the tomatoes, curry powder, and salt. Stir well. Mix the flour with 2 tablespoons of water and add to the skillet along with the pepper flakes; mix well. Cook over low heat for 1 hour, adding ½ cup of coconut milk every 15 minutes. Add the chicken pieces, cover, and cook another 10 to 15 minutes, until the sauce thickens. Serve with white rice.

NOTE: After cooking the chicken you can remove the skin and bones and cut into large pieces before adding to the curry sauce.

Chicken with Peanut Sauce

Caril de Amendoim e Galinha
4 to 6 servings

Suzette Honwana, *wife of the Mozambican writer Luis Bernado Honwana, prepared this dish for me in 1978. It is one of her favorite ways to prepare chicken. The word* caril *in this recipe means "sauce," not curry, even though the latter is the literal translation of that Portuguese word. This sauce can also be made with fish, shrimp, crab, or beef. If beef is used, cut it into cubes and cook it in lightly salted water before adding to the sauce. Serve with white rice and Manioc Purée (page 69).*

4 cups roasted unsalted peanuts (no skins)
1 chicken (4 pounds) cut into 8 serving pieces, or eight bone-in thighs
6 medium tomatoes, chopped
2 medium onions, chopped
1 teaspoon salt
Chopped piripiri peppers, or red pepper flakes, to taste

Place the peanuts and 2 cups of water in a blender or food processor and pulse to a paste. Transfer the paste to a large bowl and add 2 quarts of water. Mix well and then strain. If the resulting mixture is thick, add more water until it is the consistency of milk.

In a large skillet, place the chicken pieces, tomatoes, onions, and salt. Place over medium heat and simmer for 5 minutes. Add the peanut liquid and bring to a boil. Reduce the heat and simmer for 1 hour, until the chicken is tender. If the sauce becomes too thick add a little water.

Add the chopped piripiri during the last 5 minutes of cooking; this will ensure that the sauce is not too spicy. If you like the sauce spicy, add the piripiri along with the onions and tomatoes. The longer the hot peppers cook, the spicier the sauce.

Mozambican Grilled Meats

Churrasco Moçambicano
4 servings

in Mozambique, churrasco *was originally prepared in the forest, and the grilled meat was almost always game that had been killed that day. If you do not have access to fresh game, a pork roast, cut into cubes, is a fine substitute. Serve with a green salad and French fries.*

3 pounds boneless wild boar, buffalo, deer, or pork roast, cut into 1-inch cubes
Bamboo skewers, soaked in water for 30 minutes
1 pound smoked beef sausage, cut into 1-inch slices
2 cloves garlic
1 teaspoon salt
¼ teaspoon black pepper
1 teaspoon ground red pepper
2 tablespoons olive oil

heat the charcoal in a grill until it turns white, or preheat a gas grill to high.

Thread the meat onto bamboo skewers, alternating with slices of sausage.

Crush the garlic and salt in a mortar. Add the pepper and cayenne. Season the meat with the garlic mixture and brush with olive oil.

Place the skewers over hot coals and grill until the meat is tender, turning frequently, about 10 minutes.

Mozambican Hot Sauce

Molho de Piripiri
Makes 1 cup

U se this sauce to enhance fish, shellfish, meat, and vegetables. It can be stored in the refrigerator for up to two months.

4 whole red chili peppers, stemmed and seeded
6 tablespoons lemon juice
5 cloves garlic
1 teaspoon salt
1 cup olive oil or butter

C ut the peppers into small pieces and place them in a food processor. Add the lemon juice, garlic, and salt. Purée the mixture, then place in a flask or jar and add the olive oil. Mix well.

OTHER USES:

FOR A MARINADE: Combine all the processed ingredients except the oil in a bowl with meat or seafood. Marinate for at least 4 hours.

FOR BASTING: Combine all the processed ingredients and the oil; brush the meat or seafood while grilling. If using to baste chicken, substitute coconut milk for the lemon juice.

FOR A TABLE SAUCE FOR COOKED MEAT OR SEAFOOD: Combine all the processed ingredients in a small pot and heat on low for 5 minutes.

Shrimp Curry Sauce

Molho de Camarão com Caril

Makes 1 cup

U se as a sauce for Shrimp and Carrot Pudding (page 307) or grilled fish. Pour it over the pudding or fish before serving.

Shells from peeled shrimp
2 tablespoons butter
2 tablespoons flour
½ cup hot milk
1 tablespoon curry powder
½ teaspoon salt
⅛ teaspoon black pepper

p lace the shrimp shells in a medium pot and add cold water to barely cover. Bring to a boil and boil for 3 minutes.

Melt the butter in a medium pot. Add the flour and stir to mix well. Cook and stir for 1 minute. Add ½ cup of shrimp liquid, the hot milk, and the curry powder; stir constantly until the mixture thickens. Season the sauce with salt and pepper.

Banana Bread with Cashews

Pão de Banana
10 to 12 servings

b ananas are plentiful in Mozambique, and this bread is just one of the many ways the fruit can be used in recipes. Cashews are also abundant in that African country situated on the shore of the Indian Ocean, and the nutlike seed of the cashew fruit gives this bread its unique flavor.

½ cup (1 stick) butter or margarine, softened
1⅓ cups sugar
3 eggs
1 cup mashed bananas (about 2)
½ teaspoon vanilla extract
2 cups all-purpose flour
2 teaspoons baking powder
¼ teaspoon baking soda
¼ teaspoon salt
3 tablespoons milk
½ cup chopped unsalted cashews

p reheat the oven to 350 degrees F. In a medium bowl, beat the butter until creamy. Add the sugar ⅓ cup at a time, beating after each addition. Add the eggs, one at a time, continuing to beat. Mix in the bananas and vanilla.

In another bowl, sift together the flour, baking powder, baking soda, and salt. Add to the butter mixture a little at a time, alternating with the milk. Fold in the cashews.

Butter and flour a 9-by-5-inch loaf pan. Pour the bread batter into the pan and bake 1 hour, or until a toothpick comes out clean. Cool in pan before unmolding.

Steamed Rice Bread

Sanna

About 12 pieces

S anna *is a bread served on holidays, especially Easter. It is made from rice that is soaked overnight and then ground. A specially designed pewter steamer is used to cook the* sanna. *Any good steamer works well, however. This variety of bread originated in Goa and was brought to Mozambique by the Indo-Portuguese who settled there as early as the seventeenth century. Serve with Pork Vindaloo (page 218) or Goan Beef and Pork Stew (page 220).*

⅓ cup grated fresh coconut
1¼ cups uncooked white rice, soaked overnight in warm water
1 packet (¼ ounce) active dry yeast
1 teaspoon sugar
1 teaspoon salt

g rind the coconut in a coffee grinder or blender until very fine. Place the coconut in a bowl and pour in ¾ cup of hot water. Mix well and set aside until the water cools to lukewarm.

Place the rice in a coffee grinder or blender and grind until it resembles coarse meal. Pour the rice meal into a large bowl and add the ground coconut, yeast, sugar, and salt. Mix well and slowly add 1 cup of warm water. Stir with a wooden spoon until the mixture forms a thick batter. Cover with a towel and set aside in a warm place for about 30 minutes.

Butter twelve 4-inch foil pie tins and pour in the batter to completely cover the bottom to a depth of about ½ inch deep. Let rise for 10 minutes. Place the tins in a steamer and steam for 15 minutes. Turn out onto a dish when cool and serve at room temperature.

African Corn Bread

Broinhas Africanas
Makes 4 to 6 rolls

broinha *is the diminutive of* broa, *the latter being the Portuguese word for peasant bread made with cornmeal. Homemade corn bread is very popular in Portugal and many of the former colonies. Each has its own variation.* Broas *are often served at holiday functions and can be made with cornmeal only or cornmeal and sweet potatoes. The ground peanuts are what makes this recipe for small corn rolls distinctively Mozambican. Serve with soups or stews.*

6 tablespoons ground
   roasted peanuts
6 tablespoons sugar
6 tablespoons finely
   ground cornmeal
1 egg
1 teaspoon ground
   cinnamon

preheat the oven to 350 degrees F.

Place all ingredients in a bowl and mix well. Shape into 2-inch balls, place on a greased cookie sheet, and bake for 15 minutes. Cool on a wire rack.

Heavenly Bacon Cake

Toucinho-do-céu Moçambicano
6 to 8 servings

W
e know that this traditional recipe comes from Portugal, but there is some dispute as to exactly where it originated. Some say it was invented by the nuns of the convent of Odivelas in Tras-os-Montes. Others say the dessert originated in the historic town of Guimarães, near Porto. No matter where it originated, it has traveled to all of the Portuguese-speaking countries and territories around the world and each one has its own version. It also seems that as the name states, an original ingredient was indeed bacon. This is the Mozambican adaptation of the original, using local ingredients.

1 cup unsalted cashews
2 cups sugar
1 cup Papaya Dessert
  (page 320)
Grated peel of ½ lemon
1 tablespoon finely ground
  cornmeal
24 egg yolks
1 egg white, beaten
1 tablespoon butter

P
reheat the oven to 300 degrees F. Toast the cashews in the oven for 10 minutes. Cool and grind; set aside.

Place the sugar in a small pot and cook until it reaches the ribbon stage (230 degrees F, or when you remove a little sugar with a skimmer and it falls in ribbons). Add the cashews, papaya purée, and lemon rind and cook another 5 minutes. Remove from the heat and let cool. Once the mixture is cool, add the cornmeal and egg yolks. Fold in the egg white.

Pour the batter into a buttered 9-inch springform pan and bake for 40 to 45 minutes, or until a toothpick inserted in the center comes out clean. Place the pan on a wire rack to cool. Let stand 5 minutes and then remove the side of the pan. Cool at least 2 hours before slicing.

Cashew Nut Cake

Bolo Polana
10 to 12 servings

polana is the name of an upscale neighborhood in Maputo, Mozambique's capital, and it is also the name of the Grand Hotel in that same city. This cake is yet another example of how the Portuguese have carried their recipes to other lands, where they were often altered with indigenous ingredients. In this case cashews, which are one of Mozambique's principal crops, give this elegant dish its unique taste.

1 pound unsalted raw cashews
1 pound white potatoes, peeled
2 cups sugar
1 cup (2 sticks) butter, softened
1 tablespoon freshly grated lemon peel
9 egg yolks
4 egg whites

Preheat the oven to 350 degrees F. Roast the cashews for 10 minutes, shaking occasionally; cool. Meanwhile, cook the potatoes in water to cover for 20 minutes; or pierce with a fork, wrap in paper towels, and microwave on high for 7 minutes.

Process the cashews in a food processor until they resemble cornmeal. Remove and place in a large bowl. Mash the potatoes or press through a ricer and add to the cashews. Cream the sugar, butter, and grated lemon peel in another bowl until light and fluffy. Mix the butter with the potato and cashew mixture. Add the egg yolks one at a time, mixing after each addition. Beat the whites into stiff peaks and fold them into the batter.

Butter a 9-inch spring-form tube pan and sprinkle with flour. Pour the batter into the pan and bake in the middle of the oven for 1 hour, or until a skewer inserted in the center comes out clean. Cool the cake on a rack for 10 minutes. Remove the sides of the pan, and using 2 large spatulas, remove the cake from the base and place on a rack to cool. Serve at room temperature.

Papaya Dessert

Doce de Papaia
Makes about 4 cups

3 pounds papaya
4½ cups sugar
¼ cup white brandy or
  aguardente

Peel the papaya; slice in half and cut the pulp into cubes. Place the pulp in a medium saucepan and add ½ cup water. Cook the papaya over medium heat until it is soft.

Meanwhile place the sugar in another pot, cover with 1½ cups water and cook over medium heat until it reaches the fine thread stage (230 degrees F on a candy thermometer or when a few drops spooned into cold water immediately form coarse threads).

Add the papaya to the sugar mixture and continue stirring until the mixture reaches the transparent stage (245 to 250 degrees F or when a wooden spoon scraped on the bottom of the pan forms a path along the bottom that can be seen).

Store in bowls or trays and cover with a piece of parchment paper soaked in the brandy.

CUISINE OF
São Tomé and
Príncipe

S ituated in the Guinea Gulf about 125 miles east of the coast of Africa and almost on the equator, are the islands of São Tomé and Príncipe. They are part of an alignment of inactive volcanic islands that also include the two former Spanish islands of Ano Bom and Fernando Pó, currently belonging to Equatorial Guinea. "Discovered" in 1472 by the Portuguese, the islands were not settled until 1485 by the Portuguese, especially Madeirenses and a few other Europeans. These settlers introduced a number of agricultural products, including sugarcane, which would become a crop of special importance. But coffee and cacao, introduced by the Portuguese in 1820, gave an economic importance to the two islands, and the archipelago eventually became the principal producer of cacao in the world. The plantations or *roças*, the name given to the large farms, were worked by slaves from Angola. When slavery was abolished, the Angolans continued to be transported to the islands to work the farms under the system of contract labor, a type of forced work used by the Portuguese in their colonies in Africa. In Mozambique, workers were also recruited to work under this system. Finally, in July 1975, São Tomé and Príncipe—after years of war with their colonizers—gained its independence.

The cuisine of São Tomé and Príncipe is obviously influenced by the people from Portugal, Angola, Mozambique, Guinea-Bissau, and workers from the east coast of Africa who were brought to the islands in servitude. The cuisine also reflects the influence of the spice trade and the fact that the Portuguese were the first carriers of some agricultural products to Africa, Asia, and South America. Many recipes such as *Bolinhos de Sardinha e Mandioca* (Sardine and Manioc Croquettes), *Sopa de Camarão* (Shrimp Soup), and *Sonhos de Banana* (Banana Dreams), reflect the Portuguese influence. Recipes such as *Arroz Crioulo* (Creole Rice) and *Ovos à Moda da Terra* (Home-Style Eggs with Tuna) have a strong Angolan influence. *Calulu* (Fish with Okra) came by way of Angola and Brazil, and *Sooa* (Boiled Fish) is originally from Portugal, but with Angolan spices.

The primary ingredients used by most island cooks are rice, sweet potatoes, and corn. Rice is usually served plain with meat in stews. Sweet potatoes are also cooked simply, cut into pieces or puréed. They were initially fed to slaves because they were familiar with them and they gave substance to their diet. Corn is either ground into powder in a large mortar and pestle or beaten in a blender and used to prepare desserts. Fish make up a large part of the diet of the islands' inhabitants and the favorites are *badejo*, grouper, corvina, and smoked white fish. The seafood consumed includes crab and octopus. Pork and chicken are also very popular, and bananas and mango are the chosen fruits. These vegetables, fruits, meats, fish, and seafood from various parts of the globe have all come together to make up São Tomé and Príncipe's unique cuisine.

Manioc and Sardine Croquettes

Bolinhos de Mandioca
8 to 10 servings

*t**hese tasty croquettes are very popular on Sào Tomé. This recipe was given to me by the mother of Alda Espirito Santo, one of São Tomé's leading poets. I visited with her in 1991 and she shared this recipe with me. In Brazil, these croquettes are made with rice instead of manioc. Manioc meal or flour can be found at most Asian, Latin American, or specialty markets.*

1 tablespoon butter
1 teaspoon salt
1½ cups manioc flour
2 eggs, or ½ cup egg substitute
½ cup grated Parmesan cheese
3 cans (4.3-ounce) skinless and boneless sardines, drained and chopped
Vegetable or canola oil for frying

*b**ring 2½ cups of water to a boil in a medium pot with the butter and salt. Add the manioc flour, stirring with a whisk until the water returns to a boil. Continue cooking for 2 minutes, stirring until the mixture forms a light paste. Remove from the heat and let cool to the touch. Add 1 egg at a time, mixing well after each addition. Add the grated cheese and the sardines. Mix well.

Using 2 tablespoons of dough form it into the shape of a small egg. Continue until all the dough is used. Pour some oil into a deep skillet to the depth of two inches. Heat the oil until a piece of dough sizzles when tested. Fry the croquettes in oil until both sides are golden brown. (You can also shape the dough into small patties and fry on both sides.) Drain on paper towels. Serve hot or at room temperature.

Mushroom Salad

Cogumelos em Salada
2 side-dish servings

*t*his salad is very easy to prepare. It is a great side dish with roast beef, pork, or grilled chicken.

1 pound fresh button
    mushrooms
3 tablespoons lemon juice
1 teaspoon salt
½ cup mayonnaise

Wipe the mushrooms clean.

Heat 1 quart of water to boiling with half of the lemon juice and the salt. Add the mushrooms and return the water to boiling. When the water begins to boil, remove the pot from the heat, drain the mushrooms, and place them in a bowl.

Add the rest of the lemon juice to the mushrooms and then the mayonnaise. Mix well and serve.

Shrimp Soup

Sopa de Camarão
2 servings

t *he waters around São Tomé and Príncipe abound with fish and seafood, and shrimp is the most sought after.*

8 ounces medium raw
  shrimp with heads,
  peeled and deveined,
  heads and shells
  reserved
1 tomato, peeled, seeded,
  and chopped
3 carrots, chopped
1 teaspoon salt
¼ cup white wine
2 cups toasted bread cubes

h eat 1 quart of water and boil the shrimp shells and heads for 5 minutes. Strain and save the shrimp broth.

Heat another quart of water and cook the shrimp until they turn pink. Drain and set aside.

To the reserved shrimp broth, add the tomatoes and carrots. Simmer over medium heat for 10 minutes, or until the carrots are tender. Cool the vegetables and purée with the broth in a blender. Return the purée to a pot and add the shrimp, salt, and white wine. Mix well. Serve in a soup terrine over toasted bread cubes.

Sweet Potato Soufflé

Soufflé de Batata Doce
4 side-dish servings

he Portuguese carried sweet potatoes from South America to other parts of the world, including Africa and Asia. In São Tomé and Príncipe, this new crop was first introduced as a staple of the plantation workers' diet because of its versatility and very appealing taste, but it soon became a favorite among people of all social strata. This recipe for sweet potato soufflé was given to me by the mother of Alda Espirito Santo, São Tomé's premier poet. It is served as a side dish with beef, pork, or poultry.

2 pounds sweet potatoes
2 eggs, separated
1 teaspoon salt
¼ teaspoon black pepper
1 tablespoon sugar

preheat the oven to 350 degrees F.

Place the sweet potatoes in water to cover and cook for about 20 minutes, or until tender. Remove the sweet potatoes from the water and let cool. Peel and place in a large bowl.

Mash the sweet potatoes with a potato masher or fork and add the egg yolks; mix well. Add the salt, pepper, and sugar. Beat the egg whites into stiff peaks and fold into the potato mixture.

Butter an 8-inch ovenproof casserole and pour in the sweet potato mixture. Bake for 25 to 30 minutes or until a toothpick comes out clean. Cool the soufflé to room temperature and serve with roasted meats or poultry.

Fried Papaya

Mamão Frito
4 side-dish servings

admittedly this appears to be an unusual way to prepare papaya. But try it! You might like it! It's absolutely divine with any roasted meat and a simple salad.

2 medium green papayas
1 large egg, beaten
3 tablespoons dry bread
   crumbs
Vegetable oil for frying

peel the papaya and cut into halves. Remove all the seeds and cut lengthwise into 1-inch slices. Dip the slices into the beaten egg and then in the bread crumbs.

Pour the oil into a deep skillet to a depth of two inches. Heat the oil over medium-high heat to 365 degrees F on a deep-frying thermometer. Fry the papaya slices in the hot oil until golden on all sides. Drain on paper towels.

Banana Purée

Angu de Banana
6 to 8 side-dish servings

in São Tomé this dish is usually served as a side dish for Fish with Okra (page 333).

10 medium ripe bananas

place the unpeeled bananas in a large pot. Cover the bananas with water and bring to a boil. Cook for 15 minutes, or until they are soft. Remove the bananas from the water and cool. Peel the bananas and mash them into a purée with a fork.

Creole Rice

Arroz Crioulo
6 to 8 servings

When I visited São Tomé in 1991, I enjoyed this dish at the Hotel Mira Mar. Later I was fortunate enough to meet Alda Espirito Santo, one of the islands greatest poets. Her mother was an excellent cook and when I mentioned the wonderful rice dish I had eaten at the hotel, Alda offered me her mother's recipe. This dish is easy to prepare and a great way to use up leftover fish, poultry, beef, and other meats.

1 teaspoon salt
2 cups uncooked white rice
2 onions, chopped
3 carrots, peeled and
    chopped
1 tablespoon butter
½ cup fish broth (see note)
8 ounces cooked and
    flaked fish, chicken,
    beef, or pork (see note)

Place the salt in 3 quarts of water and bring to a boil. Add the rice, onions, and carrots. Cover and cook for 17 minutes. Drain the rice and vegetables and place in a bowl. Add the butter, mix well, and let cool. Refrigerate.

When ready to serve, heat the fish broth in a large saucepan, and then add the rice mixture and the flaked fish. Mix well and cook over low heat until all the liquid has evaporated. Serve hot.

NOTE: If you are serving the rice with poultry, add ½ cup tomato sauce to the mixture as you reheat it and 1 cup leftover shredded chicken or turkey.

If you are serving the rice with beef or pork, add ½ cup beef broth to the rice and 1 cup cut-up leftover beef or pork.

Beans, São Tomé-Style

Feijão à Moda da Terra
4 servings

beans play a large part in the diet of the São Tomense. This is a recipe that is savored throughout the country. It could be considered São Tomé's feijoada and it calls for fish instead of pork and beef. Begin the recipe a day in advance of serving as the beans must soak overnight.

2 cups (1 pound) dried
    kidney beans, washed
    and sorted
¾ cup palm oil
1 large onion, chopped
2 cloves garlic
2 tablespoons tomato sauce
1 bay leaf
1 malagueta pepper,
    minced
1-inch piece fresh ginger,
    peeled and grated
Salt and pepper to taste
12 ounces grouper fillet,
    flaked
1 can (6-ounce) water-
    packed tuna
1 pound fresh spinach,
    washed

refrigerate the beans overnight in cold water to cover. The following day, drain the beans and rinse well. Place the beans in a pot with fresh water to cover, bring to a boil, cover, and reduce the heat to a simmer. Cook the beans for 1½ hours or until tender.

Meanwhile, in a large pot, place the palm oil, onion, garlic, tomato sauce, bay leaf, malagueta pepper, ginger, and salt and pepper to taste. Sauté until the onion is soft.

Add the grouper and tuna fish and simmer for 2 minutes. Add the beans with their water and the spinach and simmer. When the fish is cooked, serve with rice or manioc flour, which should be mixed with the juice from the dish in your plate.

Banana Omelet

Omeleta de Banana

2 servings

banana omelets are great for breakfast, or serve them accompanied by salads for a light lunch or supper.

5 medium green bananas
1 tablespoon butter or olive oil
6 large eggs, or 1½ cups egg substitute
2 tablespoons flour

peel the bananas and cut them into ½-inch slices.

Heat the butter in a medium nonstick skillet over medium heat. Add the bananas and sauté until lightly golden on both sides.

Beat the eggs with the flour to form a slightly thick paste. Lower the heat and pour the eggs over the bananas. Cover the pan and cook for 2 minutes, or until the bottom of the omelet is golden and the top is set.

Invert the omelet onto a plate and slide it back into the pan to cook the other side. When the underside is golden, remove from the pan onto a platter, cut it into wedges and serve hot.

Sweet Potato Omelet

Omeleta com Batata Doce
2 to 4 servings

*t*his might seem like an unusual combination, but I'm sure that you will agree it is very tasty. Serve it for breakfast, or as a light lunch with a salad.

2 medium sweet potatoes, peeled and grated
6 eggs
½ cup whole milk
1 clove garlic, minced
1 teaspoon salt
2 tablespoons olive oil or butter

*p*lace the grated sweet potatoes in a large bowl. Beat the eggs with the milk until frothy. Add the egg mixture to the grated sweet potatoes. Season with the garlic and salt and mix well.

Melt the butter in a 10-inch skillet or omelet pan over medium-low heat. When the butter has melted, add the egg mixture, stir, and let cook for 10 minutes, covered, until the mixture has browned lightly on the underside.

Place a 12-inch plate over the pan, invert the omelet onto the dish, and slide it back into the pan. Cook on the underside for 5 minutes more or until golden. Serve hot.

Tuna Frittata

Pastelão de Atum

2 servings

t his dish is yet another example of the Portuguese influence on the local cuisine. On the islands of São Tomé and Príncipe, clever cooks took the pastelão, which is a kind of Portuguese frittata and modified it to local tastes by using tuna, palm oil, and hot sauce. The palm oil and hot sauce are an African influence. To make this dish "heart healthy," use egg substitute instead of eggs and use half olive oil and half palm oil.

6 eggs, or 1½ cups egg substitute
1 can (6-ounce) water-packed tuna, drained and flaked
¼ cup dry bread crumbs
1 teaspoon dried oregano leaves, crushed
½ medium onion, chopped
1 teaspoon salt
1 teaspoon hot sauce
⅓ cup palm oil

b eat the eggs in a large bowl until fluffy. Add the tuna, bread crumbs, oregano, onion, salt, and hot sauce.

Heat the palm oil in a 10-inch nonstick skillet. When the oil is hot but not smoking, add the egg mixture, lower the heat, cover, and let the frittata cook for 3 minutes or until set. Cover with a plate, and invert the frittata onto the plate. Slide it back into the pan and cook for another 2 minutes, until the underside is golden. Cut into quarters and serve with a green salad for lunch.

Fish with Okra

Calulu de Peixe
4 to 6 servings

O n Ash Wednesday, the people of São Tomé celebrate O Dia do Bocado (*literally, the "Day of a Mouthful"*). It is traditional to serve calulu on this day. The government has decreed it to be a half-day holiday, on which the family gathers in the home of the eldest member, usually the grandmother. It is customary to spread a tablecloth on the floor over a straw mat, on which the food is placed. Family members sit around the food. They begin with a prayer, sing religious songs, and then tell stories about the life of Christ. The high point comes when the matriarch accepts the first spoonful of calulu. At this point the banquet begins. This is a symbolic act that gives the holiday its name. In both São Tomé and Angola, chicken pieces are often used instead of fish in this dish.

3 pounds grouper fillets, cut into serving pieces
1 teaspoon salt
3 tablespoons lemon juice
2 large onions, chopped
4 cloves garlic, minced
2 medium eggplants, peeled and cut into ½-inch slices
1 pound collard greens, cut into ¼-inch strips
3 medium tomatoes, peeled, seeded, and chopped
3 malagueta peppers, seeded and chopped
26 okra pods, thinly sliced, or 2 frozen packages (10-ounce) sliced okra
1 bay leaf
1 cup palm oil
¼ cup all-purpose flour
¼ cup fresh whole basil leaves

S eason the fish pieces with salt and lemon juice and set aside for 20 minutes.

In a large skillet combine the onions, garlic, eggplants, collard greens, tomatoes, malagueta peppers, okra, and bay leaf. Pour the palm oil over all; cover and bring to a boil. Stir with a wooden spoon and cook for 5 minutes. Add the fish and enough water to cover the mixture. Reduce the heat to a simmer and continue cooking until the fish flakes, about 20 minutes. Remove the fish to a plate.

Mix the flour into a little cold water and add to the sauce. Stir well and let simmer for 5 minutes to thicken the sauce. Continue stirring to prevent the sauce from sticking, adding more water if necessary. Finally add the basil. Serve the fish with the sauce and vegetables.

VARIATION: After placing the fish fillets on top of the vegetables, add 2 bouillon cubes to the water that covers the mixture. This will make a richer broth.

Boiled Fish, São Tomé-Style

Sooa
4 servings

this recipe, whose name is a word in Forro (the language spoken by the Forro people), seems to be a mixture of a Portuguese dish with African spices. Boiled fish, a typical Portuguese dish, is prepared with tomatoes and onions. The palm oil and the pimenta-malagueta are of African origin. The fish used in this recipe are sea bream or corvina, and the seafood used is shrimp or squid. Serve hot with Creole Rice (page 328).

2 teaspoons salt
1 pound medium raw
  shrimp, peeled
⅓ cup palm oil
2 medium onions, thinly
  sliced
2 tomatoes, peeled, seeded,
  and chopped
1 bay leaf
1 teaspoon dried marjoram
1 teaspoon black pepper
Chopped pimenta–
  malagueta chilis to
  taste
3 small eggplants, peeled
  and thinly sliced
2 pounds corvina or sea
  bream

in a large pot, heat 2 quarts of water with one teaspoon of the salt to boiling. Add the shrimp and cook until the shrimp just turn pink. Remove the shrimp and save the water.

In another pot, heat the palm oil with the onions. When the onions are soft add the tomatoes, bay leaf, marjoram, the remaining teaspoon of salt, pepper, pimenta-malagueta, and eggplants. Stir and simmer for 2 minutes.

Add the fish and enough shrimp water to cook the fish. When the fish is cooked through, add the shrimp. Mix well and simmer another 2 minutes. Serve hot.

Shrimp and Smoked Fish with Collards

Izogó
4 to 6 servings

i zogó *might not be the national dish of São Tomé and Príncipe, but it is enjoyed throughout the country. It is very similar to a dish in Guinea-Bissau called* maafe, *which is made with spinach instead of collards.* Izogó *calls for manioc, which thickens the broth and gives the dish an especially nice texture and exotic taste.*

10 collard green leaves, washed and stemmed
1 teaspoon salt
1 tablespoon olive oil
¼ cup palm oil
2 medium onions, chopped
3 medium tomatoes, peeled and seeded
3 cloves garlic, chopped
1 pound smoked fish, skinned, boned, and shredded
1 bay leaf
3 whole piripiri or chili peppers, seeded and chopped
8 ounces medium raw shrimp, peeled
¼ cup finely ground manioc flour
¼ teaspoon black pepper

Stack the collard green leaves and roll them tightly like a cigar. Cut the leaves into ¼-inch slices. Place the shredded leaves in a pot of boiling water with the salt and olive oil and cook for 5 minutes. Drain the collard greens and set aside.

In a large skillet, heat the palm oil. Add the onions, tomatoes, garlic, smoked fish, bay leaf, piripiri, and shrimp. Stir well and add the collard greens and 2 cups of water or enough to barely cover the mixture. Simmer covered for 30 minutes. Add the manioc flour and pepper and stir to thicken. Serve with white rice or grilled bananas.

Chicken Stew
with Okra

Calulu de Galinha
4 to 5 servings

i n 1992, I sampled calulu, *a traditional dish, at the Hotel Miramar in São Tomé city. The greens used in the recipe,* mussua, *are native to São Tomé but are similar to the Portuguese* couve galega. *When I make this dish at home I often substitute collards, which are closest to the* couve galega *and do not significantly alter the taste of the original dish. Serve with a purée of cooked bananas (page 327).*

½ cup palm oil
10 whole okra, trimmed
   and sliced into ½-inch
   pieces
2 medium onions, thinly
   sliced
1 chicken (about 3 pounds),
   cut into 8 serving pieces
2 medium tomatoes,
   peeled, seeded, and
   chopped
2 small eggplants, peeled
   and cubed
1 pound collard greens,
   thinly sliced
1 teaspoon salt
1 teaspoon black pepper
1 small red chili pepper, or
   1 tablespoon red
   pepper flakes
1 bay leaf
2 tablespoons flour

h eat the palm oil in a large pot. Add the okra and onions and sauté for 3 minutes.

Add the chicken pieces, tomatoes, eggplants, collard greens, salt, pepper, chili pepper, and bay leaf. Add water to cover and bring to a boil. Reduce the heat and simmer for 2 to 3 hours.

Mix the flour with a little of the broth and add to the pot. Let simmer another 15 minutes to let the broth thicken.

Chicken with Plantains

Frango com Banana-pão
4 to 6 servings

b anana-pão *is a fruit that is common to the islands of São Tomé and Príncipe, as well as Guinea-Bissau, Angola, and Brazil, where it is known as* banana da terra. *The closest thing available here is the plantain, which I have used with great results. This recipe combines plantains with chicken for an exotic taste.*

5 tablespoons vegetable oil
1 large chicken (about 4
    pounds), cut into 8
    serving pieces
1 large onion, chopped
3 tomatoes, peeled and
    chopped
2 teaspoons salt
½ teaspoon black pepper
6 green plantains, peeled
½ cup chopped fresh
    parsley

i n a large pot or casserole, heat the vegetable oil. Add the chicken pieces and brown on all sides. Add the onion and tomatoes. Season the chicken with 1 teaspoon of the salt and the pepper. Cook covered, over low heat for 1 hour, occasionally adding 1 tablespoon of cold water to keep the chicken from browning.

Meanwhile, cut each plantain in half lengthwise and cook them in boiling water with the remaining 1 teaspoon salt. After 10 minutes, remove the plantains from the water and add them to the casserole with the chicken. Cook another 10 minutes. Taste for seasonings. Serve the chicken on a large platter surrounded by the plantains and sprinkled with the parsley.

Stewed Chicken

Galinha Refogada
4 servings

This is another popular way to prepare chicken throughout the islands. The basic recipe for stewed chicken is of Portuguese origin and the addition of palm oil and piripiri is the African influence. This dish can also be prepared with beef or pork.

1 whole chicken (about 3 pounds)
1 teaspoon salt
2 medium onions, thinly sliced
1 clove garlic, minced
3 medium, ripe tomatoes, peeled and seeded
1 bay leaf
½ cup palm oil
1 piripiri pepper, seeded and chopped
1 pound spinach, washed
Salt and pepper to taste

Rinse the chicken and place it in a pot with water to cover. Add one teaspoon of salt and bring to a boil. When the water begins to boil, remove the chicken and let it cool. Save the water. Cut the chicken into 8 serving pieces.

In another pot, place the onions, garlic, tomatoes, bay leaf, palm oil, and piripiri. Add the chicken pieces and a little of the reserved water. Layer the spinach leaves over the chicken, cover the pot, and place it over medium heat to cook for 30 minutes, or until the chicken is tender. Add salt and pepper to taste. Serve the chicken in the same pot it cooked in accompanied by cooked bananas.

Meat Loaf, São Tomé-Style

Pão de Carne
4 servings

Pão de carne *is made with leftover meats such as roast beef, pot roast, steak, or a combination of beef and pork. Jan Hartman, former public affairs officer at the U.S. embassy in Luanda, Angola, and in São Tomé, passed this recipe to me. Ms. Hartman's cook, a native of São Tomé, went with her to Angola, where she regularly prepares this treat.*

MEAT LOAF:

1 pound leftover cooked
    meats
½ cup parsley leaves
1 medium onion
2 cloves garlic, chopped
3 slices bread, toasted
2 medium eggs
3 tablespoons butter,
    softened, plus extra for
    topping
½ teaspoon black pepper
½ teaspoon ground nutmeg
1 tablespoon tomato sauce
2 tablespoons powdered milk
1 tablespoon brandy, or ½
    cup white wine

TOMATO SAUCE:

4 large tomatoes
2 cloves garlic, minced
1 tablespoon flour
1 teaspoon salt
¼ teaspoon black pepper
1 tablespoon butter

Preheat the oven to 350 degrees F.

Remove any bones and cut the meats into large cubes. Put the meat through a meat grinder along with the parsley, onion, garlic, and bread. Set aside.

Break the eggs into a large bowl and add the 3 tablespoons butter, pepper, nutmeg, and tomato sauce. Beat well and add to the meat mixture along with the powdered milk. Add a little water until you have a smooth mixture. Add the brandy or white wine.

Butter a 9-by-5-inch loaf pan and ladle in the meat mixture. Butter the top and cover with foil or parchment paper so that it doesn't dry out. Bake for 30 minutes, or until the meat loaf comes away from the sides of the pan. Remove from the oven and invert onto a serving dish.

While the loaf is baking, place the tomatoes in boiling water to loosen skins. Peel, seed, chop, and place them in a blender with the garlic and purée. Place the purée in a pot over medium heat and add the flour, salt, pepper, and butter. Stir and simmer for 3 minutes, until thickened. Serve with the meat loaf.

Orange-Flavored Biscuits

Biscoitos de Laranja
Makes 24 pieces

t hese tasty orange biscuits are very popular on the African islands of São Tomé and Príncipe.

6 egg yolks
3 egg whites
1¾ cups sugar
½ cup (1 stick) butter, melted
1 cup orange juice
1 tablespoon grated orange peel
1¾ cups all-purpose flour

p reheat the oven to 375 degrees F. Beat the egg yolks, egg whites, and sugar together until creamy.

In a separate bowl, mix the butter, orange juice, and grated orange peel. Add in the flour, ½ cup at a time. Combine the flour mixture with the egg mixture. Mix well and press onto a 10-by-15-inch buttered baking sheet. Bake for 15 minutes until golden.

Remove the biscuit from the oven, invert onto a wire rack, and cool. Cut into 2-inch strips and place on a baking sheet. Return to the oven to toast, turning over to brown evenly. These will keep in an airtight container for 1 week.

Sweet Corn

Milho Doce
6 to 8 servings

this dish is traditionally served for the festival of Ash Wednesday during the celebration of O Dia do Bocado *(see* Calulu de Peixe, *page 333).* As explained in the calulu recipe, this meal begins with the oldest member of the family sampling the calulu. This sweet corn is one of the desserts served with the meal.

3 cups fresh corn kernels
1 teaspoon salt
¼ cup grated fresh coconut
1 teaspoon grated lime peel
1 tablespoon butter
Sugar to taste

place the corn in a blender and pulse just to break up the kernels (5 seconds). Place the kernels in a pot with water to cover and the salt and bring to a boil. Cook for 5 minutes, drain, reserving water.

Place the grated coconut and 4 cups of the hot liquid from cooking the corn in a large bowl and mix well. Strain the coconut to result in coconut milk. Add the coconut milk to the reserved corn with the lime peel. Place this mixture in a pot and bring to a boil. Add the butter and the sugar, stirring so that the mixture doesn't stick to the bottom of the pan. Cook until the mixture thickens. Pour the corn mixture into a serving dish and serve immediately.

Banana Dreams

Sonhos de Banana

Makes 12 pieces

*t*his dessert, without the bananas, was taken by the Portuguese to Brazil and later to its colonies in Africa. The banana, a fruit which originated in Asia, was later introduced to São Tomé and added to this recipe. Today the banana is a main crop in the islands.

8 ounces bananas (about 2 medium), peeled
½ cup milk
1 egg, beaten
½ cup all-purpose flour
2 tablespoons sugar
Vegetable oil for frying
¼ cup ground cinnamon
¼ cup sugar

*m*ash the bananas with a fork until they form a purée. Add the milk, beaten egg, flour, and sugar. Incorporate all the ingredients well.

Pour some oil into a deep skillet to a depth of two inches. Heat it over medium-high heat to 365 degrees on a deep-frying thermometer. Fry spoonfuls of the banana mixture in the hot oil until golden. Drain on paper towels. Sprinkle with a mixture of the sugar and cinnamon while still warm. Serve at room temperature.

Pineapple Orangeade

Laranjada de Ananás

Makes 1 quart

*t*his refreshing drink is often served at breakfast, lunch, or with an afternoon snack. Children love the taste.

½ pineapple, peeled and cubed (2 cups)
¼ cup sugar
2 cups orange juice

*p*lace the pineapple in a food processor. Add the sugar and purée. Strain the mixture and press through a sieve to retrieve all the juice. Add the orange juice to the pineapple juice with ¼ cup of water. Mix well and chill. Serve in chilled glasses.

Cocoa Liqueur

Licor de Cacau
Makes about 1 quart

his drink should rest for at least two months before consuming. So plan the preparation of this liqueur far enough in advance to be ready for that special event.

1 quart whole milk
2¼ cups sugar
⅔ cup unsweetened cocoa
powder
2 cups grain alcohol

our the milk and sugar into a large pot and place over medium heat. When the milk is warm, add the cocoa, stir well, reduce the heat, and simmer until the liquid is reduced to 3 cups, about 30 minutes. Cool completely.

Add the alcohol to the cooled milk (see note). Pour the mixture into a clean bottle and cork. Place in a dark cool place for 12 to 15 days. Then strain the liqueur and pour it into a quart wine bottle and cork. Let the liqueur sit for 6 weeks before consuming. This drink is about 98% proof. Serve in liqueur glasses.

NOTE: Grain alcohol is highly flammable. Be sure to keep it away from the heat. The milk mixture should be completely cool before adding the alcohol.

Suggested Menus

HOLIDAY APPETIZER AND DESSERT BUFFET:
Codfish Croquettes – Portugal (page 9)
Creamy Shrimp Turnovers – Angola (page 60)
Chicken Turnovers – Mozambique (page 290)
Manioc and Sardine Croquettes – São Tomé and Príncipe (page 323)
Broccoli Fritters – Goa (page 224)
Pork Balls – Macao (page 247)
Minced Meat Croquettes – Malacca (page 273)
Cream Tartlets – Portugal (page 57)
Chocolate Bonbons – Brazil (page 133)

BRAZILIAN PARTY BUFFET:
Black-Eyed Pea Fritters – *Acarajé* (page 91)
Chicken Pastries – *Empadinhas de Galinha* (page 93)
Heart of Palm Pastries – *Pastéis de Palmito* (page 96)
Collard Greens Minas Gerais-Style – *Couve à Mineira* (page 105)
Brazilian Bean Stew – *Feijoada à Brasileira* (page 102)
Chicken Bahian-Style – *Xinxim de Galinha* (page 120)
Toasted Manioc Meal with Palm Oil – *Farofa de Azeite-de-dendem*
    (page 107)
Hot Pepper and Lemon Sauce – *Molho de Pimenta e Limão* (page 124)
Golden Dessert – *Quindims* (page 129)
Rum Drink – *Caipirinha* (page 136)
Demitasse Coffee – *Cafezinho* (page 136)

ANGOLAN DINNER:
Collard Greens in Peanut Sauce – *Couves Cozidos com Oleo-de-Palma e
    Amendoim* (page 66)
Angolan-Style Chicken – *Muamba de Galinha* (page 75)
Baked Bananas – *Bananas Assadas* (page 84)

MOZAMBICAN DINNER PARTY BUFFET:

Peanut Balls – *Almondegas de Amendoim* (page 289)
Seafood Salad – *Salada de Mariscos* (page 293)
Chicken Curry, Mozambican-Style – *Caril de Galinha à Moçambicana* (page 310)
Collard Greens with Peanut Sauce – *Matapa Saboroso* (page 298)
Green Rice – *Arroz Verde* (page 302)
Grilled Chicken, African-Style – *Frango à Cafreal* (page 309)
Mozambican Hot Sauce – *Molho de Piripiri* (page 313)
Heavenly Bacon Cake – *Toucinho-do-céu Moçambicano* (page 318)
Cashew Nut Cake – *Bolo Polana* (page 319)

MACANESE FAT TEA:

Pork Balls – *Boullettes* (page 247)
Half-Moon Pastries – *Chilicote* (page 248)
Eggs Stuffed with Ground Meat – *Ovos Recheados com Minche* (page 249)
Fish Torte, Macao-Style – *Empada de Peixe* (page 256)
Stuffed Crab – *Caranguejo em Casquinha* (page 257)
Sweet Potato Pudding – *Batatada* (page 267)
Bean Balls Rolled in Sesame Seeds – *Fritos de Sésame e Feijão* (page 268)

CAPE VERDEAN BRUNCH BUFFET:

Pastry with the Devil Inside – *Pastel com o Diabo Dentro* (page 142)
Manioc Tart with Beef Filling – *Empadão de Puré de Mandioca com Carne* (page 144)
Prawns with Hot Sauce – *Gambas com Piripiri* (page 141)
Bean Stew Cape Verdean-Style – *Cachupa Rica* (page 150)
Cape Verdean Corn Bread – *Broa Cabo Verdeana* (page 166)
Honey Cake – *Bolo de Mel* (page 164)

GOAN BUFFET:

Fish Puffs – *Sonhos de Peixe* (page 195)
Broccoli Fritters – *Pakode* (page 197)
Miniature Pork Pies – *Empadinhas de Porco* (page 198)
Goan Rice – *Arroz Pilau* (page 204)
Fish Curry – *Caril de Peixe* (page 210)
Pork Vindaloo – *Vindaloo de Porco* (page 218)
Goan Flat Bread – *Apas* (page 223)
Banana Fritters – *Filhós* (page 224)

Glossary

ACARAJÉ The black-eyed pea fritter that is very popular in Brazil, especially in Salvador, Bahia. In Nigeria, from whence Yoruba slaves brought the recipe, the fritter is called *acará*. The Brazilian term derives from the fact that women hawking the fritters on the streets of Salvador would cry "*Je abará*." *Je* is the Yoruba word for "eat." The batter is made by peeling and grinding the peas and mixing them with ground onions, dried shrimp, and garlic.

ACHAR Vegetables preserved in vinegar and salt. It is of Persian origin and was introduced to Macao by way of India.

AÇORDA Dry soup made with peasant bread. This soup is usually seasoned with olive oil, garlic, cilantro, and eggs. The best-known *açordas* are made with seafood, principally shrimp or codfish. It is very popular in Portugal and Madeira.

AGUARDENTE A brandy that is made from the continuous distillation of wine. It is very popular in Portugal and other Portuguese-speaking countries.

ALENTEJO The large expanse of southern Portugal that stretches from the Atlantic Ocean to the western border of Spain. Much of the architecture and cuisine reflect the region's Moorish heritage.

AMTAN MIREM An essential seasoning in the preparation of many Goan dishes. It consists of malagueta peppers ground with garlic, cumin, tamarind, vinegar, and coriander.

APA A small roll or pastry that originated in India.

ARROZ CARREGADO Rice sautéed in lard and then cooked in water and placed in a mold. It is very popular in Macau.

ARROZ GORDO Stir-fried rice with chicken, beef, and pork; very popular in Macao.

BACALHAU Also known as salt cod, this fish is salted at sea and brought back to the mainland to air dry. The Portuguese took salt cod to Brazil, its African colonies, and to territories in the Far East. It has become a part of each of these local cuisines.

BALCHÃO The *balchão* of Macau is a paste made from ground shrimp with salt, brandy, and chili pepper. The term is Indo-Portuguese and derived from Malaysia.

BATIDA A popular Brazilian drink made with *cachaça* and served over crushed ice with a bit of lime juice.

BOULETTE A type of meatball or croquette made with pork.

BRINGE A dish made with duck that is fried and then stewed.

BUDO A vegetable preserve that usually accompanies the main dish.

CACHAÇA A brandy (i.e., *aguardente*) distilled from sugarcane juice. *Cachaça* is often translated as "white rum" although the latter is distilled from molasses. This very Brazilian liquor is usually served as a brandy or in the cocktails known as *batidas* and *caipirinhas*.

CALDEIRADA A substantial fish or seafood stew that is popular in Portugal and many of the former colonies and territories.

CAMARÃO SECO Fresh-caught shrimp that are skewered and left to dry in the sun. They are ultimately ground and used in Afro-Brazilian dishes.

CANDOMBLÉ A word of African origin from the Angolan Bantu language, Kimbundu, that refers to the Afro-Brazilian religion practiced in Bahia, Brazil.

CANJICA In Angola it is a vegetable dish made with beans and corn; in Brazil it is a dessert made with corn, coconut, sugar, and cinnamon.

CARIL An Indian condiment composed of various spices, mainly saffron. Also known as curry.

CARIOCA A person from the city of Rio de Janeiro. The term also refers to a cup of coffee to which a little hot water has been added.

CARNE SECA Beef that is salted and dried in the sun or air. It is used in many Brazilian dishes such as *feijoada*.

CHABÉU Fruit from the African palm, from which palm oil is extracted.

CHAMUÇA A type of pastry stuffed with chicken, beef, or shrimp that originated in Goa and was taken to Mozambique.

CHILICOTE A type of pastry shaped like a half moon that is stuffed with vegetables and pork.

CHOURIÇO Dried sausages made from pork, paprika, garlic, salt, chili peppers, and red or white wine.

CHURRASCO The Brazilian equivalent of barbecue. It is meat grilled over a charcoal fire and is also popular in Portugal and other Portuguese-speaking countries.

CONSOADA Dinner served on Christmas Eve in Portuguese households.

COZIDO Roughly equivalent to "stew," a dish in which meats and vegetables are covered with water and simmered. The meats and vegetables are removed and the broth is served separately as soup.

CUSCUZ or **COUSCOUS** A dish of Arabian origin that was brought to Portugal and Africa by the Moors. The Africans took the dish to Brazil where it became very popular in the southern part of the country, particularly São Paulo.

DÃO A brand name of wine from the northwest region of Portugal. It is also the name of that region, which is famous for its wines.

DENDEM (also spelled **DENDÊ**) The oil extracted from the fruit of the African palm tree. In Africa the tree is found from the Gambia region to Angola, where it grows to between 45 and 60 feet tall. In Brazil the oil is used in many Afro-Brazilian dishes associated with the Condomblé or Macumba religions.

DIABO A Portuguese word for devil and a typical dish from Macao that is made with ground roasted meats, onions, tomatoes, saffron, mustard, pickles, and port wine.

EMPADA or **EMPADINHAS** A pastry popular in Macao made from thick dough that is stuffed with fish and seasoned with saffron and olives. In Portugal and Brazil, empadas or empadinhas (small pastries) are made with chicken, cheese, shrimp, or beef.

ESCABECHE A vegetable sauce used as a marinade for fish, poultry, and meats. It is made with a mixture of olive oil, onion, garlic, tomatoes, green peppers, and vinegar.

ESPARREGADO A dish made with spinach (*esparrago*) or other greens pounded in a mortar and seasoned with olive oil, garlic, and vinegar.

ESPETADA Skewered chunks of beef, chicken, or pork that are grilled over hot coals.

FARINHA DE MANDIOCA The flour made from the manioc root. It can be toasted to sprinkle over the beans and meats of a *feijoada, moqueça,* or stew.

FAROFA See Mandioca.

FEIJOADA A bean stew popular in most of the Portuguese-speaking countries. Each country has its own version, so ingredients vary somewhat.

FILHÓS Small balls made from flour and eggs and fried in oil. They are then rolled in sugar and cinnamon and are usually served at festive occasions and holidays.

FRANGO À CAFREAL Literally translated means "Chicken Kaffir-Style." Kaffir is a pejorative term for black Africans. Immediately after independence, the tendency was to avoid *cafreal* as a reminder of colonization and to call the dish *Frango à Africana.* Despite the negative connotations, Mozambicans have returned to calling the dish by its original name.

FUBA A type of purée made from manioc flour or corn flour.

GINDUNGO An Angolan word for the hot chili pepper.

GRÃO-DE-BICO A Portuguese word for chickpea or garbanzo bean.

KOKUM A type of prune with a sour taste, found in Macao.

KRILL A very small shrimp with long whiskers found in the Strait of Malacca. It is used for relishes and to make fritters.

LACASSÁ The name of rice flour in Macao. The name also applies to a Macanese soup made with rice flour noodles, shrimp, and chili pepper. It is traditionally served on Christmas Eve.

LINGÜIÇA A type of Portuguese sausage made from pork that is highly seasoned with chili peppers and then smoked.

MACUMBA The name by which the Afro-Brazilian religion is known in Rio de Janeiro.

MALAGUETA A hot pepper used in Brazilian cooking. It is called piripiri in the former African colonies.

MANDIOCA/MANIOC A tuber also called "yucca" or "cassava" in the United States, is consumed in large quantities in Brazil and Angola. In Bahia and Rio it is known as *aipim*. It can be fried, boiled, or mashed, and is often used in stews.

MATANÇA DO PORCO This is literally translated as "The Killing of the Pig," which is an annual gastronomical ritual that began in the Minho province of Portugal and was later taken to the Azore Islands by those early settlers. The pig is slaughtered in December and sausages and the meat are hung to be smoked. The first meat (sausages) is eaten at Carnival. This killing usually supplies the family with enough meat for the year.

MIÚDOS Cow and pig viscera, mainly the liver, gizzard, heart, and kidneys. They are usually cooked and then sautéed with rice or other ingredients.

MOQUECA A word that is probably of Brazilian-Indian origin for a type of stew made with fish or seafood and seasoned with onions, green peppers, tomatoes, palm oil, malagueta peppers, and coconut milk.

PAIO A smoked pork sausage that is similar to Canadian bacon. It is used in Brazilian *feijoada* and other dishes.

PALMITO The heart of the palm tree, used in stews, salads, and as an empada filling throughout Brazil.

PALM OIL A red oil extracted from the fruit of the African palm tree that gives the Afro-Brazilian food a unique flavor and color. Also known as *dendé* or *dendem*.

PARIDA The Portuguese word for a woman who has just given birth. In the Sephardic Jewish community in Old Portugal, the new mother was served *fritas de parida*, a kind of French toast sprinkled with cinnamon and orange-flavored syrup. When the Jews fled the Iberian Peninsula during the Inquisition, they took many of their customs and recipes with them to Brazil, Cape Verde, and Angola.

PASTEL A type of pastry that is stuffed with either a sweet or salty filling.

PASTELINHA Small pastry balls. In Macao they are prepared with ground pork, cheese, slivered almonds, garlic, saffron, and lard and baked. The term also applies to any small pastry with a filling.

PIMENTA-MALAGUETA A small red hot pepper originally grown in Brazil and later transported to Angola, Mozambique, and other parts of Africa.

PIRIPIRI A variety of the *pimenta malagueta* that is native to Asia and Africa.

PORTO A Portuguese sweet wine that is usually served as an after-dinner drink. It is produced in the Douro region in the northwestern part of Portugal.

QUEIJADA A small cake the size of a cupcake that is made with goat cheese, eggs, milk, and sugar.

QUIABO Okra or lady fingers, an essential vegetable in many of the Afro-Brazilian dishes served during the religious festivals of Condomblé. It is also an important ingredient in dishes in other Portuguese-speaking countries such as Guinea-Bissau, Angola, and Mozambique.

RABANADA A slice of bread that has been soaked in milk, wine, or sugar syrup, dipped in egg, fried, and sprinkled with sugar and cinnamon. It is traditionally served at the *consoada* on Christmas Eve. In the past, it was also called *fatia dourada* (golden slice), or *fatia-de-parida* (slice for the mother who has given birth).

REFOGADO A sauté of vegetables, usually onions, tomatoes, and green peppers cooked until the onions are translucent. The sauce is the basis for many dishes.

RISSOL A pastry stuffed with a creamy shrimp sauce that is popular in Portugal and many of the Portuguese-speaking countries.

ROUPA-VELHA A dish made with leftovers, literally means "old clothes." In the Minho region of Portugal it is a favorite lunch dish on Christmas Day, made with leftover bacalhau, collards, and potatoes from the consoada. This mixture is sautéed with a *refogado* (mixture of onions and tomatoes).

SALPICÃO A Portuguese smoked pork tenderloin that has been highly seasoned with wine, red peppers, and other spices.

SARAPATEL A specialty dish that is popular in Brazil, Goa, Timor, and Portugal. It is made from pork tripe and prepared with the blood of the pig. The dish originated in the Alentejo region of Portugal and traveled to Brazil and other former colonies.

SEPHARDIM The descendents of Jews who lived on the Iberian Peninsula before their expulsion in 1497. Sephardic Jews were exiled to or went voluntarily to the four corners of the earth including Brazil, Angola, and Cape Verde. Many of their customs and traditions, including food cultures, merged with those of the Sephardims' new homelands.

SUTATE A soy sauce, very popular in the cuisine of Macao.

TAMARINDO A fruit with a pod that contains several large seeds that are surrounded by a prune-like skin that, when dried, is used in Goan, Malaccan, and Macanese cooking. Many curries and fish dishes require tamarind juice, which is obtained by soaking the pulp in warm water.

TOUCINHO A fresh or salted pork belly that can be used in stews or fried like bacon.

VINDALOO or **VINHO-D'ALHO** A type of marinade made with vinegar or wine, garlic, bay leaf, salt, and pepper. It is used in Portuguese cooking and the ingredients vary from region to region. Vindaloo is a Goan word and vinho-d'alho is Portuguese. The dish is popular in both countries.

XEREM A purée made from cornmeal that is eaten with certain dishes in Cape Verde.

Ingredient Sources

CALIFORNIA
Liborio Markets Brazilian
Products
864 S. Vermont Avenue
Los Angeles, CA 90005
(213) 386-1458

Mo Hotta, Mo Betta
P.O. Box 4136
San Luis Obispo, CA 93403
(800) 462-3220,
Fax (805) 545-8389
www.mohotta.com

ILLINOIS
El Mercado Meat Market
3767 N. Southport Ave.
Chicago, IL 60613
(312) 477-5020

MINNESOTA
El Burrito Mercado
Latin American Foods
175 Cesar Chavez Street
St. Paul, MN 55107
(651) 227-2192
www.elburritomercado.com

El Jalepeño Market
Latin American Foods
1430 E. 66th St.
Richfield, MN 55417
(612) 869-2022

Brazilian Connection
5757 Sanibel Dr.
Minnatonka, MN 55343
(952) 935-2708
brazilianconnectioncompany.com

Groceries of the Orient
7520 Lyndale Ave. S.
Richfield, MN
(612) 861-1023

MISSOURI
La Tropicana Market
5001 Lindenwood Street
St. Louis, MO 63109
(314) 353-7328
www.latropicana.com

NEW JERSEY
Seabra Super Market
260 Lafayette Street
Newark, NJ 07105
(973) 589-8606

NEW YORK
M & M Market and Deli
529 Broome Street
New York, NY 10013
(212) 219-2619

Grand Street Deli and
Mini Market
42 Grand Street
New York, NY 10013
(212) 625-3248

NEW MEXICO
Bueño Foods
2001 4th Street S.W.
Albuquerque, NM 87102
(505) 243-2722
www.buenofoods.com

RHODE ISLAND
Gaipo's Meat Market
1075 South Broadway
East Providence, RI
02914
(401) 438-3545

Carniçaria International
756 Lonsdale Avenue
Central Falls, RI 02863
(401) 728-9000

TENNESSEE
The Global Market
918 Vine Street
Nashville, TN 37203
(615) 242-8593

International Grocery
Store
900 8th Ave. N.
(Farmer's Market)
Nashville, TN 37208
(615) 254-1697

VIRGINIA
European Foods
Import-Export, Inc.
2700 North Pershing Dr.
Arlington, VA 22201
(703) 524-2856,
(703) 524-6800
Fax: (703) 524-6801

Bibliography

Anderson, Jean. *The Food of Portugal*. New York: Morrow, 1986.

Andrade, Margarette de. *Braxilian Cookery, Traditional and Modern*. Rio de Janeiro: A Casa do Livro Eldorado, 1975.

Angel, Gilda. *Sephardic Holiday Cooking*. Mount Vernon, New York: Decalogue Books, 1986.

Angelo, Alda de Carvalho. *Fragmentos do Oriente (Contos, Viagens, Culinária)*. São Paulo: Edition by the author, 1965.

Avila, Deolinda Maria. *Foods of the Azores Islands*. Paulo Alto, California: Moonlith Press, eighth printing, 1990.

Baljekar, Mridula. *A Taste of Goa*. Singapore: Craftprint, 1995.

Barbosa, Veranúbia. *Uma Receita de Saúde*. Bahia, Salvador: Edição do autor, 2001.

Bello, António Maria de Oliveira. *Culinária Portuguesa*. Lisboa: Edição do autor, 1933.

Brandão, Darwin. *A Cozinha Baiana*. Rio de Janeiro: Editora Letrase Artes, 1965.

Brandão, Estela. *Arte e Economia: Culinária*. Porto: Livaria Simões Lopes, 1937.

Cardosa, Zita. *Segredos de Cozinha, Madeira e Porto Santo*. Madeira: Zita Cardosa, 1994.

Carrascalão, Natália. *Vamos Jantar à Timor*. Macau: Tipografia Chan Heng, 1998.

Cascudo, Luis da Câmara. *A Cozinha Africana no Brasil*. Luanda: Impresa Nacional De Angola, 1964.

Chantre, Lourdes Ribeiro de Almeida. *Cozinha de Cabo Verde*. Imprensa Nacional, Empresa Pública de Bissau e Impresso na Imprensa Nacional em Bolama, 1979.

Chantre, Maria de Lourdes. *Cozinha de Cabo Verde*. Lisboa: Editorial Presença, 1989.

Chantre, Maria de Lourdes. *111 Receitas de Cozinha Africana*. Lisboa: Publicações Europa-América, 1981.

Chilcote, Ronald H. *Portuguese Africa*. Englewood Cliffs, New Jersey: Prentice-Hall, Inc., 1967.

Correia, Carlota Mesquita. *Livro de Cozinha Goesa*. Margão, Índia: Tipografia Progresso, 1963.

Costa, Paloma Jorge Amado. *O Livro de Cozinha de Pedro Archanjo*. São Paulo: Editora Maltese, 1994.

Cozinha e Doçaria do Ultramar Português. Lisboa: Agencia-Geral do Ultramar, 1969.

Cozinha Moçambicana. Fundo de Turismo. Lourenço Marques: Empresa Moderna, 1975.

Culinária de Inhamban. Comissão Executiva das Comemorações dos 260 anos da Implantação da Cidade de Inhambane, Maputo: Governo Provincial de Inhambane, 1988.

David, Suzy. *The Sephardic Kosher Kitchen*. Middle Village, New York: Jonathan David Publishers, Inc., 1984.

Emilio, Cecilia Cardoza. *Azorean Folk Customs*. San Diego, California: Portuguese Historical Center, Fifth Edition, 1996.

Fernandes, Caloca. *Viagem Gastronômica através do Brasil*. São Paulo: Editora SENAC, 2000.

Fernandes, Joyce. *Goan Cookbook*. Goa: Bhates Publishing Co., 1990.

Fernandez, Rafi. *Malaysian Cookery*. London: Penguin Books Ltd., 1985

Fraser, Linda. *Comida Indiana*. São Paulo: Editora Manole Ltda., 1997.

Frazão, Márcia. *A Cozinha da Bruxa*. Rio de Janeiro: Bertrand Brasil S.A., 1993.

Goldberg, Betty S. *International Cooking for the Kosher Home*. Middle Village, New York: Jonathan David Publishers, Inc., 1990.

Gomes, Augusto. *Cozinha Tradicional da Ilha de São Miguel*. São Miguel: Região Autónoma dos Açores, 1987.

Goucha, Manuel Luis. *Chefe-Mate!* Lisboa: Publicações Dom Quixote, 1986.

Guedes, Francisco. *Receitas Portuguesas...os pratos típicos de todos as regiões*. Lisboa: Publicações Dom Quixote, 2000.

Guillermoprieto, Alma. *Samba*. New York: Vintage Books, 1990.

Guimarães, Manuel. *Historias de Ler e Comer*. Lisboa: VEGA, 1991.

Hamilton, Cherie Y. *Cuisines of Portuguese Encounters*. New York: Hippocrene Books, Inc., 2001.

Hamilton, Cherie Y. *A Culinary Journey.* New York: Hippocrene Books, Inc., 2005.

Hamilton, Cherie Y. *Os Sabores da Lusofonia: Encontros de Culturas*. Brazil: Senac São Paulo, 2005.

História Geral de Cabo Verde. Lisboa: Instituto de Investigação Cientifica Tropical, 1988.

Houaiss, Antonio. *Minhas Receitas Brasileiras*. São Paulo: Art Editora, 1990.

Hyman, Mavis. *Indian-Jewish Cooking*. London: Hyman, 1992.

Japiassu, Moacir. *Dando de Bom!* São Paulo: Ática S.A., 1995.

Jorge, Graça Pacheco. *A Cozinha de Macau da Casa do Meu Avo*. Macau: Instituto Cultural de Macau, 1992.

Jyrkinen, Anna Riitta et al. *Mathapa*. Hyvinkää, Finlándia e Maputo: Gummerus Kirjapaino Oy, 1992.

Kadunc, Alexandre. *Comida de Santo*. São Paulo: Tríade Editorial, 1989.

Lamas, Jõao António Ferreira Lamas. *A Culinária dos Macaenses*. Lisboa: Fundação Oriente, 1995.

Liebman, Malvina W. *Jewish Cooking from Boston to Baghdad*. Cold Spring, New York: NightinGale Resources, 1989.

Lobo, Helena Gama. *Receitas da Bahia*. São Paulo: Companhia Editora Nacional, 1959.

Lobo, Isabela Margarida. *Petisquera Saboroso di Macau*. Macau: Direcção dos Serviços De Turismo, 1989.

Lora, Irmã Maria Isabel. *Doces Conventuais*. Lisboa: Publicações Dom Quixote, Ltd., 1998.

Maciel, Elise Antonette. *Goan Cookery Book*. Sutton, England: Maslands Ltd., 1983.

Maranhão, Liêdo. *Cozinha de Pobre*. Recife: Edições Bagaço, 1992.

Marbeck, Celine J. *Cuzinhia Cristang*, A Malacca-Portuguese Cookbook. Malaysia: Tropical Press SDN. BHD., 1998.

Marks, Gil. *The World of Jewish Cooking*. New York: First Fireside Edition, Simon and Schuster, Inc., 1999.

Mazzei, Celia e Celma. *A Cozinha Caipira de Celia & Celma*. Rio de Janeiro: Nova Fronteira, 1994.

A Cozinha em São Tomé e Príncipe. Ministério da Saúde. Cruz Vermelha: 1981.

Netto, Joaquim da Costa Pinto. *Caderno de Comidas Baianas*. Rio de Janeiro: Tempo Brasileiro; Salvador: Fundação Cultural do Estado da Bahia, 1986.

Nogueira, Ilda Farinha. *Alimentação*. Lourenço Marques: Serviço Extra-Escolar, 1966.

Paixão, Nica. *A Taste of Portugal*. Lisbon: Marques Augusto Editora, 2003.

Querino, Manuel. *A Arte Culinaria na Bahia*. Salvador, Bahia: Livraria Progresso Editora, 1951. (Primeira edição, 1928).

Radke, Linda Foster. *Kosher Kettle*. Chandler, Arizona: Five Star Publications, 1996.

Ribas, Oscar. *Alimentação Regional Angolana*. Angola: Centro de Informação e Turismo de Angola, 1971.

Roden, Claudia. *The Book of Jewish Food*. New York: Alfred Knopf, Inc., 1996.

Rowan, Marielle. *Hoje Temos...Receitas de Moçambique*. Maputo: Edição do autor, 1996.

Santos, Aldaci Dada dos. *Tempero da Dada*. Salvador, Bahia: Editora Corrupio, 1998.

Santos, Ana de Sousa. *A Alimentação do Muxiluanda*. Luanda: Cooperação Portuguesa, Embaixada de Portugal, 1996.

Santos, Yara dos. *Cabo Verde—Tradição e Sabores*. Lisboa: Produções Editorials, Lda., 2003.

Sarvis, Shirley. *A Taste of Portugal*. New York: Charles Scribner's Sons, 1967.

As Nossas Receitas. Secretariado Nacional da OMM. Maputo: Edição do Instituto Nacional de Livro e do Disco, 1981.

Receitas à Moda Antiga. Selecções do Reader's Digest. Lisboa: 1997.

Senna, Maria Celestina de Mello e. *Cozinha de Macau*. Lisboa: VEGA, 1998.

Somma, Iolanda. *Pratos Típicos, regionais do Brasil*. Rio de Janeiro: Ediouro, 1979.

Tesouros da Cozinha Tradicional Portuguesa. Edição de Selecções do Reader's Digest. Lisbon: 1984.

Vieira, Edite. *The Taste of Portugal*. London: Grub Street, 1995.

Recipes by Country

CAPE VERDE

CABO VERDE

MACAO

MACAU

PORTUGAL

PORTUGAL

SÃO TOMÉ AND PRÍNCIPE

SÃO TOMÉ E PRÍNCIPE

Índice de Receitas em Portuguese

English Recipe Index

East Timor Bean Stew (East Timor), 178

Eggs with Navy Beans and Beef (Portugal), 19

Ground Beef Pie (Brazil), 100

Manioc Tart with Beef Filling (Cape Verde), 144–145

Meat and Bread Soup, Macao-Style (Macao), 252

Meat and Vegetable Stew (Brazil), 122–123

Minced Meat Croquettes (Malacca), 273

Minced Meat, Macao-Style (Macao), 262–263

Mountain Rice (Brazil), 110

Rice Hausa-Style (Brazil), 108–109

Rice Soup (Angola), 64

Sephardic Hash (Brazil), 121

Steak, Dom Pedro-Style (Portugal), 41

Steamed Meat Dumplings (East Timor), 171

Stewed Beef (Angola), 79

Beer Rolls (Brazil), 128

Beet Salad (Mozambique), 292

BELL PEPPERS

Fish and Vegetable Stew (East Timor), 179

Fish Stew (Angola), 70

Fried Fish and Manioc Stew (Mozambique), 296

Goat-Meat Stew (Angola), 78

Guinean Fish Stew (Guinea-Bissau), 229

Mussel and Vegetable Kabobs (Portugal), 35

Portuguese Salad (Portugal), 13

Sephardic Hash (Brazil), 121

Spicy Roasted Vegetables (Goa), 207

BEVERAGES

Banana Liqueur (Cape Verde), 167

Cocoa Liqueur (São Tomé and Príncipe), 343

Coconut Milk Drink (Cape Verde), 168

Demitasse Coffee (Brazil), 136

Mulled Wine (Portugal), 54

Paulista Rum Drink (Brazil), 137

Pineapple Orangeade (São Tomé and Príncipe), 342

Punch (Portugal), 55

Rum Drink (Brazil), 136

BLACK-EYED PEA(S)

Black-Eyed Pea Fritters (Brazil), 91

Black-Eyed Pea Salad (Portugal), 12

Mountain Meal (East Timor), 176

BOAR, WILD

Mozambican Grilled Meats (Mozambique), 312

Bonbons, Chocolate (Brazil), 133

BRAZIL

cuisine of, about, 85–87

recipes, 88–137

BRAZILIAN CASHEWS. *See* CASHEW(S)

BRAZIL NUTS

Dreams (Brazil), 132

Shrimp with Manioc Purée (Brazil), 118–119

BREAD. *See also* FRITTERS AND CROQUETTES

African Corn Bread (Mozambique), 317

Azorean Holy Ghost Soup (Portugal), 20–21

Banana Bread with Cashews (Mozambique), 315

Beer Rolls (Brazil), 128

Bread and Cilantro Soup from the Alentejo Region (Portugal), 23

Cape Verdean Corn Bread (Cape Verde), 166

Eggs Poached in Red Wine (Goa), 209

Goan Flat Bread (Goa), 223

Home-Style Bread (Portugal), 46

Meat and Bread Soup, Macao-Style (Macao), 252

Also by Cherie Y. Hamilton...

Brazil
A Culinary Journey

The recipes presented in *Brazil: A Culinary Journey* provide a glimpse into the surprisingly diverse repertoire of Brazilian cooking, from the heavily African-influenced cuisine of the Northeast to the cookery of the southern region, which has been shaped by European immigration. More than 130 recipes range from *Feijoada*, Brazil's national dish of beans, rice, and various meats (in its many regional variations), to lesser-known dishes, such as Shrimp

and Bread Pudding, Crab Soup, and Banana Brittle. The wonderful cookbook is both a voyage through the country's five regions, as well as a tour in recipes of the nation's history.

205 PAGES · 6 x 9½ · ISBN 0-7818-1080-9 · $24.95HC · (113)

Portuguese-interest titles from Hippocrene...

**Brazilian Portuguese-English/
English-Brazilian Portuguese Children's Picture Dictionary**
112 PAGES · 8½ x 11 · ISBN 0-7818-1131-7 · $14.95PB · (318)

**Brazilian Portuguese-English/
English-Brazilian Portuguese Dictionary & Phrasebook**
OVER 6,000 ENTRIES · 266 PAGES · 3½ x 7¼ · ISBN 0-7818-1007-8 · $12.95PB · (23)

Instant Brazilian Portuguese Vocabulary Builder
214 PAGES · 6 x 9 · ISBN 0-7818-1138-4 · $19.95PB · (281)

Portuguese-English/English-Portuguese Practical Dictionary
30,000 ENTRIES · 709 PAGES · 4¼ x 7 · ISBN 0-8705-2980-3 · $19.95PB · (477)

Prices subject to change without prior notice. To purchase Hippocrene Books contact your local bookstore, visit www.hippocrenebooks.com, call (718) 454-2366, or write to: HIPPOCRENE BOOKS, 171 Madison Avenue, New York, NY 10016. Please enclose check or money order, adding $5.00 shipping (UPS) for the first book, and $.50 for each additional book.